# The Humanistic Tradition

Third Edition

# 5 Romanticism, Realism, and the Nineteenth-Century World

# The Humanistic Tradition

THIRD EDITION

# 5 Romanticism, Realism, and the Nineteenth-Century World

Gloria K. Fiero

New York St. Louis San Francisco Auckland Bogotá Caracas
Lisbon London Madrid Mexico City Milan Montreal New Delhi
San Juan Singapore Sydney Tokyo Toronto

*McGraw-Hill*
*A Division of The* ***McGraw-Hill*** *Companies*

**THE HUMANISTIC TRADITION, BOOK 5**



Permissions Acknowledgments appear on page 139, and on this page by reference.

Library of Congress Catalog Card Number: 97–071267

ISBN 0–697–34072–4

Editorial Director *Phillip Butcher*
Senior Sponsoring Editor *Cynthia Ward*
Director of Marketing *Margaret Metz*
National Sales Manager *Jerry Arni*

This book was designed and produced by
CALMANN & KING LTD
71 Great Russell Street, London WC1B 3BN

Editor *Ursula Payne*
Designer *Karen Osborne*
Cover Designer *Karen Stafford*
Timeline Designer *Richard Foenander*
Picture Researcher *Carrie Haines*
Maps by Oxford Illustrators Ltd.

Developmental Editing by M. J. Kelly for McGraw-Hill

Typeset by Fakenham Photosetting, Norfolk
Printed in Hong Kong

10 9 8 7 6 5 4 3 2 1

http://www.mhhe.com

*Front cover*
Main image: Charles-Henri-Joseph Cordier, detail of *African in Algerian Costume*, ca. 1856–1857. Bronze and onyx, complete sculpture 37¾ × 26 × 14 in. Musée d'Orsay, Paris. Photo: © R.M.N., Paris.
Insets: (top) Marie-Louise-Elisabeth Vigée-Lebrun, detail of *Marie Antoinette*, 1788. Oil on canvas, full image 12 ft. 1½ in. × 6 ft. 3½ in. Musée de Versailles. Giraudon/Art Resource, New York.
(center) Marisol Escobar, detail of *Women and Dog*, 1964. Wood, plaster, synthetic polymer, and miscellaneous items, full assemblage 72¼ × 73 × 30 15/16 in. Collection of the Whitney Museum of American Art, New York. Purchase, with funds from the Friends of the Whitney Museum of American Art (64.17 a–g). Photo: Robert E. Mates, N.J. © Marisol Escobar/DACS, London VAGA, New York 1997.
(bottom) Toshusai Sharaku, *Bust Portrait of the Actor Segawa Tomisaburo as Yadorigi, the Wife of Ogishi Kurando*, 1794–1795. Woodblock print, 14½ × 9¼ in. Photograph © 1997, The Art Institute of Chicago, All Rights Reserved. Clarence Buckingham Collection, 1928.1056.

*Frontispiece*
Henri de Toulouse-Lautrec, detail of *At The Moulin-Rouge*, 1892–1895. Oil on canvas, full image 4 ft. ⅜ in. × 4 ft. 7¼ in. Photograph © 1993, The Art Institute of Chicago. All Rights Reserved. Helen Birch Bartlett Memorial Collection (1928.610).

# Series Contents

# Book 5
# Contents

## MUSIC LISTENING SELECTIONS



## MAPS

# Preface

"It's the most curious thing I ever saw in all my life!"exclaimed Lewis Carroll's Alice in Wonderland, as she watched the Cheshire Cat slowly disappear, leaving only the outline of a broad smile. "I've often seen a cat without a grin, but a grin without a cat!" A student who encounters an ancient Greek epic, a Yoruba mask, or a Mozart opera—lacking any context for these works—might be equally baffled. It may be helpful, therefore, to begin by explaining how the artifacts (the "grin") of the humanistic tradition relate to the larger and more elusive phenomenon (the "cat") of human culture.

## The Humanistic Tradition and the Humanities

In its broadest sense, the term *humanistic tradition* refers to humankind's cultural legacy—the sum total of the significant ideas and achievements handed down from generation to generation. This tradition is the product of responses to conditions that have confronted all people throughout history. Since the beginnings of life on earth, human beings have tried to ensure their own survival by achieving harmony with nature. They have attempted to come to terms with the inevitable realities of disease and death. They have endeavored to establish ways of living collectively and communally. And they have persisted in the desire to understand themselves and their place in the universe. In response to these ever-present and universal challenges—*survival, communality,* and *self-knowledge*—human beings have created and transmitted the tools of science and technology, social and cultural institutions, religious and philosophic systems, and various forms of personal expression, the sum total of which we call culture.

Even the most ambitious survey cannot assess all manifestations of the humanistic tradition. This book therefore focuses on the creative legacy referred to collectively as *the humanities*: literature, philosophy, history (in its literary dimension), architecture, the visual arts (including photography and film), music, and dance. Selected examples from each of these disciplines constitute our *primary sources*. Primary sources (that is, works original to the age that produced them) provide first-hand evidence of human inventiveness and ingenuity. The primary sources in this text have been chosen on the basis of their authority, their beauty, and their enduring value. They are, simply stated, the great works of their time and, in some cases, of all time. Universal in their appeal, they have been transmitted from generation to generation. Such works are, as well, the landmark examples of a specific time and place: They offer insight into the ideas and values of the society in which they were produced. The drawings of Leonardo da Vinci, for example, reveal a passionate determination to understand the operations and functions of nature. And while Leonardo's talents far exceeded those of the average individual of his time, his achievements may be viewed as a mirror of the robust curiosity that characterized his time and place—the age of the Renaissance in Italy. *The Humanistic Tradition* surveys such landmark works, but joins "the grin" to "the cat" by examining them within their political, economic, and social contexts.

*The Humanistic Tradition* explores a living legacy. History confirms that the humanities are integral forms of a given culture's values, ambitions, and beliefs. Poetry, painting, philosophy, and music are not, generally speaking, products of unstructured leisure or indulgent individuality; rather, they are tangible expressions of the human quest for the good (one might even say the "complete") life. Throughout history, these forms of expression have served the domains of the sacred, the ceremonial, and the communal. And even in the waning days of the twentieth century, as many time-honored traditions have come under assault, the arts retain their power to awaken our imagination in the quest for survival, communality, and self-knowledge.

## The Scope of the Humanistic Tradition

The humanistic tradition is not the exclusive achievement of any one geographic region, race, or class of human beings. For that reason, this text assumes a global and multicultural rather than exclusively Western perspective. At the same time, Western contributions are emphasized, first, because the audience for these books is predominantly Western, but also because in recent centuries the West has exercised a dominant influence on the course and substance of global history. Clearly, the humanistic tradition belongs to all of humankind, and the best way to understand the Western contribution to that tradition is to examine it in the arena of world culture.

As a survey, *The Humanistic Tradition* cannot provide an exhaustive analysis of our creative legacy. The critical reader will discover many gaps. Some aspects of culture that receive extended examination in traditional Western humanities surveys have been pared down to make room for the too often neglected contributions of Islam, Africa, and Asia. This book is necessarily selective—it omits many major figures and treats others only briefly. Primary sources are arranged, for the most part, chronologically, but they are presented as manifestations of *the informing ideas of the age* in which they were produced. The intent is to examine the evidence of the humanistic tradition thematically and topically, rather than to compile a series of mini-histories of the individual arts.

## Studying the Humanistic Tradition

To study the creative record is to engage in a dialogue with the past, one that brings us face to face with the values of our ancestors, and, ultimately, with our own. This dialogue is (or should be) a source of personal revelation and delight; like Alice in Wonderland, our strange, new encounters will be enriched according to the degree of curiosity and patience we bring to them. Just as lasting friendships with special people are cultivated by extended familiarity, so our appreciation of a painting, a play, or a symphony depends on close attention and repeated contact. There are no shortcuts to the study of the humanistic tradition, but there are some techniques that may be helpful. It should be useful, for instance, to approach each primary source from the triple perspective of its *text*, its *context*, and its *subtext*.

*The Text*: The *text* of any primary source refers to its *medium* (that is, what it is made of), its *form* (its outward shape), and its *content* (the subject it describes). All literature, for example, whether intended to be spoken or read, depends on the medium of words—the American poet Robert Frost once defined literature as "performance in words." Literary form varies according to the manner in which words are arranged. So poetry, which shares with music and dance rhythmic organization, may be distinguished from prose, which normally lacks regular rhythmic pattern. The main purpose of prose is to convey information, to narrate, and to describe; poetry, by its freedom from conventional patterns of grammar, provides unique opportunities for the expression of intense emotions. Philosophy (the search for truth through reasoned analysis) and history (the record of the past) make use of prose to analyze and communicate ideas and information. In literature, as in most kinds of expression, content and form are usually interrelated. The subject matter or the form of a literary work determines its *genre*. For instance, a long narrative poem recounting the adventures of a hero constitutes an *epic*, while a formal, dignified speech in praise of a person or thing constitutes a *eulogy*.

The visual arts—painting, sculpture, architecture, and photography—employ a wide variety of media, such as wood, clay, colored pigments, marble, granite, steel, and (more recently) plastic, neon, film, and computers. The form or outward shape of a work of art depends on the manner in which the artist manipulates the formal elements of color, line, texture, and space. Unlike words, these formal elements lack denotative meaning. The artist may manipulate form to describe and interpret the visible world (as in such genres as portraiture and landscape painting); to generate fantastic and imaginative kinds of imagery; or to create imagery that is nonrepresentational—without identifiable subject matter. In general, however, the visual arts are spatial, that is, they operate and are apprehended in space.

The medium of music is sound. Like literature, music is durational: It unfolds over the period of time in which it occurs. The formal elements of music are melody, rhythm, harmony, and tone color—elements that also characterize the oral life of literature. As with the visual arts, the formal elements of music are without symbolic content, but while literature, painting, and sculpture may imitate or describe nature, music is almost always nonrepresentational—it rarely has meaning beyond the sound itself. For that reason, music is the most difficult of the arts to describe in words. It is also (in the view of some) the most affective of the arts. Dance, the artform that makes the human body itself a medium of expression, resembles music in that it is temporal and performance-oriented. Like music, dance exploits rhythm as a formal tool, but, like painting and sculpture, it unfolds in space as well as time.

In analyzing the text of a work of literature, art, or music, we ask how its formal elements contribute to its meaning and affective power. We examine the ways in which the artist manipulates medium and form to achieve a characteristic manner of execution and expression that we call *style*. And we try to determine the extent to which a style reflects the personal vision of the artist and the larger vision of his or her time and place. Comparing the styles of various artworks from a single era, we may discover that they share certain defining features and characteristics. Similarities (both formal and stylistic) between, for instance, golden age Greek temples and Greek tragedies, between Chinese lyric poems and landscape paintings, and between postmodern fiction and pop sculpture, prompt us to seek the unifying moral and aesthetic values of the cultures in which they were produced.

*The Context*: We use the word *context* to describe the historical and cultural environment. To determine the context, we ask: In what time and place did the artifact originate? How did it function within the society in which it was created? Was the purpose of the piece decorative, didactic, magical, propagandistic? Did it serve the religious or political needs of the community? Sometimes our answers to these questions are mere guesses. Nevertheless, understanding the function of an artifact often serves to clarify the nature of its form (and vice versa). For instance, much of the literature produced prior to the fifteenth century was spoken or sung rather than read; for that reason, such literature tends to feature repetition and rhyme, devices that facilitate memorization. We can assume that literary works embellished with frequent repetitions, such as the *Epic of Gilgamesh* and the Hebrew Bible, were products of an oral tradition. Determining the original function of an artwork also permits us to assess its significance in its own time and place: The paintings on the walls of Paleolithic caves, which are among the most compelling animal illustrations in the history of world art, are not "artworks" in the modern sense of the term but, rather, magical signs that accompanied hunting rituals, the performance of which was essential to the survival of the community. Understanding the relationship between text and context is one of the principal concerns of any inquiry into the humanistic tradition.

*The Subtext*: The *subtext* of the literary or artistic object refers to its secondary and implied meanings. The subtext embraces the emotional or intellectual messages embedded in, or implied by, a work of art. The epic poems of the ancient Greeks, for instance, which glorify prowess and physical courage in battle, suggest that such virtues are exclusively male. The state portraits of the seventeenth-century French ruler Louis XIV carry the subtext of unassailable and absolute power. In our own century, Andy Warhol's serial adaptations of soup cans and Coca-Cola bottles offer wry commentary on the supermarket mentality of postmodern American culture. Identifying the implicit message of an artwork helps us to determine the values and customs of the age in which it was produced and to assess those values against others.

## Beyond *The Humanistic Tradition*

This book offers only small, enticing samples from an enormous cultural buffet. To dine more fully, students are encouraged to go beyond the sampling presented at this table; and for the most sumptuous feasting, nothing can substitute for first-hand experience. Students, therefore, should make every effort to supplement this book with visits to art museums and galleries, concert halls, theaters, and libraries. *The Humanistic Tradition* is designed for students who may or may not be able to read music, but who surely are able to cultivate an appreciation of music in performance. The clefs that appear in the text refer to the forty-five Music Listening Selections found on two accompanying cassettes, available from the publishers. Lists of suggestions for further reading are included at the end of each chapter, while a selected general bibliography of humanities resources appears at the end of each book.

## The Third Edition

On the threshold of the new millennium, this third edition of *The Humanistic Tradition* brings increased attention to the theme of global cross-cultural encounter and, in particular, to the interaction of the West with the cultures of Islam, East Asia, and Africa. In this connection, literary selections by Ibn Battuta, Shen Fu, Iqbal, and other non-Western writers have been added. New Western readings include selections from the works of Hernán Cortés, Jonathan Swift, Mary Shelley, Ralph Waldo Emerson, Alice Walker, Malcolm X, and Seamus Heaney. Japanese theater, the transatlantic slave trade, Islamic literature, and contemporary computer art are among the topics that receive expanded treatment in this edition.

The third edition also features two new study aids, both of which are designed to facilitate an appreciation of the arts in relation to their time and place: *Science and Technology Boxes*, which appear throughout the chapters, list key scientific and technological developments that have directly or indirectly affected the history of culture. *Locator Maps* (keyed to the map that appears on p. xii) assist readers in linking specific cultural events with the geographic region in which they occurred. This edition also expands on the number of color illustrations and large color maps, renumbers the Readings by book, and updates the Suggestions for Reading and Selected General Bibliography. Finally, in the transcription of the Chinese language, the older Wade-Giles system has been replaced by the more modern Hanyu Pinyin.

## A Note to Instructors

The key to successful classroom use of *The Humanistic Tradition* is *selectivity*. Although students may be assigned to read whole chapters that focus on a topic or theme, as well as complete works that supplement the abridged readings, the classroom should be the stage for a selective treatment of a single example or a set of examples. The organization of this textbook is designed to emphasize themes that cut across geographic boundaries—themes whose universal significance prompts students to evaluate and compare rather than simply memorize and repeat lists of names and places. In an effort to assist readers in achieving global cultural literacy, every effort has been made to resist isolating (or "ghettoizing") individual cultures and to avoid the inevitable biases we bring to our evaluation of relatively unfamiliar cultures.

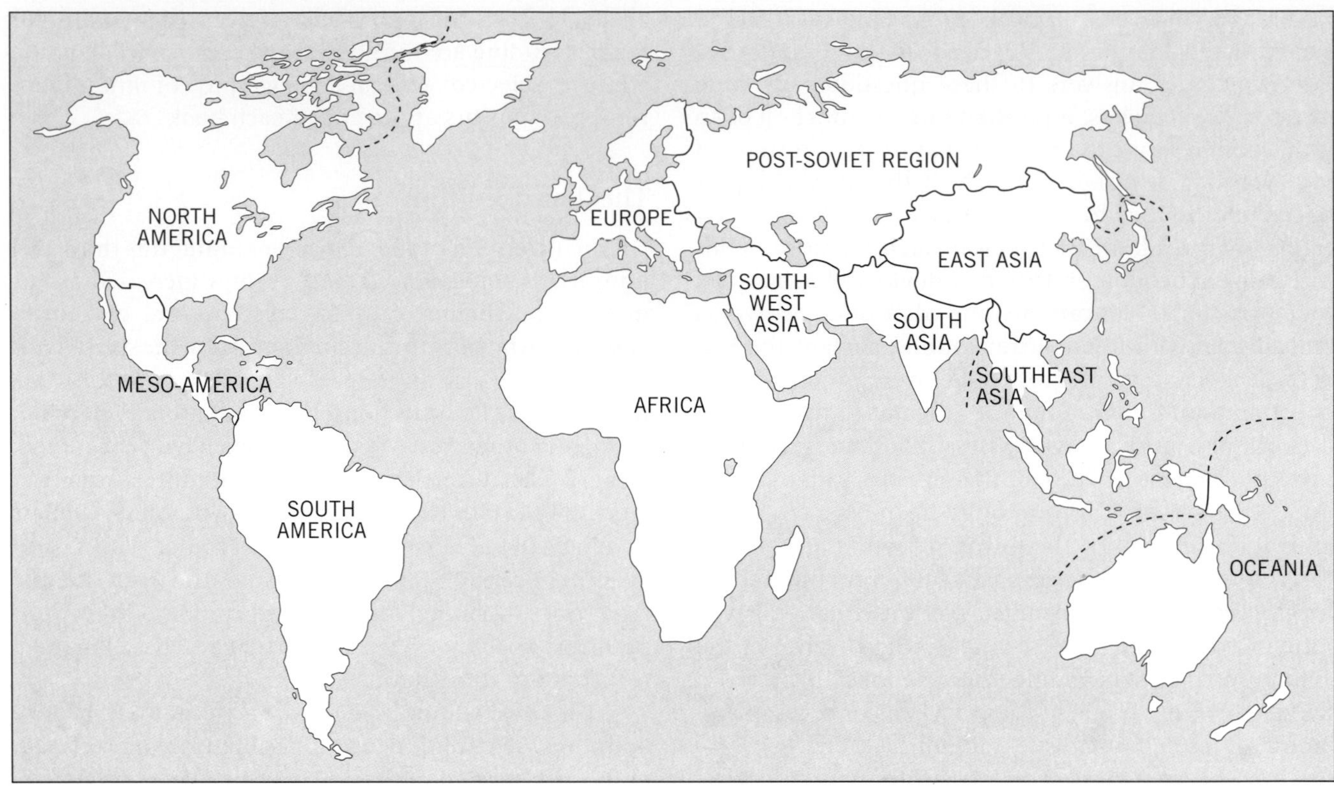


Keymap Indicating Areas Shown as White Highlights on the Locator Maps.

## Acknowledgments

Writing *The Humanistic Tradition* has been an exercise in humility. Without the assistance of learned friends and colleagues, assembling a book of this breadth would have been an impossible task. James H. Dormon read all parts of the manuscript and made extensive and substantive editorial suggestions; as his colleague, best friend, and wife, I am most deeply indebted to him. I owe thanks to the following faculty members of the University of Southwestern Louisiana: for literature, Allen David Barry, Darrell Bourque, C. Harry Bruder, John W. Fiero, Emilio F. Garcia, Doris Meriwether, and Patricia K. Rickels; for history, Ora-Wes S. Cady, John Moore, Bradley Pollack, and Thomas D. Schoonover; for philosophy, Steve Giambrone and Robert T. Kirkpatrick; for geography, Tim Reilly; for the sciences, Mark Konikoff and John R. Meriwether; and for music, James Burke and Robert F. Schmalz.

The following readers and viewers generously shared their insights in matters of content and style: Michael K. Aakhus (University of Southern Indiana), Vaughan B. Baker (University of Southwestern Louisiana), Katherine Charlton (Mt. San Antonio Community College), Bessie Chronaki (Central Piedmont Community College), Debora A. Drehen (Florida Community College—Jacksonville), Paula Drewek (Macomb Community College), William C. Gentry (Henderson State University), Kenneth Ganza (Colby College), Ellen Hofman (Highline Community College), Burton Raffel (University of Southwestern Louisiana), Frank La Rosa (San Diego City College), George Rogers (Stonehill College), Douglas P. Sjoquist (Lansing Community College), Howard V. Starks (Southeastern Oklahoma State University), Ann Wakefield (Academy of the Sacred Heart—Grand Coteau), Sylvia White (Florida Community College—Jacksonville), and Audrey Wilson (Florida State University).

In the preparation of the third edition, I have benefited from the suggestions and comments generously offered by numerous readers, only some of whom are listed below. Rodney D. Boyd (Collin County Community College), Arnold Bradford (Northern Virginia Community College), Patricia L. Brace (Southwest State University), Orville V. Clark (University of Wisconsin—Green Bay), Carolyn Copeland (Bethune Cookman), Susan Cornett (St. Petersburg Junior College—Tarpon Center), Anthony M. Coyne (University of North Carolina), Kenneth Ganza (Colby College), Margaret Hasselman (Virginia Polytechnic Institute and State University), Victor Hébert (Fayetteville State University), Ellen Hofmann (Highline Community College), Enid Housty (Hampton University), Mabel Khawaja (Hampton University), James W. Mock (University of Central Oklahoma), Lewis Parkhill (East Central University), Joseph G. Rahme (University of Michigan—

Flint), David Simmons (Brevard Community College), J. Paul De Vierville (St. Phillip's College), Bertha L. Wise (Oklahoma City Community College), and Jon Young (Fayetteville State University). I am grateful to Julia Girouard, who provided research assistance for the third edition, to Professor Timothy Reilly, who kindly helped with the Locator Keymap, and to Professor Sabruta Dasgupta (University of Southwestern Louisiana), who generously assisted in the preparation of the Science and Technology Boxes in books 4 and 5.

The burden of preparing the third edition has been lightened by the assistance of M. J. Kelly, Developmental Editor, and by the editorial vigilance of Ursula Payne at Calmann & King.

### *SUPPLEMENTS FOR THE INSTRUCTOR AND THE STUDENT*

A number of useful supplements are available to instructors and students using *The Humanistic Tradition.* Please contact your sales representative or call 1-800-338-5371 to obtain these resources, or to ask for further details.

**Audiocassettes**
Two ninety-minute audiocassettes containing a total of forty-five musical selections have been designed exclusively for use with *The Humanistic Tradition.* Cassette One corresponds to the music listening selections discussed in books 1–3 and Cassette Two contains the music in books 4–6. Each selection on the cassettes is discussed in the text and includes a voice introduction for easier location. Instructors may obtain copies of the cassettes for classroom use by calling 1-800-338-5371. Individual cassettes may be purchased separately; however, upon the request of instructors who place book orders, Cassette One or Two can be packaged with any of the six texts, so that students may use the musical examples *along with* the text.

**Slide Sets**
A set of fifty book-specific slides is available to adopters of *The Humanistic Tradition.* These slides have been especially selected to include many of the less well-known images in the books, and will be a useful complement to your present slide resources. A larger set of two hundred book-specific slides is available for purchase from Sandak, Inc. For further information, please contact Sandak, 180 Harvard Avenue, Stamford, CT 06902 (phone 1-800-343-2806, fax 203-967-2445).

**Instructor's Resource Manual**
The Instructor's Resource Manual is designed to assist instructors as they plan and prepare for classes. Course outlines and sample syllabuses for both semester and quarter systems are included. The chapter summaries emphasize key themes and topics that give focus to the primary source readings. The study questions for each chapter may be removed and copied as handouts for student discussion or written assignments. A Test Item File follows each chapter along with a correlation list that directs instructors to the appropriate music examples, slides, transparencies, and software sections of the other supplements. A list of suggested videotapes, recordings, videodiscs, and their suppliers is included.

**MicroTest III**
The questions in the Test Item File are available on MicroTest III, a powerful but easy-to-use test generating program. MicroTest is available for DOS, Windows, and Macintosh personal computers. With MicroTest, an instructor can easily select the questions from the Test Item File and print a test and answer key. You can customize questions, headings, and instructions and add or import questions of your own.

**Humanities Transparencies**
A set of seventy-one acetate transparencies is available with *The Humanistic Tradition.* These show examples of art concepts, architectural styles, art media, maps, musical notation, musical styles, and musical elements.

***Culture 3.0* CD-ROM**
*Culture 3.0* CD-ROM is a unique Macintosh reference tool that emphasizes the interaction of varied disciplines. It contains 40 historical maps, 120 signature melodies, 50,000 hypertext links, and 170 essays on topics ranging from Greek gods and goddesses to the Cold War. Thirty-two CultureGrids are arranged chronologically from the biblical era to the twentieth century, organizing people, places, and events by country, discipline, and generation. (*Culture 2.0* is also available in a seven-disk set for Mac and IBM.)

**Student Study Guides, Volumes 1 and 2**
Written by Gloria K. Fiero, two new Student Study Guides are now available to help students gain a better understanding of subjects found in *The Humanistic Tradition.* Volume 1 accompanies books 1–3 and Volume 2 accompanies books 4–6. Each chapter contains: a Chapter Objective; a Chapter Outline; Key Terms, Names, and Dates; Vocabulary Building; Multiple Choice Questions; and Essay Questions. Many chapters also contain a Visual/Spatial Exercise and Bonus Material. At the end of each Part, Synthesis material helps students draw together ideas from a set of chapters.

***The Art Historian* CD-ROM, Volumes 1 and 2**
This flexible two-volume series on dual platform (Mac and Windows) CD-ROMs is designed to supplement introductory level art history education. Volume 1 covers ancient and medieval art, and Volume 2 covers Renaissance to modern art. The images included on the CD were gathered from over three hundred museums, galleries, and private collections throughout the world, and the text and test questions were written by current scholars from universities across the United States. With *The Art Historian*, students may listen to multimedia presentations, review full-color high-resolution images, and test their knowledge with flashcards and essay questions. *The Art Historian* is flexible, allowing students to take notes, compare two images on the screen at the same time, and create personalized collections of images for study and review. With *The Art Historian*, we place the power of multimedia *and* art at your fingertips.

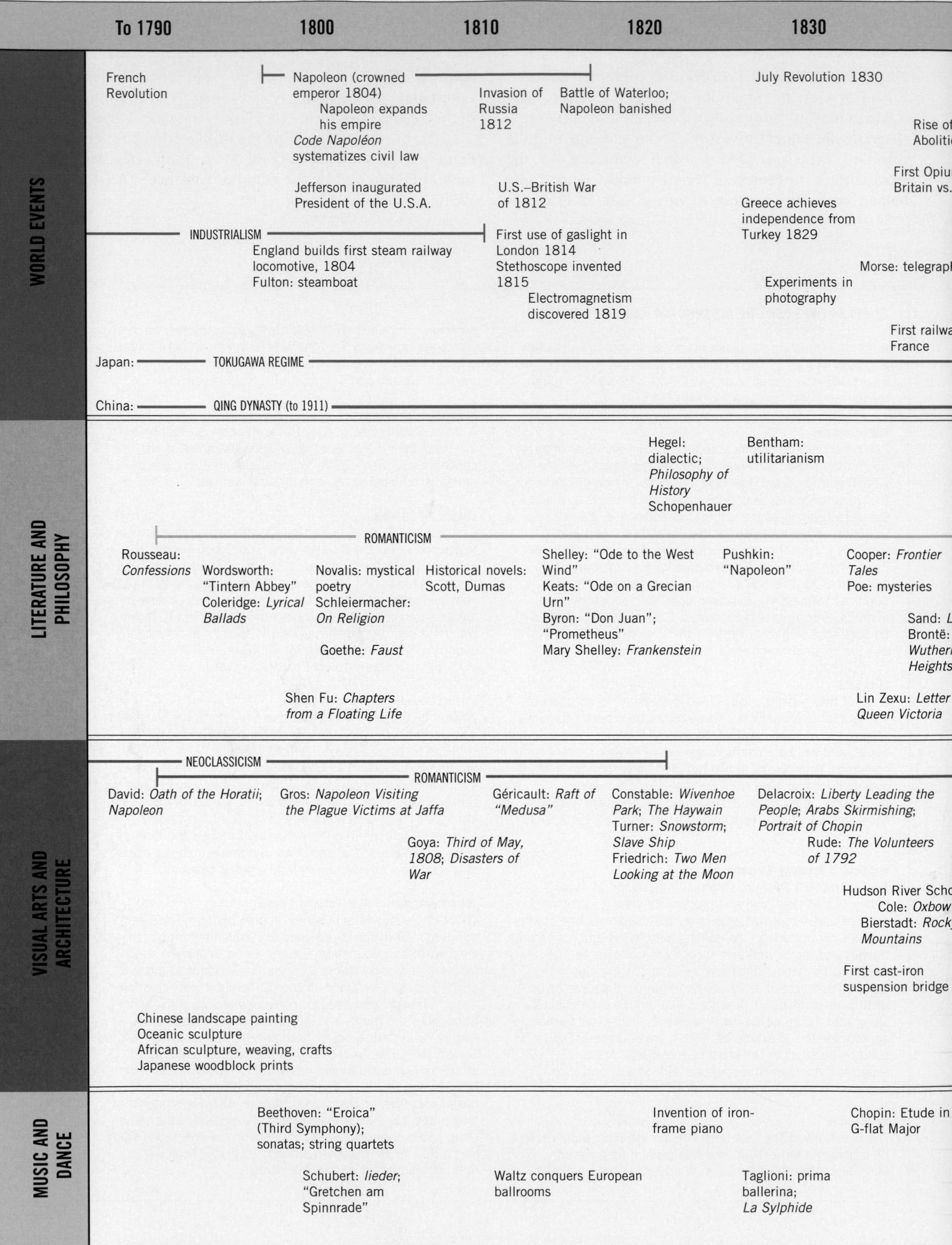

To 1790
1800
1810
1820
1830
WORLD EVENTS
French Revolution
Napoleon (crowned emperor 1804)
Napoleon expands his empire
*Code Napoléon* systematizes civil law
Invasion of Russia 1812
Battle of Waterloo; Napoleon banished
July Revolution 1830
Rise of Aboliti
Jefferson inaugurated President of the U.S.A.
U.S.–British War of 1812
First Opiu Britain vs.
Greece achieves independence from Turkey 1829
INDUSTRIALISM
England builds first steam railway locomotive, 1804
Fulton: steamboat
First use of gaslight in London 1814
Stethoscope invented 1815
Electromagnetism discovered 1819
Experiments in photography
Morse: telegrap
First railwa France
Japan: TOKUGAWA REGIME
China: QING DYNASTY (to 1911)
LITERATURE AND PHILOSOPHY
Hegel: dialectic; *Philosophy of History*
Schopenhauer
Bentham: utilitarianism
ROMANTICISM
Rousseau: *Confessions*
Wordsworth: "Tintern Abbey"
Coleridge: *Lyrical Ballads*
Novalis: mystical poetry
Schleiermacher: *On Religion*
Goethe: *Faust*
Historical novels: Scott, Dumas
Shelley: "Ode to the West Wind"
Keats: "Ode on a Grecian Urn"
Byron: "Don Juan"; "Prometheus"
Mary Shelley: *Frankenstein*
Pushkin: "Napoleon"
Cooper: *Frontier Tales*
Poe: mysteries
Sand: *L*
Brontë: *Wuther Heights*
Shen Fu: *Chapters from a Floating Life*
Lin Zexu: *Letter Queen Victoria*
VISUAL ARTS AND ARCHITECTURE
NEOCLASSICISM
ROMANTICISM
David: *Oath of the Horatii*; *Napoleon*
Gros: *Napoleon Visiting the Plague Victims at Jaffa*
Géricault: *Raft of "Medusa"*
Goya: *Third of May, 1808*; *Disasters of War*
Constable: *Wivenhoe Park*; *The Haywain*
Turner: *Snowstorm*; *Slave Ship*
Friedrich: *Two Men Looking at the Moon*
Delacroix: *Liberty Leading the People*; *Arabs Skirmishing*; *Portrait of Chopin*
Rude: *The Volunteers of 1792*
Hudson River Scho
Cole: *Oxbow*
Bierstadt: *Rock Mountains*
First cast-iron suspension bridge
Chinese landscape painting
Oceanic sculpture
African sculpture, weaving, crafts
Japanese woodblock prints
MUSIC AND DANCE
Beethoven: "Eroica" (Third Symphony); sonatas; string quartets
Schubert: *lieder*; "Gretchen am Spinnrade"
Waltz conquers European ballrooms
Invention of iron-frame piano
Taglioni: prima ballerina; *La Sylphide*
Chopin: Etude in G-flat Major

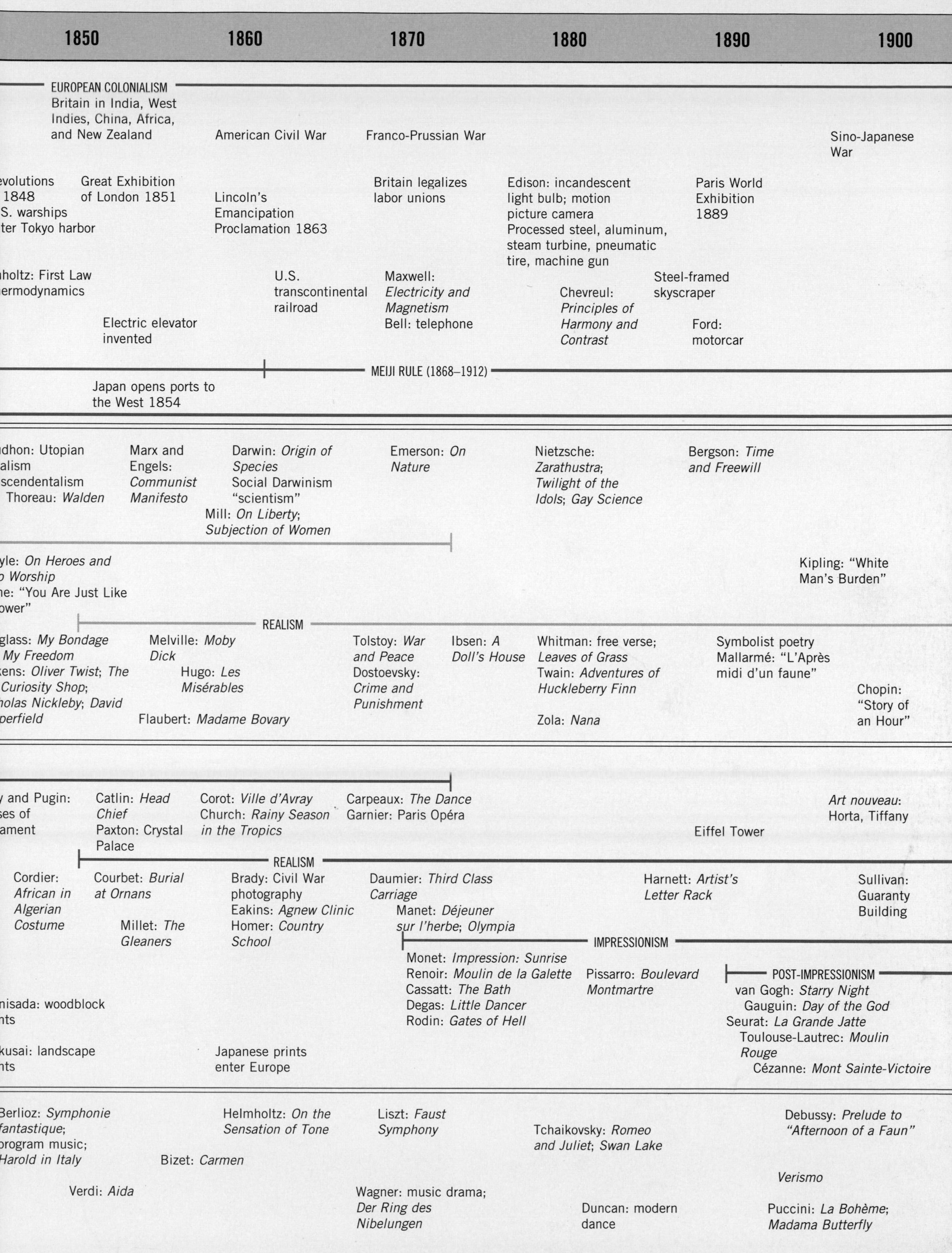

1850
1860
1870
1880
1890
1900
EUROPEAN COLONIALISM
Britain in India, West Indies, China, Africa, and New Zealand
American Civil War
Franco-Prussian War
Sino-Japanese War
evolutions 1848
.S. warships nter Tokyo harbor
Great Exhibition of London 1851
Lincoln's Emancipation Proclamation 1863
Britain legalizes labor unions
Edison: incandescent light bulb; motion picture camera
Processed steel, aluminum, steam turbine, pneumatic tire, machine gun
Paris World Exhibition 1889
nholtz: First Law hermodynamics
U.S. transcontinental railroad
Maxwell: Electricity and Magnetism
Bell: telephone
Chevreul: Principles of Harmony and Contrast
Steel-framed skyscraper
Electric elevator invented
Ford: motorcar
MEIJI RULE (1868–1912)
Japan opens ports to the West 1854
udhon: Utopian ialism
nscendentalism
Thoreau: Walden
Marx and Engels: Communist Manifesto
Darwin: Origin of Species
Social Darwinism "scientism"
Mill: On Liberty; Subjection of Women
Emerson: On Nature
Nietzsche: Zarathustra; Twilight of the Idols; Gay Science
Bergson: Time and Freewill
lyle: On Heroes and o Worship
ne: "You Are Just Like ower"
Kipling: "White Man's Burden"
REALISM
glass: My Bondage My Freedom
kens: Oliver Twist; The Curiosity Shop; holas Nickleby; David perfield
Melville: Moby Dick
Hugo: Les Misérables
Flaubert: Madame Bovary
Tolstoy: War and Peace
Dostoevsky: Crime and Punishment
Ibsen: A Doll's House
Whitman: free verse; Leaves of Grass
Twain: Adventures of Huckleberry Finn
Zola: Nana
Symbolist poetry
Mallarmé: "L'Après midi d'un faune"
Chopin: "Story of an Hour"
y and Pugin: ses of iament
Catlin: Head Chief
Paxton: Crystal Palace
Corot: Ville d'Avray
Church: Rainy Season in the Tropics
Carpeaux: The Dance
Garnier: Paris Opéra
Eiffel Tower
Art nouveau: Horta, Tiffany
REALISM
Cordier: African in Algerian Costume
Courbet: Burial at Ornans
Millet: The Gleaners
Brady: Civil War photography
Eakins: Agnew Clinic
Homer: Country School
Daumier: Third Class Carriage
Manet: Déjeuner sur l'herbe; Olympia
Harnett: Artist's Letter Rack
Sullivan: Guaranty Building
IMPRESSIONISM
Monet: Impression: Sunrise
Renoir: Moulin de la Galette
Cassatt: The Bath
Degas: Little Dancer
Rodin: Gates of Hell
Pissarro: Boulevard Montmartre
POST-IMPRESSIONISM
van Gogh: Starry Night
Gauguin: Day of the God
Seurat: La Grande Jatte
Toulouse-Lautrec: Moulin Rouge
Cézanne: Mont Sainte-Victoire
nisada: woodblock nts
kusai: landscape nts
Japanese prints enter Europe
Berlioz: Symphonie fantastique; program music; Harold in Italy
Helmholtz: On the Sensation of Tone
Liszt: Faust Symphony
Tchaikovsky: Romeo and Juliet; Swan Lake
Debussy: Prelude to "Afternoon of a Faun"
Bizet: Carmen
Verdi: Aida
Wagner: music drama; Der Ring des Nibelungen
Duncan: modern dance
Verismo
Puccini: La Bohème; Madama Butterfly

# PART I
# THE ROMANTIC ERA

Two fundamental developments influenced the cultural vitality of the nineteenth century. The first was the transformation of the West from an agricultural to an industrially based society. The second was the extension of European dominion over much of the rest of the world. This controlling presence of Europeans in Asia and Africa contributed to an eclipsing of native cultural expression in those areas. With the exception of Japan, the regions beyond the West generated few new forms of artistic expression in the nineteenth century and certainly none comparable to those produced in previous centuries. This circumstance also explains why our examination of the nineteenth century assumes an almost exclusively Western focus.

During the nineteenth century, the population of Europe doubled in size, and material culture changed more radically than it had in the previous one thousand years. The application of science to practical invention had already sparked the beginnings of the Industrial Revolution—the mass production of material goods by machines. The first phase of this revolution occurred in mid-eighteenth-century England, with the development of the steam engine and the machinery for spinning and weaving textiles. As the increased production of coal, iron, and steel encouraged the further expansion of industry and commerce, the revolution gained momentum. Industrialization involved a shift from the production of goods in homes and workshops to manufacture in factories, mills, and mines. It demanded enormous investments of capital and the efforts of a large labor force; it stimulated growth in Europe's urban centers. And clearly, industrialism provided the basis for the West's controlling influence over the rest of the world.

If industrialism was the primary force that shaped nineteenth-century Western culture, the second was nationalism. Nationalism—the exaltation of the state—involved the patriotic identification of individuals with a territory that embraced a common language and history. As people began to identify political sovereignty with the nation rather than with the person of the ruler, they sought greater freedom from the autocratic political and economic restraints of the old ruling orders. They also rejected the efforts of other nations to control their destiny. Such sentiments underlay the revolutionary outbursts that were chronic and continuous throughout the nineteenth century. European nationalism spurred the drive toward unification within the Germanies and among the Italian provinces and gave rise to a pervasive militarism in the individual states of the West. In the course of the century, England, France, Germany, Belgium, and the United States increased in political, economic, and military strength; and Germany and Italy finally reached the status of unified nation-states.

The nineteenth century is often called "the romantic era." *Romanticism* may be defined as a movement in the history of culture, as an aesthetic style, and

(opposite) John Constable, detail of *Wivenhoe Park, Essex*, 1816. Oil on canvas, full image 22⅛ × 39⅞ in. © 1998 Board of Trustees, National Gallery of Art, Washington, D.C. Widener Collection.

as an attitude or spirit. As a movement, romanticism involved a revolt against convention and authority and a search for freedom in personal, political, and artistic life. The romantics reacted against the orderly and systematic worldview of the Enlightenment, the rationalism of Enlightenment culture, and the impersonality of growing industrialism. Estranged from traditional religious beliefs, the romantics looked upon nature as the dwelling place of God. They worked to revive their nations' history and to liberate the oppressed peoples of the earth.

As an artistic style, romanticism was a reaction against the neoclassical quest for order and intellectual control. Romantics favored the free expression of the imagination and the liberation of the emotions. In preference to aesthetic objectivity and formalism, romantics chose subjectivity and the spontaneous outpouring of feeling. They cultivated a taste for the exotic, the ecstatic, and the fantastic. Finally, as an attitude, romanticism may be seen as an effort to glorify the individual self by way of intuition and a reliance upon the senses. Romantics did not reject the value of reason; rather, they regarded the emotions as equally important to human experience. Sentimentality, nostalgia, melancholy, and longing were all characteristic of the romantic cast of mind.

The romantics saw themselves as the heroes and visionaries of their time. They freed themselves from exclusive dependence on the patronage of Church and state and tended to pursue fiercely individualistic paths to creativity—paths that often alienated them from society. The lives and works of the romantics were marked by deep subjectivity—one might even say by self-indulgence. If the perceptions and passions of the romantics were intense, their desire to devise a language adequate to that intensity of feeling often drove them to frustration, despair, and, in the case of an unusual number of them, to an early death—the painters Gros and Géricault, the composers Chopin and Schubert, and the poets Byron, Shelley, and Keats all died before the age of forty.

Chapter 27, "The Romantic View of Nature," explores the centrality of nature and the natural in nineteenth-century literature, philosophy, science, and art. It examines nature as a source of inspiration in the poetry of Wordsworth, Shelley, Keats, Emerson, and Whitman, in the autobiography of Shen Fu, and in the intellectual achievements of Thoreau, Hegel, and Darwin. Eastern and Western landscape paintings, and the evidence of Native American artifacts in which nature and the natural are dominant themes, provide instructive parallels with these literary selections. Chapter 28 deals with the role of the hero in literature and life. Mary Shelley's *Frankenstein*, Byron's *Prometheus*, and Goethe's *Faust* provide opportunities for a consideration of the ways in which *fictional* heroes symbolized individual and nationalistic ideals. Napoleon's diary and Douglass' autobiographical slave narrative offer valuable insights into the views of *historical* heroes—European and American respectively—on matters of liberty and the exercise of the imagination. Finally, the chapter examines the romantic female stereotype, as conceived by male and modified by female writers of the age. Chapter 29, "The Romantic Style in Art and Music," surveys the characteristic features of romantic painting, sculpture, architecture, music, and dance. The heroic themes of Gros and Géricault, the impassioned invocations to liberty in the works of Goya, Delacroix, and Rude, and neomedievalism in architecture are among the principal topics in this chapter. The wealth of music by Beethoven, Schubert, Berlioz, and Chopin and the flowering of ballet and opera illustrate the vitality of European romanticism.

# 27
# The Romantic View of Nature

One of the central features of nineteenth-century romanticism was its love affair with nature and the natural. The romantics generally reacted against the artificiality of Enlightenment culture and the dismal effects of growing industrialism. In rural nature, they found a practical refuge from urban blight, smoke-belching factories, and poverty-ridden slums. Aesthetically, they perceived in nature, with all its shifting moods and rhythms, a metaphor for the romantic imagination. They looked to nature as the source of solace, inspiration, and self-discovery. In a broader sense, the romantic view of nature was nothing short of religious. With Rousseau, the romantics held that humans were by nature good but were corrupted by society (see chapter 25). "Natural man" was one who was close to nature and unspoiled by social institutions. To such Enlightenment figures as Locke, Pope, and Jefferson, nature had meant universal order, but to nineteenth-century romantics, nature was the source of divine ecstasy and the medium of the mystical bond that united God with the human soul. Romantics perceived unspoiled nature as the wellspring of all truth; many even viewed God and the natural universe as one. Such **pantheism**—more typical of Asian than of Western religious philosophy—characterized the writings of many European and American romantics, but it is most clearly exemplified in the poetry of William Wordsworth.

## *Nature and the Natural in European Literature*

### Wordsworth and the Poetry of Nature

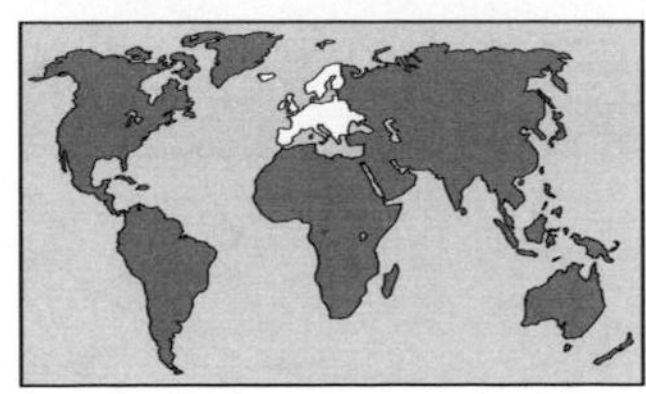

Born in the Lake District of England, William Wordsworth (1770–1850) was the leading nature poet of the nineteenth century. Wordsworth dated the beginning of his career as a poet from the time—at age fourteen—when he was struck by the image of tree boughs silhouetted against a bright evening sky. Thereafter, "the infinite variety of natural appearances" became the principal source of his inspiration and the primary subject of his poetry. Wordsworth's consciousness of nature was part of his larger belief that, through the senses, the individual could commune with elemental and divine universal forces.

In 1798, Wordsworth and his British contemporary Samuel Taylor Coleridge (1772–1834) produced the *Lyrical Ballads*, the literary work that marked the birth of the romantic movement in England. When the *Lyrical Ballads* appeared in a second edition in 1800, Wordsworth added a preface that formally explained the aims of romantic poetry. In this manifesto, Wordsworth defined poetry as "the spontaneous overflow of powerful feelings," which takes its origin "from emotion recollected in tranquillity." According to Wordsworth, the object of the poet was "to choose incidents and situations from common life [and] to throw over them a certain colouring of the imagination . . . and above all, to make these incidents and situations interesting by tracing in them, truly though not ostentatiously, the primary laws of our nature." Wordsworth championed a poetic language that resembled "the real language of men in a state of vivid sensation." Although he did not always abide by his own precepts, his rejection of the artificial diction of neoclassical verse in favor of "the real language of men" anticipated a new, more natural voice in poetry—one informed by childhood memories and deeply felt experiences recollected in tranquillity. Wordsworth's verse reflects the romantic poet's fondness for **lyric poetry**, which—like art song—describes deep personal feeling.

One of the most inspired poems in the *Lyrical Ballads* is "Lines Composed a Few Miles Above Tintern Abbey," the product of Wordsworth's visit to the ruins of a medieval monastery situated on the banks of the Wye River in Southwest England

**Figure 27.1** J. M. W. Turner, *Interior of Tintern Abbey*, 1794. Watercolor, 12⅝ × 9⅞ in.

(Figure 27.1). The 159-line poem constitutes a paean to nature. Wordsworth begins by describing the sensations evoked by the countryside itself; he then muses on the pleasures and the solace that these memories provide as they are called up in recollection. The heart of the poem, however, is a joyous celebration of nature's moral value: Nature allows the poet to "see into the life of things" (line 49), infuses him with "the still, sad music of humanity" (line 91), and ultimately brings him into the presence of the divine spirit. Nature, he exults, is the "anchor" of his purest thoughts, the "nurse" and "guardian" of his heart and soul (lines 109–110). In the final portion of the extract (lines 111–134), Wordsworth shares with his "dearest Friend," his sister Dorothy, the joys of his mystical communion with nature and humankind. In "Tintern Abbey," Wordsworth established three of the key motifs of nineteenth-century romanticism: the redemptive power of nature, the idea of nature's sympathy with humankind, and the view that one who is close to nature is close to God.

### READING 5.1

## From Wordsworth's "Lines Composed a Few Miles Above Tintern Abbey"

Five years have passed; five summers, with the length
Of five long winters! and again I hear
These waters, rolling from their mountain-springs
With a soft inland murmur. Once again
Do I behold these steep and lofty cliffs,
That on a wild secluded scene impress
Thoughts of more deep seclusion; and connect
The landscape with the quiet of the sky.
The day is come when I again repose
Here, under this dark sycamore, and view
These plots of cottage-ground, these orchard tufts,
Which at this season, with their unripe fruits,
Are clad in one green hue, and lose themselves
'Mid groves and copses. Once again I see
These hedge-rows, hardly hedge-rows, little lines
Of sportive wood run wild: these pastoral farms,
Green to the very door; and wreaths of smoke
Sent up, in silence, from among the trees!
With some uncertain notice, as might seem
Of vagrant dwellers in the houseless woods,
Or of some Hermit's cave, where by his fire
The hermit sits alone.
                                        These beauteous forms,
Through a long absence, have not been to me
As is a landscape to a blind man's eye;
But oft, in lonely rooms, and 'mid the din
Of towns and cities, I have owed to them
In hours of weariness, sensations sweet,
Felt in the blood, and felt along the heart;
And passing even into my purer mind,
With tranquil restoration:—feelings too
Of unremembered pleasure: such, perhaps,
As have no slight or trivial influence
On that best portion of a good man's life,
His little, nameless, unremembered acts
Of kindness and of love. Nor less, I trust,
To them I may have owed another gift,
Of aspect more sublime; that blessed mood,
In which the burthen[1] of the mystery,
In which the heavy and the weary weight
Of all this unintelligible world,
Is lightened—that serene and blessed mood,
In which the affections gently lead us on—
Until, the breath of this corporeal frame
And even the motion of our human blood
Almost suspended, we are laid asleep
In body, and become a living soul;
While with an eye made quiet by the power
Of harmony, and the deep power of joy,
We see into the life of things.
                                        If this
Be but a vain belief, yet, oh! how oft—
In darkness and amid the many shapes
Of joyless daylight; when the fretful stir
Unprofitable, and the fever of the world,
Have hung upon the beatings of my heart—
How oft, in spirit, have I turned to thee,
O sylvan[2] Wye! thou wanderer through the woods,
How often has my spirit turned to thee!

And now, with gleams of half-extinguished thought,
With many recognitions dim and faint,
And somewhat of a sad perplexity,
The picture of the mind revives again;
While here I stand, not only with the sense
Of present pleasure, but with pleasing thoughts
That in this moment there is life and food
For future years. And so I dare to hope,
Though changed, no doubt, from what I was when first
I came among these hills; when like a roe
I bounded o'er the mountains, by the sides
Of the deep rivers, and the lonely streams,
Wherever nature led: more like a man
Flying from something that he dreads than one
Who sought the thing he loved. For nature then
(The coarser pleasures of my boyish days,
And their glad animal movements all gone by)
To me was all in all—I cannot paint
What then I was. The sounding cataract[3]
Haunted me like a passion; the tall rock,
The mountain, and the deep and gloomy wood,
Their colours and their forms, were then to me
An appetite; a feeling and a love,
That had no need of a remoter charm,
By thought supplied, nor any interest
Unborrowed from the eye. That time is past,
And all its aching joys are now no more,
And all its dizzy raptures. Not for this
Faint I, nor mourn nor murmur; other gifts
Have followed; for such loss, I would believe,
Abundant recompense. For I have learned

[1] Burden.
[2] Wooded.
[3] A descent of water over a steep surface.

To look on nature, not as in the hour
Of thoughtless youth; but hearing oftentimes
The still, sad music of humanity,
Nor harsh nor grating, though of ample power
To chasten and subdue. And I have felt
A presence that disturbs me with the joy
Of elevated thoughts; a sense sublime
Of something far more deeply interfused,
Whose dwelling is the light of setting suns,
And the round ocean and the living air,
And the blue sky, and in the mind of man:
A motion and a spirit, that impels
All thinking things, all objects of all thought,
And rolls through all things. Therefore am I still
A lover of the meadows and the woods,
And mountains; and of all that we behold
From this green earth; of all the mighty world
Of eye, and ear—both what they half create,
And what perceive; well pleased to recognize
In nature and the language of the sense,
The anchor of my purest thoughts, the nurse,
The guide, the guardian of my heart, and soul
Of all my moral being.
Nor perchance,
If I were not thus taught, should I the more
Suffer my genial spirits to decay:
For thou art with me here upon the banks
Of this fair river; thou my dearest Friend,[4]
My dear, dear Friend; and in thy voice I catch
The language of my former heart, and read
My former pleasures in the shooting lights
Of thy wild eyes. Oh! yet a little while
May I behold in thee what I was once,
My dear, dear Sister! and this prayer I make,
Knowing that Nature never did betray
The heart that loved her; 'tis her privilege,
Through all the years of this our life, to lead
From joy to joy: for she can so inform
The mind that is within us, so impress
With quietness and beauty, and so feed
With lofty thoughts, that neither evil tongues,
Rash judgments, nor the sneers of selfish men,
Nor greetings where no kindness is, nor all
The dreary intercourse of daily life,
Shall e'er prevail against us, or disturb
Our cheerful faith, that all which we behold
Is full of blessings. . . .

◆

[4]Wordsworth's sister, Dorothy.

**1769** James Watt (Scottish) patents the first steam engine
**1787** the first power loom revolutionizes the weaving industry
**1805** earliest use of morphine (extracted from opium) to relieve pain
**1814** coal is transported by locomotive for the first time in England

## The Poetry of Shelley

Like Wordsworth, the British poet Percy Bysshe Shelley (1792–1822) embraced nature as the source of sublime truth, but his volcanic personality led him to engage the natural world with greater intensity and deeper melancholy than his older contemporary. A prolific writer and a passionate champion of human liberty, Shelley led a life that had all the features of the romantic hero (see chapter 28). Defiant and unconventional even in his youth, Shelley provoked the reading public with a treatise entitled *The Necessity of Atheism* (1811), the circulation of which led to his expulsion from Oxford University. He was outspoken in his opposition to marriage, a union that he viewed as hostile to human happiness. Moreover, he was as unconventional in his deeds as in his discourse: While married to one woman (Harriet Westbrook), with whom he had two children, he ran off with another (Mary Godwin). A harsh critic of England's rulers, he went into permanent exile in Italy in 1818 and died there four years later in a boating accident.

Shelley's *Defence of Poetry*, a manifesto of the poet's function in society, hails poets as "the unacknowledged legislators of the world." According to Shelley, poets take their authority from nature, the fountainhead of inspiration. Shelley finds in nature's moods, metaphors for insubstantial, yet potent, human states. In "Ode to the West Wind" he appeals to the wind, a symbol of creativity, to drive his visions throughout the universe, as the wind drives leaves over the earth (stanza 1), clouds through the air (stanza 2), and waves on the seas (stanza 3). In the final stanza, Shelley compares the poet to a lyre, whose "mighty harmonies," stirred by the wind of creativity, will awaken the world. By means of language that is itself musical, Shelley defends the notion of poetry as the music of the soul. Consider, for instance, his frequent use of the exclamatory "O" and the effective use of **assonance** and **tone color** in lines 38 to 40: "while far below/The sea-blooms and the oozy woods which wear/The sapless foliage of the ocean, know."

### READING 5.2

### Shelley's "Ode to the West Wind"

**1**

O wild West Wind, thou breath of Autumn's being,
Thou, from whose unseen presence the leaves dead
Are driven, like ghosts from an enchanter fleeing,

Yellow, and black, and pale, and hectic red,
Pestilence-stricken multitudes: O thou,
Who chariotest to their dark wintry bed

The wingéd seeds, where they lie cold and low,
Each like a corpse within its grave, until
Thine azure sister of the spring shall blow

Her clarion o'er the dreaming earth, and fill
(Driving sweet buds like flocks to feed in air)
With living hues and odours plain and hill:

Wild Spirit, which art moving everywhere;
Destroyer and preserver; hear, oh, hear!

**2**

Thou on whose stream, 'mid the steep sky's commotion,
Loose clouds like earth's decaying leaves are shed,
Shook from the tangled boughs of Heaven and Ocean,

Angels of rain and lightning: there are spread
On the blue surface of thine aëry surge,
Like the bright hair uplifted from the head

Of some fierce Maenad,[1] even from the dim verge
Of the horizon to the zenith's height,
The locks of the approaching storm. Thou dirge

Of the dying year, to which this closing night
Will be the dome of a vast sepulchre,[2]
Vaulted with all thy congregated might

Of vapours, from whose solid atmosphere
Black rain, and fire, and hail will burst: O, hear!

**3**

Thou who didst waken from his summer dreams
The blue Mediterranean, where he lay,
Lulled by the coil of his crystalline streams,

Beside a pumice isle in Baiae's bay,[3]
And saw in sleep old palaces and towers
Quivering within the wave's intenser day,

All overgrown with azure moss and flowers
So sweet, the sense faints picturing them! Thou
For whose path the Atlantic's level powers

Cleave themselves into chasms, while far below
The sea-blooms and the oozy woods which wear
The sapless foliage of the ocean, know

Thy voice, and suddenly grow grey with fear,
And tremble and despoil themselves: O, hear!

**4**

If I were a dead leaf thou mightest bear;
If I were a swift cloud to fly with thee;
A wave to pant beneath thy power, and share

The impulse of thy strength, only less free
Than thou, O uncontrollable! If even
I were as in my boyhood, and could be

The comrade of thy wanderings over heaven,
As then, when to outstrip thy skiey speed
Scarce seemed a vision; I would ne'er have striven

As thus with thee in prayer in my sore need.
Oh! lift me as a wave, a leaf, a cloud!
I fall upon the thorns of life! I bleed!

A heavy weight of hours has chained and bowed
One too like thee: tameless, and swift, and proud.

[1]A female attendant of Dionysus; a bacchante (see chapter 26).
[2]Tomb.
[3]An ancient resort in Southwest Italy.

**5**

Make me thy lyre, even as the forest is:
What if my leaves are falling like its own!
The tumult of thy mighty harmonies

Will take from both a deep, autumnal tone,
Sweet though in sadness. Be thou, spirit fierce,
My spirit! Be thou me, impetuous one!

Drive my dead thoughts over the universe
Like withered leaves to quicken a new birth!
And, by the incantation of this verse,

Scatter, as from an unextinguished hearth
Ashes and sparks, my words among mankind!
Be through my lips to unawakened earth

The trumpet of a prophecy! O, Wind,
If Winter comes, can Spring be far behind?

◆

## The Poetry of Keats

The poetry of John Keats (1795–1821), the third of the great British nature poets, shares the elegiac mood of romantic landscape painting. Keats lamented the transience of life's pleasures, even as he anticipated the brevity of life. He lost both his mother and his brother to tuberculosis, and he himself succumbed to that disease at the age of twenty-five. The threat of imminent death seems to have produced in Keats a heightened awareness of the virtues of beauty, human love, and friendship. Keats perceived these phenomena as fleeting forms of a higher reality that might be made permanent only in art. For Keats, art was the great balm of the poet. Art was more than a response to the human experience of love and nature; it was the transmuted product of the imagination, a higher form of nature itself. These ideas are central to Keats' "Ode on a Grecian Urn." The poem was inspired by ancient Greek artifacts Keats had seen among those brought to London by Lord Elgin in 1816 and placed on display in the British Museum (see chapter 6).

In the "Ode," Keats contemplates a Greek vase (much like the one pictured in Figure **27.2**), whose delicately drawn figures immortalize life's fleeting pleasures. The boughs of trees pictured on such a vase will never shed their leaves, the fair youths will never grow old, the music of the pipes and timbrels will never cease to play, and the lovers will never cease to love. The "little town by river" and the other pastoral vignettes in the poem probably did not belong to any one existing Greek vase; yet Keats describes the imaginary urn (his metaphoric "Cold Pastoral") as a symbol of all great works of art, which, because of their unchanging beauty, remain eternally "true." The poem concludes with the joyous pronouncement that beauty and truth are one.

**Figure 27.2** Sisyphus painter, South Italian volute krater with women making music and centaur fight, late fifth century B.C.E. Red-figure pottery. Staatliche Antikensammlungen und Glyptothek, Munich.

## READING 5.3

## Keats' "Ode on a Grecian Urn"

**1**

Thou still unravished bride of quietness,
  Thou foster-child of Silence and slow Time,
Sylvan historian, who canst thus express
  A flowery tale more sweetly than our rhyme:
What leaf-fringed[1] legend haunts about thy shape
  Of deities or mortals, or of both,
    In Tempe[2] or the dales of Arcady?[3]
  What men or gods are these? What maidens loth?
What mad pursuit? What struggle to escape?
    What pipes and timbrels? What wild ecstasy?

**2**

Heard melodies are sweet, but those unheard
  Are sweeter; therefore, ye soft pipes, play on;
Not to the sensual ear, but, more endeared,
  Pipe to the spirit ditties of no tone:
Fair youth, beneath the trees, thou canst not leave
  Thy song, nor ever can those trees be bare;
    Bold Lover, never, never canst thou kiss,
Though winning near the goal—yet, do not grieve;
    She cannot fade, though thou hast not thy bliss,
  For ever wilt thou love, and she be fair!

**3**

Ah, happy, happy boughs! that cannot shed
  Your leaves, nor ever bid the Spring adieu;
And, happy melodist, unweariéd,
  For ever piping songs for ever new;
More happy love! more happy, happy love!
  For ever warm and still to be enjoyed,
    For ever panting, and for ever young;
All breathing human passion far above,
  That leaves a heart high-sorrowful and cloyed,
    A burning forehead, and a parching tongue.

[1]A reference to the common Greek practice of bordering the vase with stylized leaf forms (see Figure 27.2).

[2]A valley sacred to Apollo between Mounts Olympus and Ossa in Thessaly, Greece.

[3]Arcadia, the pastoral regions of ancient Greece (see Poussin's *Arcadian Shepherds*, in chapter 23).

**4**

Who are these coming to the sacrifice?
  To what green altar, O mysterious priest,
Lead'st thou that heifer lowing at the skies,
  And all her silken flanks with garlands drest?
What little town by river or sea shore,
  Or mountain-built with peaceful citadel,
    Is emptied of this folk, this pious morn?
And, little town, thy streets for evermore
  Will silent be; and not a soul to tell
    Why thou art desolate, can e'er return.

**5**

O Attic[4] shape! Fair attitude! with brede[5]
  Of marble men and maidens overwrought,
With forest branches and the trodden weed;
  Thou, silent form, dost tease us out of thought
As doth eternity: Cold Pastoral!
  When old age shall this generation waste,
    Thou shalt remain, in midst of other woe
Than ours, a friend to man, to whom thou say'st,
  "Beauty is truth, truth beauty,"—that is all
    Ye know on earth, and all ye need to know.

◆

[4]Attica, a region in Southeastern Greece dominated by Athens.
[5]Embroidered border.

## *Nature and the Natural in Asian Literature*

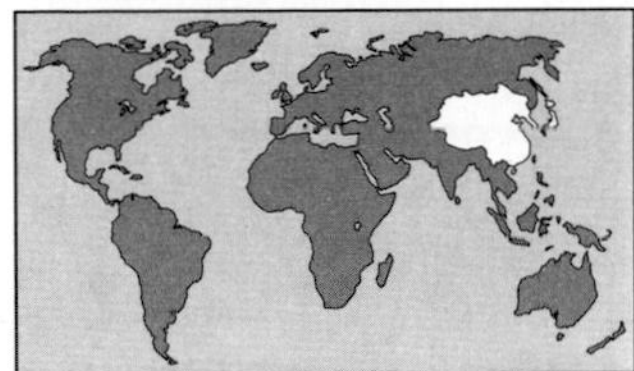

Wordsworth, Shelley, and Keats made nature a major theme in European romantic poetry; however, nature and the natural landscape had dominated the literary arts of East Asia for centuries (see chapter 14). Asian writers, immersed in Buddhist pantheism (the belief that a divine spirit pervades all things in the universe), valued the natural landscape as a symbol of the oneness of man and nature. Chinese poets of the Tang dynasty (618–907 C.E.), a Golden Age of Chinese poetry, embraced nature as a source of solitary joy and private meditation. They exalted China's mountainous landscape and changing

**Figure 27.3** Shen Zhou, *Poet on a Mountain Top*, from the "Landscape Album" series, ca. 1495–1500. Album leaf mounted as a handscroll: ink on paper or ink and light color on paper, 15¼ × 23¾ in. The Nelson-Atkins Museum of Art, Kansas City, Missouri. Purchase: Nelson Trust.

seasons as metaphors for human moods and feelings. In poems that resemble intimate diary entries (often inscribed directly on landscape scrolls or album leaves), Chinese poets cultivated the art of nature poetry—an art that has survived well into modern times. These lines were written in the late fifteenth century by Shen Zhou (1427–1509), on a landscape that he himself painted (Figure **27.3**):

> White clouds encircle the waist of the hills like a
>   belt;
> A stony ledge soars into the void, a narrow path
>   into space.
> Alone, I lean on my thornwood staff and gaze
>   calmly into the distance,
> About to play my flute in reply to the song of this
>   mountain stream.*

Although Asian poets anticipated the romantic engagement with nature, Eastern and Western styles of poetry differed considerably. Asian poets translated nature's moods by way of only a few carefully chosen words, evoking the subtlest of analogies between the natural landscape and the human condition. The European romantics, on the other hand, generally built up a series of richly detailed pictorial images through which they might explore the redemptive or affective powers of nature. Whereas Chinese poets tried to record natural appearance with some immediacy, the English romantics felt bound to distill the experience of the senses by way of the intellect, to discover moral analogues, and to put personal feelings at the service of human instruction and improvement. But despite the differences, the nature poetry of both East and West addresses an enduring theme in the humanistic tradition: the value of nature in helping human beings escape the artificial confines of the material world. Moreover, such poetry suggests that humans and human life processes are extensions of the patterns and rhythms that govern the cosmos itself.

Although no literary movement in Chinese history has been designated "romantic," there are clear examples of the romantic sensibility in Chinese literature of the nineteenth century, especially in those works that exalt the emotional identification of the individual with nature. The Chinese writer Shen Fu (1763–1809) shares with Wordsworth, Shelley, and Keats the reflective view of nature and a heightened sensitivity to its transient moods. A bohemian spirit, Shen Fu failed the district civil examinations that guaranteed financial success for Chinese intellectuals. Often in debt and expelled from his family by an overbearing father, he found brief but profound joy in his marriage to a neighbor's daughter,

*Translated by Daniel Bryant.

**Figure 27.4** Chinese water pot, probably eighteenth century. Jade, 6 × 4½ in. © The Board of Trustees of the Victoria and Albert Museum, London.

Zhen Yuen. Shen Fu's autobiography, *Six Chapters from a Floating Life* (1809), is a confessional record of their life together, a life in which poverty is balanced by the pleasures of married love and an abiding affection for nature. In the following excerpt from Shen's autobiography—a favorite with Chinese readers to this day—the writer describes the simple pleasures he and Zhen Yuen derived from growing flowers and designing "rockeries": natural arrangements of rocks and soil which resemble miniature gardens, like the decorative jade objects produced at this time (Figure **27.4**). The tender story of the destruction of the "Place of Falling Flowers," the couple's tiny version of the natural landscape, anticipates the central event of Shen's intimate life history: the death of his beloved wife. The story also functions as a reminder that all of nature is fragile and impermanent.

## READING 5.4

## From Shen Fu's *Six Chapters from a Floating Life*

As a young man I was excessively fond of flowers and loved to prune and shape potted plants and trees. When I met Chang Lan-p'o he began to teach me the art of training branches and supporting joints, and after I had mastered these skills, he showed me how to graft flowers. Later on, I also learned the placing of stones and designing of rockeries.

The orchid we considered the peerless flower, selecting it as much for its subtle and delicate fragrance as for its beauty and grace. Fine varieties of orchids were very difficult to find, especially those worthy of being recorded in the Botanical Register. When Lan-p'o was dying he gave me a pot of spring orchids of the lotus type, with broad white centres, perfectly even "shoulders," and very slender stems. As the plant was a classic specimen of its type, I treasured its perfection like a piece of ancient jade. Yuen took care of it whenever my work as yamen secretary[1] called me away from home. She always watered it herself and the plant flourished, producing a luxuriant growth of leaves and flowers.

One morning, about two years later, it suddenly withered and died. When I dug up the roots to inspect them, I saw that they were as white as jade, with many new shoots beginning to sprout. At first, I could not understand it. Was I just too unlucky, I wondered, to possess and enjoy such beauty? Sighing despondently, I dismissed the matter from my mind. But some time later I found out what had really happened. It seemed that a person who had asked for a cutting from the plant and had been refused, had then poured boiling water on it and killed it. After that, I vowed never to grow orchids again.

Azaleas were my second choice. Although the flowers had no fragrance they were very beautiful and lasted a long time. The plants were easy to trim and to train, but Yuen loved the green of the branches and leaves so much that she would not let me cut them back, and this made it difficult for me to train them to correct shapes. Unfortunately, Yuen felt this way about all the potted plants that she enjoyed.

Every year, in the autumn, I became completely devoted to the chrysanthemum. I loved to arrange the cut flowers in vases but did not like the potted plants. Not that I did not think the potted flowers beautiful, but our house having no garden, it was impossible for me to grow the plants myself, and those for sale at the market were overgrown and untrained; not at all what I would have chosen.

One day, as I was sweeping my ancestral graves in the hills, I found some very unusual stones with interesting streaks and lines running through them. I talked to Yuen about them when I went home.

"When Hsuan-chou stones are mixed with putty and arranged in white-stone dishes, the putty and stones blend well and the effect is very harmonious," I remarked. "These yellow stones from the hills are rugged and old-looking, but if we mix them with putty the yellow and white won't blend. All the seams and gaps will show up and the arrangement will look spotty. I wonder what else we could use instead of putty?"

"Why not pick out some of the poor, uninteresting stones and pound them to powder," Yuen said. "If we mix the powdered stones with the putty while it is still damp, the colour will probably match when it dries."

After doing as she suggested, we took a rectangular I-hsing pottery dish and piled the stones and putty into a miniature mountain peak on the left side of it, with a rocky crag jutting out towards the right. On the surface of the mountain, we made criss-cross marks in the style of the rocks painted by Ni Tsan[2] of the Yuan dynasty. This gave an effect of perspective and the finished arrangement looked very realistic—a precipitous cliff rising sharply from the rocks at the river's edge. Making a hollow in one corner of the dish, we filled it with river mud and planted it with duck-weed. Among the rocks we planted "clouds of the pine trees," bindweed. It was several days before the whole thing was finished.

Before the end of autumn the bindweed had spread all over the mountain and hung like wistaria from the rocky cliff. The flowers, when they bloomed, were a beautiful clear red. The duckweed, too, had sprouted luxuriantly from the mud and was now a mass of snowy white. Seeing the beauty of the contrasting red and white, we could easily imagine ourselves in Fairyland.

Setting the dish under the eaves, we started discussing what should be done next, developing many themes: "Here there should be a lake with a pavilion—" "This spot calls for a thatched summerhouse—" "This is the perfect place for the six-character inscription 'Place of Falling Flowers and Flowing Water' "—"Here we could build our house—here go fishing—here enjoy the view"; becoming, by this time, so much a part of the tiny landscape, with its hills and ravines, that it seemed to us as if we were really going to move there to live.

One night, a couple of mis-begotten cats, fighting over food, fell off the eaves and hit the dish, knocking it off its stand and smashing it to fragments in an instant. Neither of us could help crying.

"Isn't it possible," I sighed, "to have even a little thing like this without incurring the envy of the gods?"

◆

[1]A government clerk.
[2]A famous landscape painter (1301–1374) of the Yuan dynasty (1279–1368).

## *Romantic Landscape Painting*

Like nature poetry, landscape painting originated in China, where it acquired specific stylistic and pictorial conventions (see chapter 14). By the thirteenth century it had overtaken figure painting in popularity and had spread to Japan and other parts of East Asia (see Figure 31.10). Throughout the history of Chinese art, the natural landscape remained an independent genre, that is, a subject *in and of itself*. Chinese landscape painting thus holds a unique place in the history of world art.

Generally speaking, portrayals of the Chinese landscape are not literal imitations of reality, but expressions of a benign natural harmony. Typically their vast and sweeping composition dwarfs all human figures and suggests the cosmic unity of air, earth, and water (see Figure 27.3). Whether vertical or horizontal in format, the composition may be "read" from various viewpoints, rather than (as is usual in the West) from a single vantage point. Often executed by scholar-officials in monochrome ink on silk, bamboo, or paper scrolls, such landscapes—like modern-day hiking expeditions—were intended as sources of personal pleasure and private retreat.

By contrast with the East, the landscape in the West developed quite late as an independent subject. Although Roman artists created elaborate landscape settings for mythological subjects, it was not until the

Renaissance—among such painters as Leonardo da Vinci, Dürer, and Brueghel—that the natural landscape became a subject in its own right. During the seventeenth century, the French academicians Poussin and Lorrain devised the ideal landscape, a genre in which nature became the theater for mythological and biblical subjects (see chapter 23). The design or composition of the painting was conceived in the studio, and key elements, such as a large foreground tree, a distant sunset, and a meandering road or stream (which might be drawn from nature), were then organized according to the prearranged design. The seventeenth-century Dutch masters Vermeer and Rembrandt, however, rejected the ideal landscape. They preferred instead empirically precise views of the physical world, thus advancing landscape painting as an independent genre (see chapter 22). Nevertheless, it was not until the nineteenth century that landscape painting became a primary vehicle for recording the artist's shifting moods and private emotions. Romantic painters translated their native affection for the countryside into scenes that ranged from the picturesque to the sublime. Like Wordsworth and Shelley, these artists discovered in nature a source of inspiration and a mirror of their own sensibilities.

## Constable and Turner

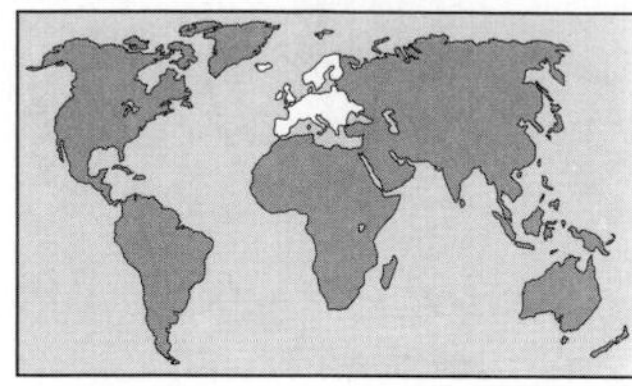

Of the many landscape painters of nineteenth-century Britain, two figures stand out: John Constable (1776–1837) and Joseph Mallord William Turner (1775–1851). Constable owed much to the Dutch masters; yet his approach to nature was uncluttered by tradition. "When I sit down to make a sketch from nature," he wrote, "the first thing I try to do is to forget that I have ever seen a picture." Constable's freshly perceived landscapes celebrate the physical beauty of the rivers, trees, and cottages of his native Suffolk countryside even as they describe the mundane labors of its inhabitants (Figure **27.5**). Like Wordsworth, who tried to illustrate "incidents and situations from common life," Constable chose to paint ordinary and humble subjects—"water escaping from mill-dams, willows, old rotten planks, slimy posts, and brickwork"—as he described them. And like Wordsworth, Constable drew on his childhood experiences as sources of inspiration. "Painting,"

**Figure 27.5** John Constable, *The Haywain*, 1821. Oil on canvas, 4 ft. 3½ in. × 6 ft. 1 in. National Gallery, London.

**Figure 27.6** John Constable, *Wivenhoe Park, Essex*, 1816. Oil on canvas, 22⅛ × 39⅞ in. © 1998 Board of Trustees, National Gallery of Art, Washington, D.C. Widener Collection.

Constable explained, "is with me but another word for feeling and I associate 'my careless boyhood' with all that lies on the banks of the Stour [River]; those scenes made me a painter, and I am grateful."

Constable brought to his landscapes a sensitive blend of empirical detail and freedom of form. Fascinated by nineteenth-century treatises on the scientific classifications of clouds, he made numerous oil studies of cloud formations, noting on the reverse of each sketch the time of the year, hour of the day, and direction of the wind. He confessed to an "over-anxiety" about his skies and feared that he might destroy "that easy appearance which nature always has in all her movements." In order to capture the "easy appearance" of nature and the fugitive effects of light and atmosphere, Constable often stippled parts of the landscape with white dots (compare Vermeer; see chapter 22)—a device critics called "Constable's snow." His finished landscapes thus record not so much the "look" of nature as its fleeting moods. In *Wivenhoe Park, Essex*, Constable depicts cattle grazing on English lawns which typically resemble well-manicured gardens (Figure **27.6**; see also Part Opener, p. xvi). From the distant horizon, the residence of the owners overlooks a verdant estate. Brilliant sunshine floods through the trees and across the fields onto a lake that is shared by swans and fishermen. But the real subject of the painting is the sky, which, with its windblown clouds, preserves the spontaneity of Constable's oil sketches.

If Constable's landscapes describe nature in its humble and contemplative guises, Turner's render nature at its most sublime. Turner began his career making topographical drawings of picturesque and architectural subjects; these he sold to engravers, who, in turn, mass-produced and marketed them in great numbers. One of these early drawings, the ruined monastery of Tintern Abbey, calls attention to the transience of worldly beauty and reflects the romantic artist's nostalgia for the Gothic past (see Figure 27.1). Between 1814 and 1830, Turner traveled extensively throughout England and the Continent, making landscape studies of the mountains and lakes of Switzerland, the breathtaking reaches of the Alps, and the picturesque cities of Italy. His systematic tours inspired hundreds of rapid pencil sketches and luminous, intimate studies executed in the spontaneous (and portable) medium of watercolor.

In contrast with the peaceful lyricism of his early landscapes, Turner's mature style investigated nature's more turbulent moods. As subjects for large-sized canvases, Turner frequently seized on natural disasters—great storms and Alpine avalanches—and human catastrophes such as shipwrecks and destructive fires. Many of Turner's seascapes treat the sea as a symbol for nature's indomitable power—a favorite romantic theme, and one that prevails in Coleridge's *Rime of the Ancient Mariner* (1798), Théodore Géricault's painting, *The Raft of the "Medusa"* (see Figure 29.4), and Herman Melville's monumental sea novel, *Moby Dick* (1851), to name only three examples. In *The Slave Ship* of 1840 (Figure **27.7**), the aesthetic effects of the glowing sunset, turbulent seas, impending storm, and fantastic fish (that appear to devour the remains of the shackled body in the right foreground) distract the viewer from

**Figure 27.7** (above) J. M. W. Turner, *The Slave Ship (Slavers Throwing Overboard the Dead and Dying: Typhon Coming On)*, 1840. Oil on canvas, $35\frac{3}{4} \times 48\frac{1}{4}$ in. The Museum of Fine Arts, Boston. Henry Lillie Pierce Fund.

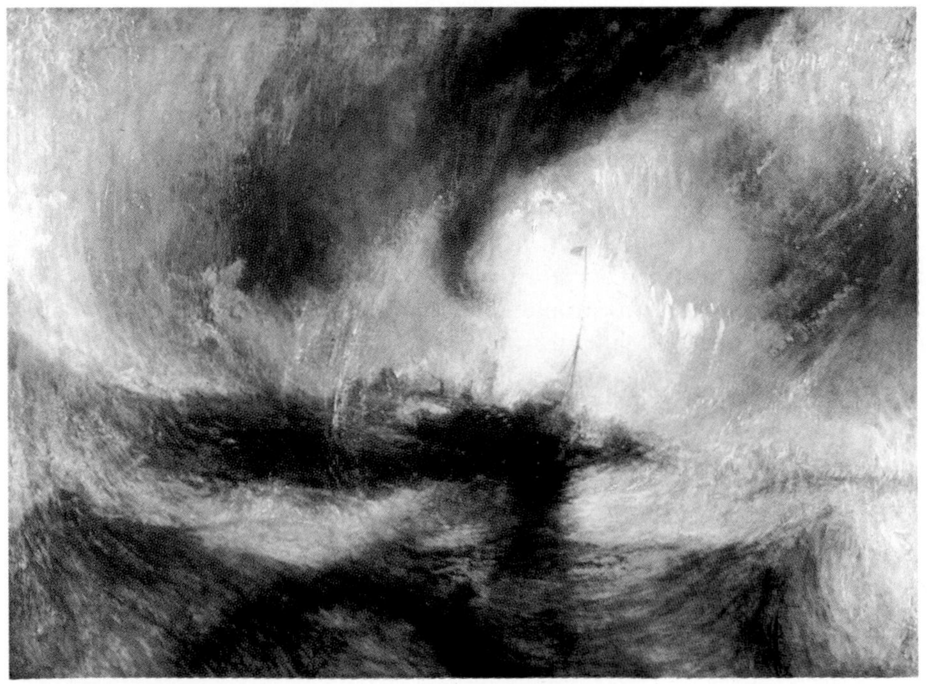

**Figure 27.8** J. M. W. Turner, *Snowstorm: Steamboat off a Harbour's Mouth*, 1842. Oil on canvas, 3 ft. × 4 ft. Tate Gallery, London.

the complex social issue boldly described in the original title: *Slavers Throwing Overboard the Dead and Dying: Typhon Coming On*. While Britain had finally abolished slavery throughout the British colonies in 1838, popular literature on the history of the slave trade published in 1839 described in some detail the notorious activity that inspired Turner's painting: the Transatlantic traders' practice of throwing overboard the dead and dying bodies of African slaves (see chapter 25). On the eve of rising British commercialism (see chapter 30), Turner seems to suggest that the human capacity for destruction rivals nature's cruelest powers.

Two years later, in *Snowstorm* (Figure **27.8**), Turner explored his own romantic engagement with nature: The sixty-seven-year-old artist claimed that, at his request, sailors lashed him to the mast of a ship caught for hours in a storm at sea so that he might "show what such a scene was like." He subtitled the painting "Steamboat off a Harbour's Mouth making Signals in Shallow Water . . . the Author was in this Storm on the Night the Ariel left Harwich." Since no ship by that name is listed in the records of the port of Harwich, Turner's imagination may have exceeded his experience. Nevertheless, as with many of Turner's late works, *Snowstorm* is an exercise in sensation and intuition. It is the imaginative transformation of an intense physical experience, which, recollected thereafter, evokes—as Wordsworth declared—"a sense sublime/Of something far more deeply interfused,/ Whose dwelling place is the light of setting suns,/And the round ocean and the living air,/And the blue sky, and in the mind of man." Indeed, Turner's "landscapes of the sublime" come closer to capturing the spirit of Wordsworth's nature mysticism than do Constable's gentler views of the physical landscape. Their expanding and contracting forms, their swirling masses of paint, and their startling bursts of color are also comparable to the impassioned rhythms and brilliant dynamics of much romantic music.

Turner's late paintings are daringly innovative. His luminous landscapes, haunted by suggestive, "empty" spaces, have more in common with Chinese landscapes than with traditional Western ones. Critics disparagingly called Turner's transparent veils of color—resembling his beloved watercolors—"tinted steam" and "soapsuds." Nevertheless, in dozens of canvases that he never dared to exhibit during his lifetime, Turner all but abandoned recognizable subject matter; these experiments in light and color anticipated (and even outreached) the French impressionists by more than three decades.

## Landscape Painting in Germany and France

Outside of England, German landscape artists took a profoundly spiritual view of nature. The paintings of Constable's contemporary, Caspar David Friedrich (1774–1840), which often include ruined Gothic

**Figure 27.9** Caspar David Friedrich, *Two Men Looking at the Moon*, 1819–1820. Oil on panel, 13¾ × 17¼ in. Gemäldegalerie Neue Meister, Dresden.

**Figure 27.10** Jean-Baptiste-Camille Corot, *Ville d'Avray*, 1870. Oil on canvas, 21⅝ × 31½ in. The Metropolitan Museum of Art, New York. Catharine Lorillard Wolfe Collection. Bequest of Catharine Lorillard Wolfe, 1887 (87.15.141). © 1980 The Metropolitan Museum of Art.

chapels and wintry graveyards, are elegiac remnants of a vanished world. In *Two Men Looking at the Moon* (Figure **27.9**), Friedrich silhouettes a craggy, half-uprooted tree against a glowing, moonlit sky. At the brink of a steep cliff, overlooking the perilous edge of the earth, stand two male figures. Somber colors add to the mood of poetic loneliness in a universe whose vast mysteries might be contemplated by what Friedrich called "our spiritual eye." As a comment on the eternal dialogue between man and nature, the painting has much in common with traditional Chinese landscapes (compare Figure 27.3).

In contrast to Friedrich, French landscape painters made unsentimental but poetic renderings of the local countryside. The artists of the Barbizon school—named after the picturesque village on the edge of the Forest of Fontainebleau near Paris—were the first to take their easels out of doors. Working directly from nature (though usually finishing the canvas in the studio), they painted modest landscapes and scenes of rural life that evoked the realists' unembellished vision of the world; the romantic-realists of the Barbizon school were highly successful in capturing nature's moods. The greatest French landscape painter of the mid-nineteenth century, Jean-Baptiste-Camille Corot (1796–1875), shared the Barbizon preference for working outdoors, but Corot brought to his landscapes a breathtaking sense of harmony and tranquillity. Corot's early landscapes, executed for the most part in Italy, are as formally composed as the paintings of Poussin and David, but they are at once simpler, more personal, and more serene. In his late canvases, Corot created luminescent landscapes that are intimate and contemplative (Figure **27.10**). Corot called them "souvenirs," that is, remembrances, to indicate that they were recollections of previous visual experiences, rather than on-the-spot accounts. These poetic landscapes, filled with feathery trees and misty rivers, and bathed in nuances of silver light, became so popular in France and elsewhere that Corot was able to sell as many canvases as he could paint. Even in his own time, forgeries of Corot's work abounded.

## *American Romanticism*

### Transcendentalism

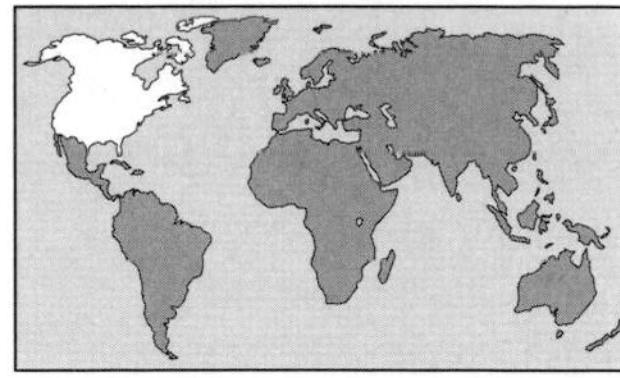

Across the Atlantic, along the eastern shores of the rapidly industrializing American continent, romanticism took hold both as an attitude of mind and as a style. Romanticism infused all aspects of nineteenth-century American culture: It distinguished the frontier tales of James Fenimore Cooper (1789–1851), the mysteries of Edgar Allan Poe (1809–1849), and the novels of Nathaniel Hawthorne (1804–1864) and Herman Melville (1819–1891). But it found its purest expression in a movement known as *transcendentalism*. The transcendentalists were a group of New England intellectuals who held that knowledge gained by way of intuition transcended or surpassed knowledge based on reason and logic. They believed that the direct experience of nature united one with God. They exalted individualism and self-reliance and urged that human beings discover their higher spiritual selves through sympathy with nature. Reacting against the material excesses of advancing industrialism, the transcendentalists embraced such antimaterialistic philosophies as neoplatonism (see chapter 16), Asian mysticism (see chapters 2 and 14), and German idealism (see chapter 25). Though the transcendentalists were the descendants of English Puritans, they sought spiritual instruction in Eastern religious philosophies that had reached the Boston area in the early nineteenth century. From Hinduism and Buddhism, the transcendentalists adopted a holistic philosophy based in pantheism: the belief that all aspects of the universe are infused with spiritual divinity. It followed as well that all living things derived their being from the same universal source and therefore shared a "universal brotherhood"—the unity of humanity, nature, and God.

The prime exemplar of the transcendentalists was Ralph Waldo Emerson (1803–1882), whose essays powerfully influenced nineteenth-century American thought. Like Wordsworth, Emerson courted nature to "see into the life of things" and to taste nature's cleansing power. In the essay entitled *Nature,* Emerson sets forth his pantheistic credo:

> In the woods is perpetual youth. Within these plantations of God, a decorum and sanctity reign, a perennial festival is dressed, and the guest sees not how he should tire of them in a thousand years. In the woods, we return to reason and faith. There I feel that nothing can befall me in life—no disgrace, no calamity (leaving my eyes), which nature cannot repair. Standing on the bare ground—my head bathed by the blithe air and uplifted into infinite space—all mean egotism vanishes. I become a transparent eyeball; I am nothing; I see all; the currents of the Universal Being circulate through me; I am part or parcel of God.*

Although best known for his essays, Emerson was a poet of considerable talent. He shared with Coleridge and Wordsworth (both of whom he had met in England) a mystic reverence for nature; but he also brought to his poetry a unique appreciation of Asian philosophy, which he had acquired by reading some of the central works of Hindu literature, including the *Bhagavad Gita* (see chapter 2). In Emerson's short poem "Brahma," the voice of the Absolute Spirit and World Creator reminds the reader that a single identity—Brahma him/her/itself—underlies all apparent differences in nature. All universal forces, explains Brahma—even death and birth ("shadow and sunlight")—are one, the knowledge of which supersedes Heaven.

**READING 5.5**

### Emerson's "Brahma"

If the red slayer[1] think he slays,
  Or if the slain think he is slain,
They know not well the subtle ways
  I keep, and pass, and turn again.

Far or forgot to me is near;
  Shadow and sunlight are the same;
The vanished gods to me appear;
  And one to me are shame and fame.

They reckon ill who leave me out;
  When me they fly, I am the wings;
I am the doubter and the doubt,
  And I the hymn the Brahmin[2] sings.

The strong gods[3] pine for my abode,
  And pine in vain the sacred Seven;[4]
But thou, meek lover of the good!
  Find me, and turn thy back on heaven.

◆

Emerson's friend Henry David Thoreau (1817–1862) carried transcendentalism to its logical end by literally returning to nature. Thoreau had completed a degree at Harvard University and made his way in the

* *The Complete Essays and Other Writings of Ralph Waldo Emerson*, ed. Brooks Atkinson. New York: The Modern Library, 1950, 6.

[1]Siva, the Hindu god who represents the destructive (and also the recreative) force in nature; with Brahma and Vishnu, one of the three central deities in the Hindu pantheon.
[2]Hindu priest.
[3]*Devas* or angelic beings.
[4]The seven highest Hindu saints.

world by tutoring, surveying, and making pencils. An avid opponent of slavery, he was jailed briefly for refusing to pay a poll tax to a proslavery government. In an influential essay on civil disobedience, he described the philosophy of passive resistance and moral idealism that he himself practiced—a philosophy embraced by the twentieth-century leaders Mohandas Karamchand Gandhi and Martin Luther King. In 1845 Thoreau abandoned urban society to live in the Massachusetts woods near Walden Pond—an experiment that lasted twenty-six months. He described his love of the natural world, his nonconformist attitude toward society, and his deep commitment to monkish simplicity in his "handbook for living," called simply *Walden*. In this intimate yet forthright diary, from which the following excerpts are drawn, Thoreau glorifies nature as innocent and beneficent—a source of joy and practical instruction.

## READING 5.6

### From Thoreau's *Walden*

Near the end of March, 1845, I borrowed an axe and went down to the woods by Walden Pond, nearest to where I intended to build my house, and began to cut down some tall, arrowy white pines, still in their youth, for timber. . . . It was a pleasant hillside where I worked, covered with pine woods, through which I looked out on the pond, and a small open field in the woods where pines and hickories were springing up. The ice in the pond was not yet dissolved, though there were some open spaces, and it was all dark-colored and saturated with water. There were some slight flurries of snow during the days that I worked there; but for the most part when I came out on to the railroad, on my way home, its yellow sand-heap stretched away gleaming in the hazy atmosphere, and the rails shone in the spring sun, and I heard the lark and pewee and other birds already come to commence another year with us. They were pleasant spring days, in which the winter of man's discontent was thawing as well as the earth, and the life that had lain torpid began to stretch itself. One day, when my axe had come off and I had cut a green hickory for a wedge, driving it with a stone, and had placed the whole to soak in a pond-hole in order to swell the wood, I saw a striped snake run into the water, and he lay on the bottom, apparently without inconvenience, as long as I stayed there, or more than a quarter of an hour; perhaps because he had not yet fairly come out of the torpid state. It appeared to me that for a like reason men remain in their present low and primitive condition; but if they should feel the influence of the spring of springs arousing them, they would of necessity rise to a higher and more ethereal life. I had previously seen the snakes on frosty mornings in my path with portions of their bodies still numb and inflexible, waiting for the sun to thaw them. On the 1st of April it rained and melted the ice, and in the early part of the day, which was very foggy, I heard a stray goose groping about over the pond and cackling as if lost, or like the spirit of the fog. . . .

I went to the woods because I wished to live deliberately, to front only the essential facts of life, and see if I could not learn what it had to teach, and not, when I came to die, discover that I had not lived. I did not wish to live what was not life, living is so dear; nor did I wish to practice resignation, unless it was quite necessary. I wanted to live deep and suck out all the marrow of life, to live so sturdily and Spartan-like as to put to rout all that was not life, to cut a broad swath and shave close, to drive life into a corner, and reduce it to its lowest terms, and, if it proved to be mean, why then to get the whole and genuine meanness of it, and publish its meanness to the world; or if it were sublime, to know it by experience, and be able to give a true account of it in my next excursion. For most men, it appears to me, are in a strange uncertainty about it, whether it is of the devil or of God, and have *somewhat hastily* concluded that it is the chief end of man here to "glorify God and enjoy him forever." . . .

Simplicity, simplicity, simplicity! I say, let your affairs be as two or three, and not a hundred or a thousand; instead of a million count half a dozen, and keep your accounts on your thumb-nail. . . . Instead of three meals a day, if it be necessary eat but one; instead of a hundred dishes, five; and reduce other things in proportion. . . .

The indescribable innocence and beneficence of Nature,—of sun and wind and rain, of summer and winter,—such health, such cheer, they afford forever! and such sympathy have they ever with our race, that all Nature would be affected, and the sun's brightness fade, and the winds would sigh humanely, and the clouds rain tears, and the woods shed their leaves and put on mourning in midsummer, if any man should ever for a just cause grieve. Shall I not have intelligence with the earth? Am I not partly leaves and vegetable mould myself? . . .

◆

## Walt Whitman's Romantic Individualism

Though technically not a transcendentalist, Walt Whitman (1818–1892; Figure **27.11**) gave voice to the transcendental worldview in his euphoric poetry. Whitman followed Emerson's advice and lived according to the motto of self-reliance. He served as a male nurse in an American Civil War hospital and wrote articles and poems that celebrated his love for the American landscape. Like Wordsworth, Whitman took everyday life as his theme, but he rejected artificial poetic diction more

**1790** the cotton mill inaugurates the Industrial Revolution in America
**1792** Eli Whitney (American) manufactures the first effective cotton gin
**1803** Robert Fulton (American) produces the first steam-powered ship
**1831** Cyrus McCormick (American) introduces the horse-drawn reaper for harvesting

completely than Wordsworth had. His natural voice bellowed a "barbaric yawp" that found ideal expression in **free verse** (poetry based on irregular rhythmic patterns rather than on the conventional use of meter). Whitman molded his bold rhythms and sonorous cadences by means of standard poetic devices, such as **alliteration**, assonance, and repetition. Whitman loved Italian opera, and his style often simulates the musical grandeur of that genre. He also loved the American landscape, a source of endless inspiration for his sprawling, cosmic images. In "Song of Myself," the longest of the lyric poems included in the autobiographical collection called *Leaves of Grass,* we come face to face with the expansive individualism that typified the romantic movement. At the same time, we are struck by Whitman's impassioned quest for unity with nature and with all humanity.

**Figure 27.11** Thomas Eakins, *Walt Whitman,* 1888. Oil on canvas, $30\frac{1}{8} \times 24\frac{1}{4}$ in. Courtesy of the Museum of American Art of the Pennsylvania Academy of the Fine Arts, Philadelphia. General Fund 1917.1.

## READING 5.7

## From Whitman's "Song of Myself"

### 1

I celebrate myself, and sing myself,
And what I assume you shall assume,
For every atom belonging to me as good belongs to you.

I loaf and invite my soul,
I learn and loaf at my ease observing a spear of summer
grass.

My tongue, every atom of my blood, form'd from this soil,
this air,
Born of parents born here from parents the same, and
their parents the same,
I, now thirty-seven years old in perfect health begin,
Hoping to cease not till death.

Creeds and schools in abeyance,
Retiring back a while sufficed at what they are, but never
forgotten,
I harbor for good or bad, I permit to speak at every hazard,
Nature without check with original energy.

### 24

Walt Whitman, a kosmos, of Manhattan the son,
Turbulent, fleshy, sensual, eating, drinking and breeding,
No sentimentalist, no stander above men and women or
apart from them,
No more modest than immodest.

Unscrew the locks from the doors!
Unscrew the doors themselves from their jambs!
Whoever degrades another degrades me,
And whatever is done or said returns at last to me.
Through me the afflatus surging and surging, through me
the current and index.

I speak the pass-word primeval, I give the sign of
democracy,
By God! I will accept nothing which all cannot have their
counterpart of on the same terms.

Through me many long dumb voices,
Voices of the interminable generations of prisoners and
slaves,
Voices of the diseas'd and despairing and of thieves and
dwarfs,
Voices of cycles of preparation and accretion,
And of the threads that connect the stars, and of wombs
and of the father-stuff,
And of the rights of them the others are down upon,
Of the deform'd, trivial, flat, foolish, despised,
Fog in the air, beetles rolling balls of dung.

Through me forbidden voices,
Voices of sexes and lusts, voices veil'd and I remove the
veil,
Voices indecent by me clarified and transfigur'd.

I do not press my fingers across my mouth,
I keep as delicate around the bowels as around the head
and heart,
Copulation is no more rank to me than death is.

I believe in the flesh and the appetites,
Seeing, hearing, feeling, are miracles, and each part and
tag of me is a miracle.

Divine am I inside and out, and I make holy whatever I
touch or am touch'd from,
The scent of these arm-pits aroma finer than prayer,
This head more than churches, bibles, and all the creeds.

. . . . . . . . . . .

**52**

The spotted hawk swoops by and accuses me, he complains of my gab and my loitering.

I too am not a bit tamed, I too am untranslatable,
I sound my barbaric yawp over the roofs of the world.

The last scud of day holds back for me,
It flings my likeness after the rest and true as any on the shadow'd wilds,
It coaxes me to the vapor and the dusk.

I depart as air, I shake my white locks at the runaway sun,
I effuse my flesh in eddies, and drift it in lacy jags.

I bequeath myself to the dirt to grow from the grass I love,
If you want me again look for me under your boot-soles.

You will hardly know who I am or what I mean,
But I shall be good health to you nevertheless,
And filter and fibre your blood.

Failing to fetch me at first keep encouraged,
Missing me one place search another,
I stop somewhere waiting for you.

◆

## American Landscape Painting

Landscape painters in America mirrored the sentiments of the transcendentalists by capturing on canvas "the indescribable innocence and beneficence of nature" (Thoreau). As with the paintings of Constable and Corot, American landscapes reveal a clear delight in natural beauty and a fascination with nature's fleeting and dramatic moods; a distinguishing feature of American landscapes is their evocation of nature as unspoiled and resplendent. Every detail of a vast panorama is captured on canvas, as if the artist felt compelled to record with photographic precision the majesty and moral power of the American continent and, at the same time, celebrate the magnitude of its untamed wilderness. Panorama and precision are features found in the topographic landscapes of the Hudson River school—a group of artists who worked chiefly in the region of upstate New York during the 1830s and 1840s. One of the leading figures of the Hudson River school was the British-born Thomas Cole (1801–1848), whose *Oxbow* offers a view of the Connecticut River near Northampton, Massachusetts (Figure **27.12**). In this landscape, Cole achieved a dramatic mood by framing

**Figure 27.12** Thomas Cole, *The Oxbow (View from Mount Holyoke, Northampton, Massachusetts, After a Thunderstorm)*, 1836. Oil on canvas, 4 ft. 3½ in. × 6 ft. 4 in. The Metropolitan Museum of Art, New York. Gift of Mrs. Russell Sage, 1908 (08.228). © 1986 The Metropolitan Museum of Art.

**Figure 27.13** Albert Bierstadt, *The Rocky Mountains, Lander's Peak*, 1863. Oil on canvas, 6 ft. 1 in. × 10 ft. ¾ in. The Metropolitan Museum of Art, New York. Rogers Fund, 1907 (07.123).


**Figure 27.14** Frederic Edwin Church, *Rainy Season in the Tropics*, 1866. Oil on canvas, 4 ft. 8¼ in. × 7 ft. ¼ in. Fine Arts Museums of San Francisco. Mildred Anna Williams Collection, 1970.9.

the brightly lit hills and curving river of the distant vista with the darker motifs of an impending thunderstorm and a blighted tree.

Intrigued by America's drive to settle the West, nineteenth-century artists made panoramic depictions of that virginal territory. Albert Bierstadt's landscape of the Rocky Mountains, which includes a Native American encampment in the foreground, reflects the German-born artist's fascination with the templelike purity of America's vast, rugged spaces along the Western frontier (Figure **27.13**). The isolated settlement, dwarfed and enshrined by snowcapped mountains, a magnificent waterfall, and a looking-glass lake—all bathed in golden light—is an American Garden of Eden, inhabited by tribes of unspoiled "noble savages." Bierstadt, who like Keats and Shelley (and numerous American artist/tourists) had toured Italy, gave new meaning to the ancient image of the idyllic landscape, in which man and nature flourish in perfect harmony. At the same time, the painting gave public evidence of the American taste for expansion and empire-building, a visible reflection of nineteenth-century American nationalism. Significantly, the size of Bierstadt's painting (some 6 × 10 feet) heralded the official establishment of landscape as a genre: Academic tradition had dictated that large canvases were appropriate only for the representation of serious themes.

Panoramic landscapes with views of exotic, faraway places were popular nineteenth-century substitutes for actual travel, and viewers were known to carry binoculars to their showings, admission to which usually required entrance fees. Such was in fact the case with the paintings of Frederic Edwin Church (1826–1900), a pupil of Thomas Cole. Church's cosmic landscapes, which regularly featured tropical storms, dazzling sunsets, erupting volcanos, and gigantic icebergs, transported gallery patrons to the remote and exotic places—Brazil, Ecuador, Newfoundland—that Church himself had visited. Called by his contemporaries "the Michelangelo of landscape art," Church invested his vistas with a heroic and quasi-religious spirit: In *Rainy Season in the Tropics* (Figure **27.14**), for instance, which he painted at the end of the American Civil War, Church uses a rainbow—the symbol of divine benevolence and restored harmony—as the unifying motif. Much like the other nineteenth-century romantics, Church conceived the landscape as the vehicle for a moralizing message—here a political one.

## America and Native Americans

The romantic fascination with unspoiled nature and "natural man" also inspired documentary studies of Native Americans (Figure **27.15**), such as those executed by the artist/ethnologist George Catlin (1796–1872). During the 1830s, Catlin went to live among the Native Americans of the Great Plains. Moved by what he called the "silent and stoic dignity" of America's tribal peoples, he recorded their lives and customs in literature, as well as in hundreds of drawings and paintings. Catlin's "Gallery of Indians," exhibited widely in mid-nineteenth-century Europe, drew more acclaim abroad than it did in his native country. Catlin popularized the image of Native Americans as people who deeply respected nature and the natural world (see chapter 19). He described native rituals designed to honor the Great Spirit (or Great Sun) and promote health and fertility. Observing that most tribes killed only as much game as was actually needed to feed themselves, Catlin brought attention to the Indians as the first ecologists.

**Figure 27.15** George Catlin, *The White Cloud, Head Chief of the Iowas*, 1844–1845. Oil on canvas, 28 × 22⅞ in. © 1998 Board of Trustees, National Gallery of Art, Washington, D.C. Paul Mellon Collection.

Harmony with nature and its living creatures, a central feature of Native American culture, was an authentic expression of the pantheistic idealism embraced by the American romantics in their own worship of nature. Following ancestral tradition, Native Americans of the nineteenth century looked upon living things—plants, animals, and human beings—as sacred parts of an all-embracing, spiritually-charged environment. Their arts, which for the most part served religious and communal purposes, reflected their need to protect the balance between these natural forces and to take spiritual advantage of their transformative and healing powers. Woodcarving, pottery, basket-weaving, beadwork embroidery, sandpainting, and other crafts make significant use of natural imagery, but do so in ways that are profoundly different from the artistic enterprises of the European and American romantics: Whereas Western artists perceived nature from "without," as a source of moral and aesthetic inspiration, Native American artists perceived nature from "within," as a resource to be harnessed and appeased. While Western artists recreated the physical appearance of the natural world as a stage for powerful human actions and emotional states, Native Americans stylized individual natural elements to adorn functional and ceremonial objects that embodied the spiritual bond between animals, plants, and humans. A polychrome water jar from the Zuni Pueblos of the American Southwest, for instance, is treated as a living being whose spirit or breath may escape from the bowl by means of an opening in the path (the double line) painted around the vessel's shoulder (Figure **27.16**). Likewise, the deer represented on the bowl bears a line that links heart and mouth—a convention that, like the spirit line, derives from prehistoric pottery decoration.

Not the panoramic landscape, but the natural forces and living creatures immediate to that landscape, preoccupied native artists. As Catlin observed while living with the Plains Indians, natural forms embellished all ceremonial objects, one of the most important of which was the carved stone pipe. Pipes were often presented as gifts to seal tribal alliances. They were believed to be charged with supernatural power, and pipe smoking—both public and private—was a sacred act. Among the Plains Indians, pipes were considered supernaturally "activated" when the stem (symbolic of male power) was joined to the bowl (symbolic of the maternal earth). Often produced jointly by men and women, Plains pipes were carved of catlinite, a red-colored stone quarried in southwestern Minnesota (and so-named because Catlin was the first to bring East samples of this distinctive mineral). Legend identified the stone variously as the flesh of a tribal people or the congealed blood of all dead Indians and dead buffalo. Catlinite pipes served in rituals for healing. They usually bear effigies of mythologically important birds, bears, or water creatures (Figure **27.17**), while those executed after the European introduction of the horse often incorporate that animal as well.

**Figure 27.16** Zuni water jar, nineteenth century. Height 9½ in. Smithsonian Institution, Washington, D.C. Photo: Peter T. Furst, Albany, New York.

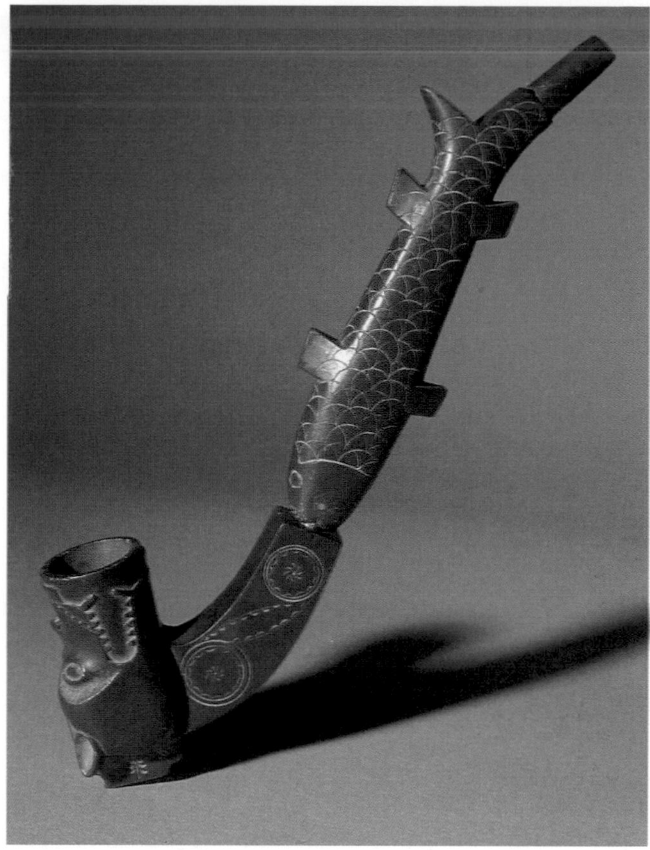

**Figure 27.17** Catlinite pipe (possibly a specialized medicine pipe or one for women's use) representing a fanged and crested water spirit, with fish effigy stem, 1850–1860. Sioux tribe, carved in Minnesota. Length 8⅝ in. Private collection. Photo: Peter T. Furst, Albany, New York.

Popularizing the culture of the Native American in literature, the American poet Henry Wadsworth Longfellow (1807–1882) offered a sentimental picture of American Indian life in his narrative poem *The Song of Hiawatha* (1885), a fictional tale based on the life of a sixteenth-century Mohawk statesman. Unfortunately, neither Longfellow nor Catlin, nor the achievements of the Indians themselves, impeded the wholesale destruction of Native American cultures. Beginning in the

1830s, under pressure from the United States government, tribes were forced to cede their homelands and their hunting grounds to white settlers and to move into unoccupied lands in the American West. The perception of the Native American as the "devil savage" ultimately prevailed over the romantic notion of the "noble savage" and came to justify America's effort to "civilize" its "savage" populations through policies (strongly criticized by Catlin and others) that forced them to take up residence on "reservations" and, more often than not, to abandon their native languages, religions, and traditions. Persecution, humiliation, outright physical attack, and the continuing effects of disease further accelerated the decline and near extinction of America's indigenous peoples.

## *Early Nineteenth-Century Thought*

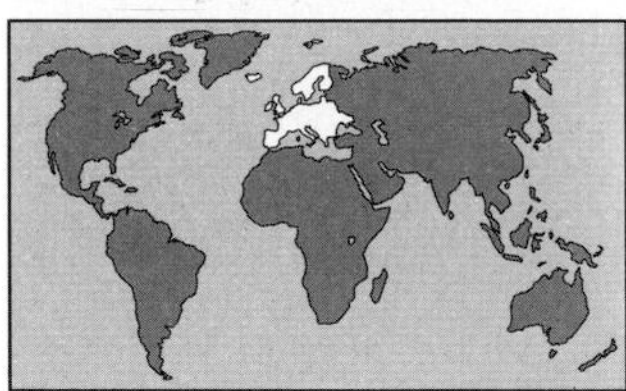

Romanticism found its formal philosophers largely among nineteenth-century German intellectuals. Gottlieb Fichte (1762–1814), Georg Wilhelm Friedrich Hegel (1770–1831), and Arthur Schopenhauer (1788–1860) followed the philosophic idealism of Immanuel Kant (see chapter 25) by exalting the role of the human mind in constructing an idea of the world. According to these thinkers, the truths of empirical experience were not self-evident, as Locke had argued, and the truths of the mind were not clear and distinct, as Descartes had held. The German idealists shared Rousseau's belief in the power of human instinct. And, much like Rousseau and the romantic poets, they viewed nature in deeply subjective terms. Schopenhauer defended the existence of a "life-will," a blind and striving impersonal force whose operations are without purpose or design, and whose activities give rise to disorder and delusion. In Schopenhauer's view, the only escape from malignant reality was selfless contemplation of the kind described in Hindu literature and the mystical treatises of Meister Eckhart (see chapter 15). Welcoming the influence of Indian religious philosophy on European intellectuals, Schopenhauer wrote, "Sanskrit literature will be no less influential for our time than Greek literature was in the fifteenth century for the Renaissance."

While Schopenhauer perceived existence as devoid of reason and burdened by constant suffering, other nineteenth-century metaphysicians moved in the direction of mysticism. Some allied with notable religious mystics such as Friedrich von Hardenberg, better known as Novalis (1772–1801). Novalis shaped the German romantic movement through poems and essays that—like the paintings of Caspar David Friedrich—expressed longing for the lost religious past. The romantic reawakening of religion embraced the doctrines of mysticism, confessional emotionalism, and pantheism, the last of which stressed (as we have seen with Emerson and Whitman) unity of god, man, and nature. According to the foremost German Protestant theologian and preacher, Friedrich E. D. Schleiermacher (1768–1834), the object of religion was "to love the spirit of the world" and "to become one with the infinite." As sentiments of spiritual fervor came to flourish, the once closely allied domains of religion, philosophy, and science moved in independent directions.

### Hegel and the Hegelian Dialectic

The most influential philosopher of the nineteenth century was Hegel. A professor of philosophy at the University of Berlin, Hegel taught that the world consisted of a single divine nature, which he termed "absolute mind" or "spirit." According to Hegel, spirit and matter were involved in an evolutionary process impelled by spirit seeking to know its own nature. Hegel explained the operation of that process, or **dialectic**, as follows: Every condition (or "thesis") confronts its opposite condition (or "antithesis"), which then generates a synthesis. The synthesis in turn produces its opposite, and so on, in a continuing evolution that moves, explained Hegel, toward the ultimate goal of spiritual freedom. For Hegel, all reality was a process that operated on the principle of the dialectic—thesis, antithesis, and synthesis—a principle that governed the realm of ideas, artistic creation, philosophic understanding . . . indeed, history itself. "Change in nature, no matter how infinitely varied it is," wrote Hegel, "shows only a cycle of constant repetition. In nature, nothing new happens under the sun."

In the dense prose work entitled *The Philosophy of History*, actually a compilation of his own and his students' lecture notes, Hegel advanced the idea that the essence of spirit is freedom, which finds its ultimate expression in the state. According to Hegel, human beings possess free will (thesis), which, though freely exercised over property, is limited by duty to the universal will (antithesis). The ultimate synthesis is a stage that is reached as individual will comes into harmony with universal duty. This last stage, which represents

**1799** paleontologist William Smith (British) theorizes that rock strata may be identified by fossils characteristic to each
**1830** Charles Lyell (British) provides foundations for the modern study of geology in his *Principles of Geology*
**1859** Darwin publishes *The Origin of Species*

real freedom, manifests itself in the concrete institutions of the state and its laws. Hegel's view of the state (and the European nation-state in particular) as the last stage in the development of spirit and the Hegelian dialectic in general had enormous influence on late nineteenth-century nationalism, as well as on the economic theories of Karl Marx (see chapter 30).

## Darwin and the Theory of Evolution

Like Hegel, the British scientist Charles Darwin (1809–1882) perceived nature as constantly changing. A naturalist in the tradition of Aristotle, Darwin spent his early career amassing enormous amounts of biological and geological data, partly as the result of a five-year voyage to South America aboard the research vessel *HMS Beagle*. Darwin's study of fossils confirmed the view of his predecessors that complex forms of life evolved from a few extremely simple organic forms. The theory of evolution did not originate with Darwin—Goethe, for example, had already suggested that all forms of plant life had evolved from a single primeval plant, and the French biologist Jean-Baptiste de Lamarck (1744–1829) showed that fossils gave evidence of perpetual change in all species. Darwin, however, substantiated the theory of evolution by explaining the process by which evolution occurred. Observing the tendency of organisms to increase rapidly over time and to preserve certain traits favorable to their survival, Darwin concluded that evolution operated by means of natural selection.

By natural selection, Darwin meant a process whereby nature "pruned away" unfavorable traits in a given species, permitting the survival of those creatures most suited to the struggle for life and for reproduction of their species. The elephant's trunk, the giraffe's neck, and the human brain were evidence of adjustments made by each of these species to its environment and proof that any trait that remained advantageous to a species' continuity would prevail in the species. Failure to develop such advantageous traits meant the ultimate extinction of less developed species, in that only the "fittest" survived.

**Figure 27.18** Spoofing evolution, a cartoon of the day portrays an apelike Charles Darwin explaining his controversial theory of evolution to an ape with the help of a mirror. The work appeared in the *London Sketch Book* in May 1874, captioned by two suitable quotations from the plays of Shakespeare: "This is the ape of form" and "Four or five descents since." Archiv für Kunst und Geschichte, Berlin.

In 1859 Darwin published his classic work, *The Origin of Species by Means of Natural Selection, or the Preservation of the Favored Races in the Struggle for Life*. Less than a year later, a commentator observed, "No scientific work that has been published within this century has excited so much general curiosity." But curiosity was among the milder responses to this publication, for Darwin's law of evolution, like Newton's law of gravity, challenged traditional ideas about nature and the world order. For centuries, Westerners had believed that God had supervised creation (as described in Scripture) and that human beings, created in God's image, were God's favored creatures. Darwin's theory of evolution by natural selection did not deny the idea of a divine Creator—indeed, Darwin initially agreed that "it is just as noble a conception of the Deity to believe that He created a few original forms capable of self-development into other and needful forms, as to believe that He required a fresh act of creation to supply the voids caused by the action of His laws." But Darwin's theory implied that natural selection, not divine will, governed natural processes. By the implication that nature and its operations were impersonal, continuous and, indeed, the only source of design in nature, the theory of natural selection challenged the creationist view (supported by the Bible) that a loving God had created a fixed and unchanging number of species. Equally troubling was Darwin's argument (clarified in his later publication, *The Descent of Man*) that the differences between humans and less complex orders of life were differences of degree, not kind, and that all creatures were related to one another by their kinship to lower forms of life (Figure **27.18**).

Clearly, Darwin's conclusions (which nurtured his own reluctant agnosticism) toppled human beings from their elevated place in the hierarchy of living creatures. If the cosmology of Copernicus and Galileo had displaced earth from the center of the solar system, Darwin's theory robbed human beings of their preeminence on that planet. At a single blow, Darwin shattered the harmonious worldviews of both Renaissance humanists and Enlightenment *philosophes*.

Yet, the theory of evolution by natural selection complemented a view of nature in keeping with romanticism, with transcendentalism, and with Asian philosophy, which presupposed an intrinsic unity of all living things. As Thoreau mused, "Am I not partly leaves and vegetable mould myself?" And numerous passages from the writings of Wordsworth, Shelley, Emerson, and Whitman exhibit a similar sort of pantheism. At the same time, Darwin's ideas encouraged the late nineteenth-century movement of "scientism" (the proposition that the methods of the natural sciences should be applied in all areas of rational investigation).

The consequences of Darwin's monumental theory were far-reaching, but his ideas were often oversimplified or misinterpreted, especially by social Darwinists, who applied his theories freely to political, economic, and social life. In the context of European efforts to colonize non-Western territories, for instance, social Darwinists justified the rapacious efforts of powerful groups of people who, seeing themselves as the "fittest," asserted their right to rule over the less powerful peoples of the world. Further, the theory of evolution provided the basis for analyzing civilizations as living organisms with stages of growth, maturity, and decline. However, since Darwin meant by "fitness" the reproductive success of the species, not simply its survival, most applications of his work to social conditions represented a distortion, if not a vulgarization, of his ideas.

Beyond the impact of the theory of evolution by natural selection, Darwin's importance lay in the curiosity and intelligence he brought to his assessment of nature and the natural. Like the romantic poets, Darwin was an eager observer of nature, which he described as vast, energetic, and unceasingly dynamic. In *The Origin of Species*, he exults:

> When we no longer look at an organic being as a savage looks at a ship, as something wholly beyond his comprehension; when we regard every production of nature as one which has had a long history; when we contemplate every complex structure and instinct as the summing up of many contrivances, each useful to the possessor, in the same way as any great mechanical invention is the summing up of the labor, the experience, the reason, and even the blunders of numerous workmen; when we thus view each organic being, how far more interesting . . . does the study of natural history become!

And in the final paragraph of his opus, Darwin brings romantic fervor to his eloquent description of nature's laws:

> It is interesting to contemplate a tangled bank, clothed with many plants of many kinds, with birds singing on the bushes, with various insects flitting about, and with worms crawling through the damp earth, and to reflect that these elaborately constructed forms, so different from each other, and dependent upon each other in so complex a manner, have all been produced by laws acting around us. These laws, taken in the largest sense, being Growth and Reproduction; Inheritance which is almost implied by reproduction; Variability from the indirect and direct action of the conditions of life, and from use and disuse; a Ratio of Increase so high as to lead to a Struggle for Life, and as a consequence to Natural Selection, entailing Divergence of Character and the Extinction of less-improved forms. Thus, from the war of nature, from famine and death, the most exalted object which we are capable of conceiving, namely, the production of the higher animals, directly follows. There is grandeur in this view of life, with its several powers, having been originally breathed by the Creator into a few forms or into one; and that, whilst this planet has gone cycling on according to the fixed law of gravity, from so simple a beginning endless forms most beautiful and most wonderful have been, and are being evolved.*

## *SUMMARY*

Nature provided both a metaphor for the romantic sensibility and a refuge from the evils of nineteenth-century industrialism and urbanization. William Wordsworth, the leading nature poet of the nineteenth century, emphasized the redemptive power of nature and characterized the English landscape as the source of sublime inspiration and moral truth. Wordsworth and

*Charles Darwin, *The Origin of Species by Means of Natural Selection, or the Preservation of the Favored Races in the Struggle for Life*, 6th ed. New York: Appleton, 1892, II, 280, 306.

his contemporaries initiated the romantic movement in England. The romantics stressed the free exercise of the imagination, the liberation of the senses, and the cultivation of a more natural language of poetic expression. Shelley compared the elemental forces of nature with the creative powers of the poet, while Keats rejoiced that nature's fleeting beauty might forever dwell in art. American romantics endowed the quest for natural simplicity with a robust spirit of individualism. The transcendentalists Emerson and Thoreau sought a union of self with nature; Walt Whitman proclaimed his untamed and "untranslatable" ego in sympathy with nature's energy.

The romantic embrace of nature and natural imagery was not confined to the West: In Chinese literature, as reflected in Shen Fu's confessional prose, and in painting, nature was a source of inspiration and personal solace. But it was among Western romantics that the landscape became an independent and publicly acclaimed subject in the visual arts. Constable's contemplative scenes of English country life and Turner's sublime vistas are the visual counterparts of the poems of Wordsworth and Shelley. The elegiac landscapes of Friedrich in Germany and Corot in France reflect the efforts of romantic artists to explore nature's moods as metaphors for human feeling. In the American landscapes of Cole, Bierstadt, and Church, nature becomes the symbol of an unspoiled and rapidly vanishing world; and in the art of George Catlin, the native populations of America are lovingly documented. Among these tribal people, yet another (less romantic but equally mystical) view of nature was at work, as evidenced in the production of magnificent nineteenth-century ceremonial objects.

The romantic view of nature extended to intellectual inquiry: German philosophers, influenced by Asian philosophy and Western mysticism, described the world in terms of powerful organic forces. Hegel proposed a dialectical model according to which all reality, all history, and all ideas moved toward perfect freedom. Darwin's *Origin of Species* argued that, by means of natural selection, all living things including man evolved from a few simple forms and that species evolved into higher forms of life or failed to survive. While the theory of natural selection displaced human beings from their central place in nature, it confirmed the romantic view of the unity of nature and humankind.

## GLOSSARY

**alliteration** a literary device involving the repetition of initial sounds in successive or closely associated words or syllables

**assonance** a literary device involving similarity in sound between vowels followed by different consonants

**dialectic** in Hegelian philosophy, the process by which every condition (or "thesis") confronts an opposite condition (or "antithesis") to resolve in synthesis

**free verse** poetry that is based on irregular rhythmic patterns rather than on the conventional and regular use of meter

**lyric poetry** "lyric" means accompanied by the lyre, hence, verse that is meant to be sung rather than spoken; poetry marked by individual and personal emotion (see also chapter 6)

**pantheism** the belief that a divine spirit pervades all things in the universe

**tone color** the distinctive quality of musical sound made by a voice, a musical instrument, or a combination of instruments; also called "timbre"

## SUGGESTIONS FOR READING

Clark, Kenneth. *Landscape into Art.* Boston: Beacon Press, 1972.

Eiseley, Loren C. *Darwin's Century: Evolution and the Men Who Discovered It.* Garden City, N.J.: Doubleday, 1958.

Furst, Peter T., and Jill L. Furst. *North American Indian Art.* New York: Rizzoli, 1982.

Green, Nicholas. *The Spectacle of Nature: Landscape and Bourgeois Culture in Nineteenth-Century France.* New York: St. Martin's Press, 1993.

Heffernan, James A. W. *The Recreation of Landscape: A Study of Wordsworth, Coleridge, Constable and Turner.* Hanover, Mass.: University Press of New England, 1985.

Himmelfarb, Gertrude. *Darwin and the Darwinian Revolution.* New York: Elephant/Ivan R. Dee, 1996.

Kroeber, Karl. *Romantic Landscape Vision: Constable and Wordsworth.* Madison, Wis.: University of Wisconsin Press, 1975.

McIntish, James. *Thoreau as Romantic Naturalist: His Shifting Stance Toward Nature.* Ithaca, N.Y.: Cornell University Press, 1974.

Penney, David W. *Art of the American Indian Frontier: The Chandler-Pohrt Collection.* Seattle: University of Washington Press, 1992.

Price, Kenneth M. *Whitman and Tradition.* New Haven: Yale University Press, 1990.

Rosenthal, Michael. *Constable: The Painter and his Landscape.* New Haven: Yale University Press, 1983.

Schenk, H. G. *The Mind of the European Romantics.* Garden City, N.Y.: Doubleday, 1969.

Schwab, Raymond. *The Oriental Renaissance: Europe's Rediscovery of India and the East 1680–1880.* New York: Columbia University Press, 1984.

Shanes, Eric. *Turner's Human Landscape.* London: Heinemann, 1990.

Wordsworth, Jonathan, and others. *William Wordsworth and the Age of English Romanticism.* New Brunswick, N.J.: Rutgers University Press, 1989.

# 28
# The Romantic Hero

As the romantics idealized nature and the natural, so they exalted the creative singularity of the individual in the person of the hero. Heroes, whether mortal or semi-divine, traditionally symbolized humanity at its best, most powerful, and most godlike. The heroes of such classics as the *Epic of Gilgamesh*, the *Mahabharata*, the *Iliad*, the *Aeneid*, the *Song of Roland*, and *Sundiata* were larger-than-life male figures with extraordinary expectations, abilities, and goals. The heroes of old embodied the shared values of the culture they represented. Likewise, the romantic hero was a figure of superhuman ambitions and extraordinary achievements. But romantic heroes differed from traditional literary heroes in that they tended to challenge rather than champion the social and moral values of their time. Their heroism lay in their dedication to the causes of liberty and equality. Egocentric and occasionally misanthropic, the heroes of the romantic era were unique personalities, rarely communal symbols. Among the most notable heroes of the era were its artists, whose powers of self-invention exalted their public and private image. Intrigued by European folklore, medieval legend, and Asian customs, romantic artists modeled themselves after the heroes of "exotic" cultures. They passionately defended the notion that artists both create and are created by their art.

Nineteenth-century intellectuals were fascinated by the nature of the heroic personality. The prose essays of Ralph Waldo Emerson (see chapter 27) describe the hero as the ultimate individual: "The sublime," wrote Emerson in a stupendous moment of self-confidence, "is excited in me by the great stoical doctrine, *obey thyself.*" Across the Atlantic, in 1841, the British historian and essayist Thomas Carlyle (1795–1881) published a series of lectures, *On Heroes and Hero-Worship*, in which he glorified hero-gods, prophets, poets, priests, men of letters, and the quasi-legendary Napoleon Bonaparte. Walter Scott (1771–1832) and Alexandre Dumas (1802–1870) wrote historical novels that described the heroic adventures of swashbuckling soldiers and maidens in distress, while Victor Hugo (1802–1885) made sentimental heroes out of egalitarian patriots in the novel *Les Misérables*. Real-life heroes challenged literary heroes in color and daring; Shaka (1787–1828), the Zulu warrior chief, changed the destiny of Southern Africa by aggressive campaigns that united all of the clans in the region to form the Zulu nation.

In America, too, the hero occupied the attention of artists: The novelists Nathaniel Hawthorne (1804–1864) and Herman Melville (1819–1891) created brooding, melancholic fictional heroes whose moral strength was tested by the forces of evil. At the same time, the Americas produced some notable real-life heroes and champions of political freedom, such as Simón Bolívar (1783–1830)—whose victories over the Spanish forces in South America won independence for Bolivia, Colombia, Ecuador, Peru, and Venezuela—and Frederick Douglass (1817–1895), the leading antislavery spokesman, whose autobiography details a heroic life of oppression and struggle.

The nineteenth century did not produce more heroes than other centuries, but it visibly exalted heroic achievement and glorified the role of the heroic imagination. While Enlightenment writers studied the social animal, the romantics explored the depths of their own souls. With a subjectivity bordering on egotism, the romantics saw *themselves* as heroes—the champions of a cult of the senses and of the heart. They eagerly embraced all means of heightening imaginative experience, including those induced by such hallucinogens as opium. "Exister, pour nous, c'est sentir" ("For us, to exist is to feel"), Rousseau had proclaimed in the late eighteenth century. And, on the first page of his *Confessions*, the prophet of romanticism anticipated the sentiments of self-conscious individualism that would drive artists of the next two generations: "I am made unlike anyone I have ever met: I will even venture to say that I am like no one in the whole world. I may be no better, but at least I am different."

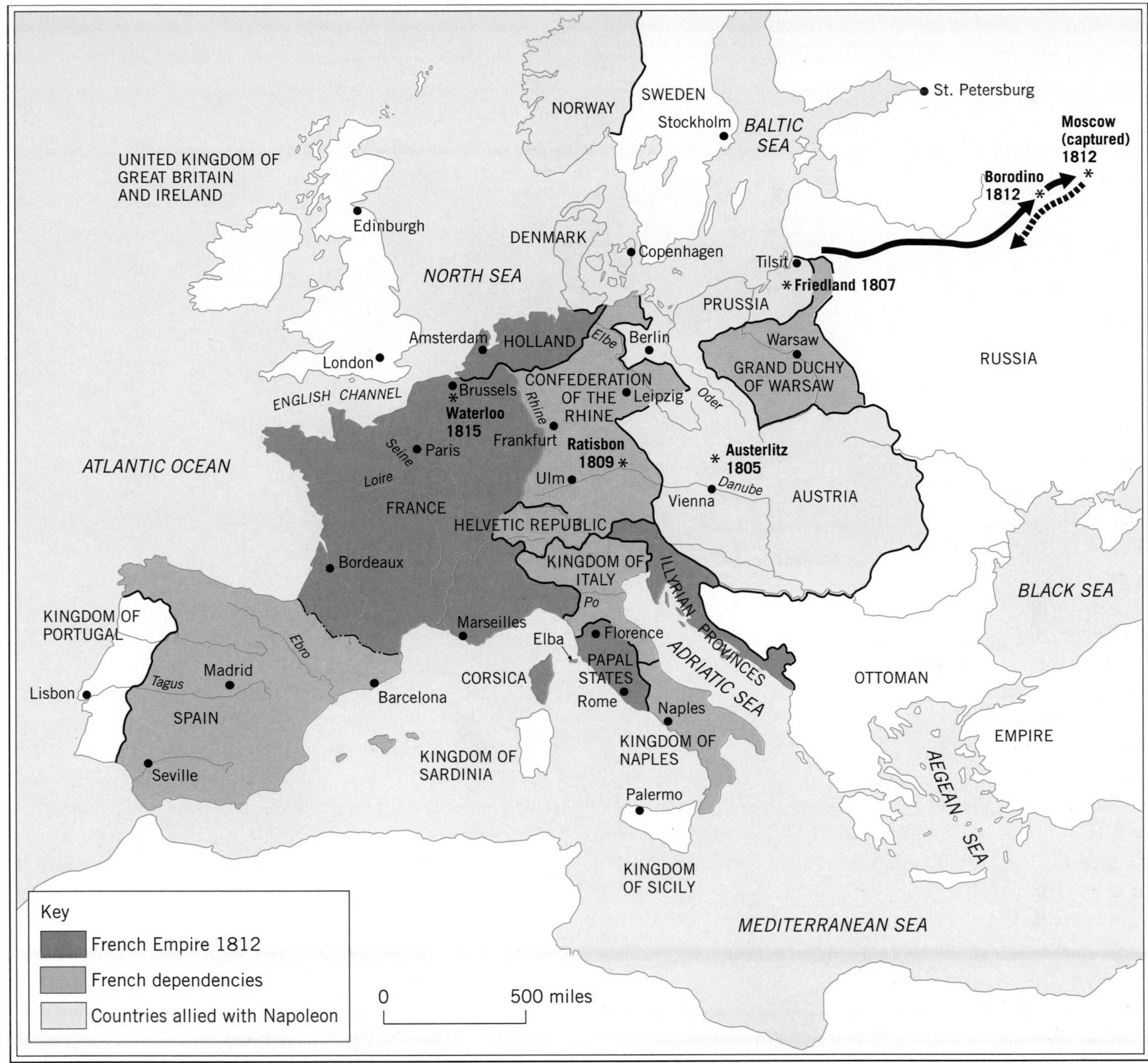


**Map 28.1** The Empire of Napoleon at Its Greatest Extent, 1812.

# *Napoleon as a Romantic Hero*

In 1799 the thirty-year-old Corsican army general Napoleon Bonaparte (1769–1821) seized control of the government of France. "The Revolution is ended," announced Napoleon when he proclaimed himself emperor in 1804. In the following ten years, Napoleon pursued a policy of conquest that brought continental Western Europe to his feet. Throughout much of the West Napoleon abolished serfdom, expropriated Church possessions, curtailed feudal privileges, and introduced French laws, institutions, and influence. Napoleon spread the revolutionary ideals of liberty, fraternity, and equality throughout the empire (Map **28.1**). He championed popular sovereignty and kindled the sentiments of nationalism. In France, Napoleon ended civil strife, reorganized the educational system, and institutionalized the system of civil law known as the *Code Napoléon*.

If Napoleon's ambitions were heroic, his military campaigns were stunning. Having conquered Italy, Egypt, Austria, Prussia, Portugal, and Spain, he pressed on to Russia where, in 1812, bitter weather and lack of food forced his armies to retreat. Only 100,000 of his army of 600,000 survived. In 1813, a coalition of European powers forced his defeat and exile to the island of Elba off the coast of Italy. A second and final defeat occurred after he escaped in 1814, raised a new army, and met the combined European forces led by the

**Figure 28.1** Jacques-Louis David, *Napoleon Crossing the Great Saint Bernard Pass*, 1800. Oil on canvas, 8 ft. 6 in. × 7 ft. 3 in. Musée National du Château de la Malmaison, Rueil-Malmaison, France. Photo: © R.M.N., Paris.

English Duke of Wellington at the battle of Waterloo. The fallen hero spent the last years of his life in exile on the barren island of Saint Helena off the west coast of Africa.

Napoleon, the first of the modern European dictators, left a distinctly neoclassical stamp upon the city of Paris (see chapter 26). However, he also became the nineteenth century's first romantic hero, as envisioned in numerous European poems and paintings, and especially in the majestic portraits of Jacques-Louis David, Napoleon's favorite artist. David's equestrian portrait of Napoleon (Figure **28.1**), which clearly draws on Roman traditions of heroic glorification, shows an idealized Napoleon who is following the path of ancient generals such as Charlemagne and Hannibal (whose names are carved in stone in the foreground). David suggests in this painting—one of five identical versions of the subject—that Napoleon's rule was one of glory and achievement. Napoleon's ideas, as expressed in his diary, were equally significant in cultivating the image of a romantic hero. The diary—an intimate record of personal reflections and feelings—became a favorite mode of expression for such nineteenth-century romantics as Delacroix, Beethoven, George Sand, and Mary Shelley. Napoleon's diary entries of 1800, 1802, and 1817, quoted in Reading 5.8, reveal some of the typical features of the romantic personality: self-conscious individualism, a sense of personal power, unbridled egotism, and a high regard for the life of the imagination.

### READING 5.8

### From Napoleon's *Diary*

Milan, June 17, 1800: . . . What a thing is imagination! Here are men who don't know me, who have never seen me, but who only knew of me, and they are moved by my presence, they would do anything for me! And this same incident arises in all centuries and in all countries! Such is fanaticism! Yes, imagination rules the world. The defect of our modern institutions is that they do not speak to the imagination. By that alone can man be governed; without it he is but a brute.

December 30, 1802: My power proceeds from my reputation, and my reputation from the victories I have won. My power would fall if I were not to support it with more glory and more victories. Conquest has made me what I am; only conquest can maintain me. . . .

Saint Helena, March 3, 1817: In spite of all the libels, I have no fear whatever about my fame. Posterity will do me justice. The truth will be known; and the good I have done will be compared with the faults I have committed. I am not uneasy as to the result. Had I succeeded, I would have died with the reputation of the greatest man that ever existed. As it is, although I have failed, I shall be considered as an extraordinary man: my elevation was unparalleled, because unaccompanied by crime. I have fought fifty pitched battles, almost all of which I have won. I have framed and carried into effect a code of laws that will bear my name to the most distant posterity. I raised myself from nothing to be the most powerful monarch in the world. Europe was at my feet. I have always been of [the] opinion that the sovereignty lay in the people.

◆

# *The Promethean Hero*

## The Promethean Myth in Literature

If Napoleon Bonaparte was nineteenth-century Europe's favorite real-life hero, Prometheus was its favorite fictional hero. Prometheus (the name means "forethought") was one of the primordial deities of Greek mythology. According to legend, Prometheus challenged the other Greek gods by stealing from their home on Mount Olympus the sacred fire, source of divine wisdom and creative inspiration, and bestowing this great gift upon humankind. As punishment, Zeus chained him to a lonely rock, where a vulture fed daily on his liver. A second, less dramatic aspect of the Prometheus story, more popular among the Romans than the Greeks, credited Prometheus with having fashioned human beings out of clay, in the manner of the Babylonian hero-god Marduk (see chapter 2).

Romantic poets embraced the figure of Prometheus as the suffering champion of humanity—a symbol of freedom and a deliverer whose noble ambitions had incurred the wrath of the gods. Percy Bysshe Shelley, whom we met in chapter 27, made Prometheus the savior-hero of his four-act play *Prometheus Unbound* (1820). In this drama, Prometheus frees the universe from the tyranny of the gods. Two years earlier, in 1818, Shelley's second wife, Mary Godwin Shelley (1797–1851), had explored yet another aspect of the Promethean legend in her novel *Frankenstein; or, The Modern Prometheus*. The daughter of William Godwin and the feminist writer Mary Wollstonecraft, Mary Shelley began to write *Frankenstein* at the age of eighteen. Framed as a series of letters, the novel relates the astonishing tale of the scientist/philosopher Victor Frankenstein, who, having discovered the secret of imparting life to inanimate matter, produces a monster endowed with supernatural strength (Figure **28.2**). A modern Prometheus, Frankenstein suffers the punishment for his ambitious designs when the creature, excluded from the normal life of ordinary mortals, betrays its creator: "I was benevolent and good," he protests, "misery made me a fiend." Like the fallen Lucifer, Frankenstein's creature becomes a figure of heroic evil. The novel, excerpts from which appear below, has become a modern classic that has inspired numerous science fiction "spin-offs," as well as cinematic and video interpretations. Ironically, however, it is not the Promethean scientist but the monster that has captured the modern imagination, even to the point of usurping the name of his creator.

## READING 5.9

## From Mary Shelley's *Frankenstein* (Chapters 4 and 5)

. . . One of the phenomena which had peculiarly attracted my attention was the structure of the human frame, and, indeed, any animal endued with life. Whence, I often asked myself, did the principle of life proceed? It was a bold question, and one which has ever been considered as a mystery: yet with how many things are we upon the brink of becoming acquainted, if cowardice or carelessness did not restrain our enquiries. I revolved these circumstances in my mind and determined thenceforth to apply myself more particularly to those branches of natural philosophy which relate to physiology. Unless I had been animated by an almost supernatural enthusiasm, my application to this study would have been irksome and almost intolerable. To examine the causes of life, we must first have recourse to death. I became acquainted with the science of anatomy, but this was not sufficient; I must also observe the natural decay and corruption of the human body. In my education my father had taken the greatest precautions that my mind should be impressed with no supernatural horrors. I do not ever remember to have trembled at a tale of superstition or to have feared the apparition of a spirit. Darkness had no effect upon my fancy, and a churchyard was to be merely the receptacle of bodies deprived of life, which, from being the seat of beauty and strength, had become food for the worm. Now I was led to examine the cause and progress of this decay and forced to spend days and nights in vaults and charnel-houses. My attention was fixed upon every object the most insupportable to the delicacy of the human feelings. I saw how the fine form of man was degraded and wasted; I beheld the corruption of death succeed to the blooming cheek of life; I saw how the worm inherited the wonders of the eye and brain. I paused, examining and analysing all the minutiae of causation, as exemplified in the change from life to death, and death to life, until from the midst of this darkness a sudden light broke in upon me—a light so brilliant and wondrous, yet so simple, that while I became dizzy with the immensity of the prospect which it illustrated, I was surprized that among so many men of genius who had directed their enquiries towards the same science, that I alone should be reserved to discover so astonishing a secret.

Remember, I am not recording the vision of a madman. The sun does not more certainly shine in the heavens than that which I now affirm is true. Some miracle might have produced it, yet the stages of the discovery were distinct and probable. After days and nights of incredible labour and fatigue, I succeeded in discovering the cause of generation and life; nay, more, I became myself capable of bestowing animation upon lifeless matter.

**Figure 28.2** The first illustration of the *Frankenstein* monster, frontispiece from the 1831 Standards Novel edition. Mary Evans Picture Library, London.

The astonishment which I had at first experienced on this discovery soon gave place to delight and rapture. After so much time spent in painful labour, to arrive at once at the summit of my desires was the most gratifying consummation of my toils. But this discovery was so great and overwhelming that all the steps by which I had been progressively led to it were obliterated, and I beheld only the result. What had been the study and desire of the wisest men since the creation of the world was now within my grasp. . . .

. . . Learn from me, if not by my precepts, at least by my example, how dangerous is the acquirement of knowledge and how much happier that man is who believes his native town to be the world, than he who aspires to become greater than his nature will allow.

When I found so astonishing a power placed within my hands, I hesitated a long time concerning the manner in which I should employ it. Although I possessed the capacity of bestowing animation, yet to prepare a frame for the reception of it, with all its intricacies of fibres, muscles, and veins, still remained a work of inconceivable difficulty and labour. I doubted at first whether I should attempt the creation of a being like myself, or one of simpler organization; but my imagination was too much exalted by my first success to permit me to doubt of my ability to give life to an animal as complex and wonderful as man. The materials at present within my command hardly appeared adequate to so arduous an undertaking, but I doubted not that I should ultimately succeed. I prepared myself for a multitude of reverses; my operations might be incessantly baffled, and at last my work be imperfect; yet when I considered the improvement which every day takes place in science and mechanics, I was encouraged to hope my present attempts would at least lay the foundations of future success. Nor could I consider the magnitude and complexity of my plan as any argument of its impracticability. It was with these feelings that I began the creation of a human being. As the minuteness of the parts formed a great hindrance to my speed, I resolved, contrary to my first intention, to make the being of a gigantic stature; that is to say, about eight feet in height, and proportionately large. After having formed this determination and having spent some months in successfully collecting and arranging my materials, I began.

No one can conceive the variety of feelings which bore me onwards, like a hurricane, in the first enthusiasm of success. Life and death appeared to be ideal bounds, which I should first break through, and pour a torrent of light into our dark world. A new species would bless me as its creator and source; many happy and excellent natures would owe their being to me. No father could claim the gratitude of his child so completely as I should deserve theirs. Pursuing these reflections, I thought that if I could bestow animation upon lifeless matter, I might in process of time (although I now found it impossible) renew life where death had apparently devoted the body to corruption.

These thoughts supported my spirits, while I pursued my undertaking with unremitting ardour. My cheek had grown pale with study, and my person had become emaciated with confinement. Sometimes, on the very brink of certainty, I failed; yet still I clung to the hope which the next day or the next hour might realize. One secret which I alone possessed was the hope to which I had dedicated myself; and the moon gazed on my midnight labours, while, with unrelaxed and breathless eagerness, I pursued nature to her hiding-places. Who shall conceive the horrors of my secret toil as I dabbled among the unhallowed damps of the grave or tortured the living animal to animate the lifeless clay? My limbs now tremble, and my eyes swim with the remembrance; but then a resistless and almost frantic impulse urged me forward; I seemed to have lost all soul or sensation but for this one pursuit. It was indeed but a passing trance, that only made me feel with renewed acuteness so soon as, the unnatural stimulus ceasing to operate, I had returned to my old habits. I collected bones from charnel-houses and disturbed, with profane fingers, the tremendous secrets of the human frame. In a solitary chamber, or rather cell, at the top of the house, and separated from all the other apartments by a gallery and staircase, I kept my workshop of filthy creation: my eyeballs were starting from their sockets in attending to the details of my employment. The dissecting room and the slaughter-house furnished many of my materials; and often did my human nature turn with loathing from my occupation, whilst, still urged on by an eagerness which perpetually increased, I brought my work near to a conclusion. . . .

It was on a dreary night of November that I beheld the accomplishment of my toils. With an anxiety that almost amounted to agony, I collected the instruments of life around me, that I might infuse a spark of being into the lifeless thing that lay at my feet. It was already one in the morning; the rain pattered dismally against the panes, and my candle was nearly burnt out, when, by the glimmer of the half-extinguished light, I saw the dull yellow eye of the creation open; it breathed hard, and a convulsive motion agitated its limbs.

How can I describe my emotions at this catastrophe, or how delineate the wretch whom with such infinite pains and care I had endeavoured to form? His limbs were in proportion, and I had selected his features as beautiful. Beautiful! Great God! His yellow skin scarcely covered the work of muscles and arteries beneath; his hair was of a lustrous black, and flowing; his teeth of pearly whiteness; but these luxuriances only formed a more horrid contrast with his watery eyes, that seemed almost of the same colour as the dun-white sockets in which they were set, his shrivelled complexion and straight black lips.

The different accidents of life are not so changeable as the feelings of human nature. I had worked hard for nearly two years, for the sole purpose of infusing life into an inanimate body. For this I had deprived myself of rest and health. I had desired it with an ardour that far exceeded moderation; but now that I had finished, the beauty of the dream vanished, and breathless horror and disgust filled my heart. Unable to endure the aspect of the being I had created, I rushed out of the room and continued a long time traversing my bedchamber, unable to compose my mind to sleep. At length lassitude succeeded to the tumult I had before endured, and I threw myself on the bed in my clothes, endeavouring to seek a few moments of forgetfulness. But it was in vain; I slept, indeed, but I was disturbed by the wildest dreams. I thought I saw Elizabeth, in the bloom of health, walking in the streets of Ingolstadt. Delighted and surprized, I embraced her, but as I imprinted the first kiss on her lips, they became livid with the hue of death; her features appeared to change, and I thought that I held the corpse of my dead mother in my arms; a shroud enveloped her form, and I saw the grave-worms crawling in the folds of the flannel. I started from my sleep with horror; a cold dew covered my forehead, my teeth chattered, and every limb became convulsed; when, by the dim and yellow light of the moon, as it forced its way through the window shutters, I beheld the wretch—the miserable monster whom I had created. He held up the curtain of the bed; and his eyes, if eyes they may be called, were fixed on me. His jaws opened, and he muttered some inarticulate sounds, while a grin wrinkled his cheeks. He might have spoken, but I did not hear; one hand was stretched out, seemingly to detain me, but I escaped and rushed downstairs. I took refuge in the courtyard belonging to the house which I inhabited, where I remained during the rest of the night, walking up and down in the greatest agitation, listening attentively, catching and fearing each sound as if it were to announce the approach of the daemoniacal corpse to which I had so miserably given life.

◆

**Figure 28.3** Thomas Phillips, *Lord Byron Sixth Baron in Albanian Costume*, 1813. Oil on canvas, 29½ × 24½ in. National Portrait Gallery, London.

## Byron and the Promethean Myth

The Promethean myth found its most passionate champion in the life and works of the British poet George Gordon, Lord Byron (1788–1824). Byron was one of the most flamboyant personalities of the age (Figure **28.3**). Dedicated to the pleasures of the senses, he was equally impassioned by the ideals of liberty and brotherhood. In his brief, mercurial life, he established the prototype of the romantic hero, often called—after Byron himself—the Byronic hero. As a young man, Byron (much like Turner) traveled restlessly throughout Europe and the Mediterranean, devouring the landscape and the major sites. A physically attractive man (despite the handicap of a club foot) with dark, brooding eyes, he engaged in numerous love affairs, including one with his half-sister, a union that produced an illegitimate daughter. In 1816, Byron abandoned an unsuccessful marriage and left England for good. He lived in Italy for a time with the Shelleys and a string of mistresses before sailing to Greece, where he died while defending the cause of Greek independence from the Turks.

Throughout his life, Byron was given to periodic bouts of creativity and dissipation. A man of violent passions, he harbored a desperate need to unbosom his innermost thoughts and feelings. In Italy, where he composed two of his greatest poems, *Childe Harold's Pilgrimage* and *Don Juan*, he described his frenzied spirit thus: "half mad . . . between metaphysics, mountains, lakes, love unextinguishable, thoughts unutterable, and the nightmare of my own delinquencies." The heroes of Byron's poems were surely autobiographical: Childe Harold, the wanderer who, alienated from society, seeks companionship in nature; Don Juan, the libertine who cannot satiate his sexual desires; and Prometheus, the god who "stole from Heaven the flame, for which he fell." Prometheus preoccupied Byron as a symbol of triumphant individualism. For Byron, capturing the imagination in art or in life was comparable to stealing the sacred fire. In a number of his poems, Byron compares the fallen Napoleon to the mythic Prometheus—symbol of heroic ambition and ungovernable passions. And, in the stirring ode called simply "Prometheus" (1816), Byron makes of the Promethean myth a parable for the romantic imagination. He begins by recalling the traditional story of the hero whose "Godlike crime was to be kind." He goes on to identify Prometheus as "a symbol and a sign" to mortals who, also "part divine," anticipate their "funereal destiny" but who, like Prometheus, must strive to defy that destiny. Byron's verses mingle defiance and hope with melancholy and despair.

### READING 5.10

### Byron's "Prometheus"

Titan! to whose immortal eyes
  The sufferings of mortality,
  Seen in their sad reality,
Were not as things that gods despise;
What was thy pity's recompense?
A silent suffering, and intense;
The rock, the vulture, and the chain,
All that the proud can feel of pain,
The agony they do not show,
The suffocating sense of woe,
  Which speaks but in its loneliness,
And then is jealous lest the sky
Should have a listener, nor will sigh
  Until its voice is echoless.
Titan! to thee the strife was given
  Between the suffering and the will,
  Which torture where they cannot kill;
And the inexorable Heaven,
And the deaf tyranny of Fate,
The ruling principle of Hate,
Which for its pleasure doth create
The things it may annihilate,
Refused thee even the boon to die:
The wretched gift eternity
Was thine—and thou hast borne it well.
All that the Thunderer[1] wrung from thee

[1]Zeus, the supreme god of the Greeks.

Was but the menace which flung back
On him the torments of thy rack;
The fate thou didst so well foresee,
But would not to appease him tell;
And in thy Silence was his Sentence,
And in his Soul a vain repentance,
And evil dread so ill dissembled,
That in his hand the lightnings trembled.

Thy Godlike crime was to be kind,
  To render with thy precepts less
  The sum of human wretchedness,
And strengthen Man with his own mind;
But baffled as thou wert from high,
Still in thy patient energy,
In the endurance, and repulse
  Of thine impenetrable Spirit,
Which Earth and Heaven could not convulse,
  A mighty lesson we inherit:
Thou art symbol and a sign
  To Mortals of their fate and force;
Like thee, Man is in part divine,
  A troubled stream from a pure source;
And Man in portions can foresee
His own funereal destiny,
His wretchedness, and his resistance,
And his sad unallied existence:
To which his Spirit may oppose
Itself—and equal to all woes,
  And a firm will, and a deep sense,
Which even in torture can descry
  Its own concenter'd recompense,[2]
Triumphant where it dares defy,
And making Death a Victory.

◆

## Pushkin: The Byron of Russia

Napoleon's invasion of Russia in 1812 was one of the most dramatic events in nineteenth-century history. Sorely outnumbered by the Grand Army of Napoleon, Russian troops resorted to a "scorched earth" policy that produced severe shortages of food for French and Russians alike. As Napoleon advanced on Moscow, leaving a trail of bloody battles, the Russians burned their own capital city. Napoleon ultimately captured Moscow, but within a few months he and his badly diminished army retreated from Russia, never to return. Deeply moved by Napoleon's role in stirring Russian patriotism, Alexander Pushkin (1799–1837)—Russia's leading lyric poet and dramatist—eulogized the hero who, as he explains in the poem "Napoleon," had "launched the Russian nation/Upon its lofty destinies."

Pushkin, whose maternal great-grandfather was a black African general, came from an old aristocratic family. Nevertheless, he claimed comradery with Russia's humble commoners and, taking pride in his African ancestry, he boasted "I am a versewright and a bookman, . . . /No financier, no titled footman,/A commoner: great on his own." Like Byron, Pushkin championed political freedom; he defended liberal causes that resulted in his banishment to South Russia and ultimately to his dismissal from the foreign service. His agonizing death, at the age of thirty-seven, was the result of wounds suffered in a duel with his wife's alleged lover. Pushkin's romantic tragedies and long narrative poems show great admiration for Shakespeare and for Pushkin's British contemporary, Byron, and earned him a reputation as "the Byron of Russia." Some of Pushkin's works, such as *Boris Godunov* (1825) and *Eugene Onegin* (1833)—modeled in part on Byron's *Don Juan*—would inspire operas by composers Modest Mussorgsky (1839–1881) and Peter Ilich Tchaikovsky (see chapter 29) respectively. The lyric poem "Napoleon" (1821), part of which follows, conveys Pushkin's gift for buoyant, energetic language and his profound respect for the figure whom he viewed as both the oppressor and the liberator of Russia.

### READING 5.11

### From Pushkin's "Napoleon"

A wondrous fate is now fulfilled,
Extinguished a majestic man.
In somber prison night was stilled
Napoleon's grim, tumultuous span.
The outlawed potentate has vanished,
Bright Nike's mighty, pampered son;
For him, from all Creation banished,
Posterity has now begun.

O hero, with whose bloodied story
Long, long the earth will still resound,
Sleep in the shadow of your glory,
The desert ocean all around . . .
A tomb of rock, in splendor riding!
The urn that holds your mortal clay,
As tribal hatreds are subsiding,
Now sends aloft a deathless ray.

How recently your eagles glowered
Atop a disenfranchised world,
And fallen sovereignties cowered
Beneath the thunderbolts you hurled!
Your banners at a word would shower
Destruction from their folds and dearth,
Yoke after yoke of ruthless power
You fitted on the tribes of earth.

. . . . . . . . . .

Vainglorious man! Where were you faring,
Who blinded that astounding mind?
How came it in designs of daring
The Russian's heart was not divined?

[2]Catch a glimpse of the Spirit's own sufficient reward.

At fiery sacrifice not guessing,
You idly fancied, tempting fate,
We would seek peace and count it blessing;
You came to fathom us too late . . .

Fight on, embattled Russia mine,
Recall the rights of ancient days!
The sun of Austerlitz,[1] decline!
And Moscow, mighty city, blaze!
Brief be the time of our dishonor,
The auspices are turning now;
Hail Moscow—Russia's blessings on her!
War to extinction, thus our vow!

The diadem of iron[2] shaking
In stiffened fingers' feeble clasp,
He stares into a chasm, quaking,
And is undone, undone at last.
Behold all Europe's legions sprawling . . .
The wintry fields' encrimsoned glow
Bore testimony to their falling
Till blood-prints melted with the snow.

. . . . . . . . . . .

Let us hold up to reprobation
Such petty-minded men as chose
With unappeasable damnation
To stir his laurel-dark repose!
Hail him! He launched the Russian nation
Upon its lofty destinies
And augured ultimate salvation
For man's long-exiled liberties.

◆

## The Abolitionists: American Prometheans

Among the most fervent champions of liberty in nineteenth-century America were those who crusaded against the institution of slavery. It is unlikely that the leaders of the abolitionist crusade against slavery regarded themselves in the image of a Napoleon or the fictional Prometheus but, as historical figures, the abolitionists were the heroes of their time. They fought against the enslavement of Africans (and their descendants), a practice that had prevailed in America since the sixteenth century. Although the abolitionists constituted only a small minority of America's population, their arguments were emotionally charged and their protests were often dramatic and telling. The most direct challenge to slavery came from the slaves themselves, and none more so than the slave rebels who—like Prometheus—mounted outright attacks against their owners and masters in their efforts to gain

**Figure 28.4** *Portrait of Frederick Douglass*, 1847. Daguerreotype. National Portrait Gallery, Smithsonian Institution, Washington, D.C. Collection William Rubel.

a prized privilege: freedom. While slave rebellions were rare in nineteenth-century America—between 1800 and 1860 only two reached the level of overt insurrection—the threat or rumor of rebellion was terrifying to slaveowners.

One of the most notable insurrections of the century took place in Southampton County, Virginia, in 1831: Nat Turner (1800–1831), a slave preacher and mystic, believed that he was divinely appointed to lead the slaves to freedom. The Turner rebellion resulted in the deaths of at least fifty-seven whites (and many more blacks, killed when the rebellion was suppressed) and the destruction of several area plantations. Following the defeat of the rebel slaves, the captive Turner explained his motives to a local attorney, who prepared a published version of his account in the so-called "Confessions of Nat Turner."

A longer, more vividly detailed autobiography, the *Narrative of the Life of Frederick Douglass: An American Slave* (1845), came from the pen of the nineteenth century's leading African-American crusader for black freedom (Figure **28.4**). Born a slave on the east coast of Maryland, Douglass had taught himself how to read and write at an early age; he escaped bondage in Baltimore in 1838 and eventually found his way to New England, where he joined the Massachusetts Antislavery Society. A powerful public speaker who captivated his audiences with the account of his life in bondage and in freedom, Douglass served as living proof of the potential of black slaves to achieve brilliantly as free persons. He wrote extensively and eloquently in support of abolition,

[1]The site of Napoleon's greatest victory where, on December 2, 1805, he defeated the combined Austrian and Russian forces, acquiring control of European lands north of Rome and making him King of Italy.
[2]The iron crown of Lombardy, dating back to the fifth century, which Napoleon had assumed some time after the Italian campaigns.

describing the "dehumanizing character of slavery" for both blacks and whites, and defending the idea that, by abandoning slavelike behavior, even slaves could determine their own lives. On occasion, he employed high irony in these accounts, as is the case with his justification of theft as a moral act if perpetrated by a slave against his master. Though it is unlikely that Douglass had in mind any reference to the Promethean theme, the parallel is not without significance. "A Slave's Right to Steal" comes from *My Bondage and My Freedom* (1855), the revised and enlarged version of Douglass' autobiography.

## READING 5.12

## From Douglass' *My Bondage and My Freedom*

. . . There were four slaves of us in the kitchen, and four whites in the great house—Thomas Auld, Mrs. Auld, Hadaway Auld (brother of Thomas Auld), and little Amanda. The names of the slaves in the kitchen, were Eliza, my sister; Priscilla, my aunt; Henry, my cousin; and myself. There were eight persons in the family. There was, each week, one half bushel of corn-meal brought from the mill; and in the kitchen, corn-meal was almost our exclusive food, for very little else was allowed us. Out of this half bushel of corn-meal, the family in the great house had a small loaf every morning; thus leaving us, in the kitchen, with not quite a half a peck of meal per week, apiece. This allowance was less than half the allowance of food on Lloyd's plantation. It was not enough to subsist upon; and we were, therefore, reduced to the wretched necessity of living at the expense of our neighbors. We were compelled either to beg, or to steal, and we did both. I frankly confess, that while I hated everything like stealing, *as such*, I nevertheless did not hesitate to take food, when I was hungry, wherever I could find it. Nor was this practice the mere result of an unreasoning instinct; it was, in my case, the result of a clear apprehension of the claims of morality. I weighed and considered the matter closely, before I ventured to satisfy my hunger by such means. Considering that my labor and person were the property of Master Thomas, and that I was by him deprived of the necessaries of life—necessaries obtained by my own labor—it was easy to deduce the right to supply myself with what was my own. It was simply appropriating what was my own to the use of my master, since the health and strength derived from such food were exerted in *his* service. To be sure, this was stealing, according to the law and gospel I heard from St. Michael's pulpit; but I had already begun to attach less importance to what dropped from that quarter, on that point, while, as yet, I retained my reverence for religion. It was not always convenient to steal from master, and the same reason why I might, innocently, steal from him, did not seem to justify me in stealing from others. In the case of my master, it was only a question of *removal*—the taking his meat out of the tub, and putting it into another; the ownership of the meat was not affected by the transaction. At first, he owned it in the *tub*, and last, he owned it in *me*. His meat house was not always open. There was a strict watch kept on that point, and the key was on a large bunch in Rowena's pocket. A great many times have we, poor creatures, been severely pinched with hunger, when meat and bread have been moulding under the lock, while the key was in the pocket of our mistress. This had been so when she *knew* we were nearly half starved; and yet, that mistress, with saintly air, would kneel with her husband, and pray each morning that a merciful God would bless them in basket and in store, and save them, at last, in his kingdom. But I proceed with the argument.

It was necessary that the right to steal from *others* should be established; and this could only rest upon a wider range of generalization than that which supposed the right to steal from my master.

It was sometime before I arrived at this clear right. The reader will get some idea of my train of reasoning, by a brief statement of the case. "I am," thought I, "not only the slave of Master Thomas, but I am the slave of society at large. Society at large has bound itself, in form and in fact, to assist Master Thomas in robbing me of my rightful liberty, and of the just reward of my labor; therefore, whatever rights I have against Master Thomas, I have, equally, against those confederated with him in robbing me of liberty. As society has marked me out as privileged plunder, on the principle of self-preservation I am justified in plundering in turn. Since each slave belongs to all; all must, therefore, belong to each."

I shall here make a profession of faith which may shock some, offend others, and be dissented from by all. It is this: Within the bounds of his just earnings, I hold that the slave is fully justified in helping himself to the *gold and silver, and the best apparel of his master, or that of any other slaveholder; and that such taking is not stealing in any just sense of that word.*

The morality of *free* society can have no application to *slave* society. Slaveholders have made it almost impossible for the slave to commit any crime, known either to the laws of God or to the laws of man. If he steals, he takes his own; if he kills his master, he imitates only the heroes of the revolution. Slaveholders I hold to be individually and collectively responsible for all the evils which grow out of the horrid relation, and I believe they will be so held at the judgment, in the sight of a just God. Make a man a slave, and you rob him of moral responsibility. . . .

◆

# *Goethe's Faust: The Quintessential Romantic Hero*

Of all literary heroes of the nineteenth century, perhaps the most compelling is Goethe's Faust. The story of Faust is based on a sixteenth-century German legend of a historical figure named Johann or Georg Faust. A traveling physician and a practitioner of black magic, he is reputed to have sold his soul to the devil in exchange for infinite knowledge and personal experience. The Faust legend became the subject of numerous dramas, the first of which was written by the English playwright Christopher Marlowe (1564–1593), who turned the story into a tragedy in which Faust loses his soul. Faust

Delacroix inv.t et Lithog.

Ch. Motte, Imp.r Editeur, à Paris.

Meph : Pourquoi tout ce vacarme ? que demande Monsieur ? qu'y a-t'il pour son service ?

**Figure 28.5** Eugène Delacroix, *Mephistopheles Appearing to Faust in His Study*, illustration for Goethe's *Faust*, 1828. Lithograph, 10¾ × 9 in. The Metropolitan Museum of Art, New York. Rogers Fund, 1917 (17.12).

was the favorite Renaissance symbol of the lust for knowledge and experience balanced against the perils of eternal damnation—a motif that figured largely in literary characterizations of Don Juan as well. In the hands of the German poet Johann Wolfgang von Goethe (1749–1832), Faust became the paradigm of Western man and—more broadly—of the human quest for knowledge, experience, and power. He was the quintessential romantic hero, the epitome of the human desire to transcend physical limitations and to master all realms of knowledge. The Faustian hero, like Prometheus or the apotheosized Napoleon, sought power that might permit him to control the world.

Goethe's *Faust* is one of the most monumental literary works of its time. Goethe conceived the piece during the 1770s, published the first version in 1790, and completed it more than forty years later; hence, *Faust* was the product of Goethe's entire career. Although ostensibly a drama, *Faust* more closely resembles an epic poem. It is written in a lyric German, with a freedom of rhyme and meter that is typical of romantic poetry. As a play, it deliberately ignores the classical unities of time and place—indeed, its shifting "cinematic" qualities make it more adaptable to modern film than to the traditional stage. Despite a cosmic breadth which compares with Milton's *Paradise Lost* or Dante's *Divine Comedy*, Goethe's *Faust* focuses more narrowly on the human condition. Goethe neither seeks to justify God's ways to humanity nor to allegorize the Christian ascent to salvation; rather, he uncovers the tragic tension between heroic aspirations and human limitations. Goethe, a student of law, medicine, theology, theater, biology, optics, and alchemy, seems to have modeled Faust after himself: Faust is a man of deep learning, a Christian, and a scientist. He is, moreover, a creative genius whose desire to know and achieve has dominated his life. But he feels stale, bored, and deeply dissatisfied with all theoretical modes of understanding. He is driven to exhaust other kinds of experience—not only intellectual but sensual, erotic, aesthetic and, finally, spiritual.

The Prologue of *Faust* is set in Heaven, where (in a manner reminiscent of the Book of Job) a wager is made between Mephistopheles (Satan) and God. Mephistopheles bets God that he can divert Faust from "the path that is true and fit." God contends that, though "men make mistakes as long as they strive," Faust will never relinquish his soul to Satan. In the first part of the tragedy, Mephistopheles proceeds to make a second pact, this one with Faust himself: If he can satisfy Faust's deepest desires and ambitions to the hero's ultimate satisfaction, then Mephistopheles will win Faust's soul. Mephistopheles lures the despairing Faust out of the study that Faust calls "This God-damned dreary hole in the wall"—away from the life of the mind and into the larger world of experience (Figure **28.5**). The newly-liberated hero then engages in a passionate love affair with a young maiden named Gretchen. Discovering the joys of the sensual life, Faust proclaims the priority of the heart ("Feeling is all!") over the mind. Faust's romance, however, has tragic consequences, including the death of Gretchen's mother, illegitimate child, brother and, ultimately, Gretchen herself. Nevertheless, at the close of Part One, Gretchen's pure and selfless love wins her salvation.

In the second part of Goethe's *Faust*—and symbolically in the life of Faust's imagination—the hero travels with Mephistopheles through a netherworld in which he meets an array of witches, sirens, and other fantastic creatures. He also encounters the ravishing Helen of Troy. Helen, the symbol of ideal beauty, acquaints Faust with the entire history and culture of humankind; but Faust remains unsated. His unquenched thirst for experience now leads him to pursue a life of action for the public good: He undertakes a vast land-reclamation project which provides habitation for millions of people. And in this endeavor—so different, it might be observed, from Candide's reclusive "garden" (see chapter 25)—the aged and near-blind Faust begins to find personal fulfillment. He dies, however, before fully realizing his dream; hence he never actually avows the satisfaction that would damn his soul to Hell. And although Mephistopheles gathers a hellish host to apprehend Faust's soul when it leaves his body, God's angels spirit his soul to Heaven.

The heroic Faust is a timeless symbol of the Western drive for consummate knowledge, experience, and the will to exert power over nature. Though it is possible to reproduce here only a small portion of Goethe's twelve-thousand-line poem, the following excerpt conveys the powerful lyricism, the verbal subtleties, and the shifts between high seriousness and comedy that make Goethe's *Faust* a literary masterpiece.

## READING 5.13

## From Goethe's *Faust*

**Prologue in Heaven**

*The Lord. The Heavenly Hosts. Mephistopheles following (the Three Archangels step forward).*

**RAPHAEL:** The chanting sun, as ever, rivals
The chanting of his brother spheres
And marches round his destined circuit—[1]
A march that thunders in our ears.
His aspect cheers the Hosts of Heaven
Though what his essence none can say;
These inconceivable creations
Keep the high state of their first day.

[1]The sun is treated here as one of the planets, all of which, according to Pythagoras, moved harmoniously in crystalline spheres.

**GABRIEL:** And swift, with inconceivable swiftness,
The earth's full splendor rolls around,
Celestial radiance alternating
With a dread night too deep to sound;
The sea against the rocks' deep bases
Comes foaming up in far-flung force,
And rock and sea go whirling onward
In the swift spheres' eternal course.

**MICHAEL:** And storms in rivalry are raging
From sea to land, from land to sea,
In frenzy forge the world a girdle
From which no inmost part is free
The blight of lightning flaming yonder
Marks where the thunder-bolt will play;
And yet Thine envoys, Lord, revere
The gentle movement of Thy day.

**CHOIR OF ANGELS:** Thine aspect cheers the Hosts of Heaven
Though what Thine essence none can say,
And all Thy loftiest creations
Keep the high state of their first day.
*(Enter Mephistopheles)*[2]

**MEPHISTOPHELES:** Since you, O Lord, once more approach and ask
If business down with us be light or heavy—
And in the past you've usually welcomed me—
That's why you see me also at your levee.
Excuse me, I can't manage lofty words—
Not though your whole court jeer and find me low;
My pathos certainly would make you laugh
Had you not left off laughing long ago.
Your suns and worlds mean nothing much to me;
How men torment themselves, that's all I see.
The little god of the world, one can't reshape, reshade him;
He is as strange to-day as that first day you made him.
His life would be not so bad, not quite,
Had you not granted him a gleam of Heaven's light;
He calls it Reason, uses it not the least
Except to be more beastly than any beast.
He seems to me—if your Honor does not mind—
Like a grasshopper—the long-legged kind—
That's always in flight and leaps as it flies along
And then in the grass strikes up its same old song.
I could only wish he confined himself to the grass!
He thrusts his nose into every filth, alas.

**LORD:** Mephistopheles, have you no other news?
Do you always come here to accuse?
Is nothing ever right in your eyes on earth?

**MEPHISTOPHELES:** No, Lord! I find things there as downright bad as ever.
I am sorry for men's days of dread and dearth;
Poor things, *my* wish to plague 'em isn't fervent.

**LORD:** Do you know Faust?

**MEPHISTOPHELES:** The Doctor?

**LORD:** Aye, my servant.[3]

**MEPHISTOPHELES:** Indeed! He serves you oddly enough, I think.
The fool has no earthly habits in meat and drink.
The ferment in him drives him wide and far,
That he is mad he too has almost guessed;
He demands of heaven each fairest star
And of earth each highest joy and best,
And all that is new and all that is far
Can bring no calm to the deep-sea swell of his breast.

**LORD:** Now he may serve me only gropingly,
Soon I shall lead him into the light.
The gardener knows when the sapling first turns green
That flowers and fruit will make the future bright.

**MEPHISTOPHELES:** What do you wager? You will lose him yet,
Provided *you* give *me* permission
To steer him gently the course I set.

**LORD:** So long as he walks the earth alive,
So long you may try what enters your head;
Men make mistakes as long as they strive.

**MEPHISTOPHELES:** I thank you for that; as regards the dead,
The dead have never taken my fancy.
I favor cheeks that are full and rosy-red;
No corpse is welcome to my house;
I work as the cat does with the mouse.

**LORD:** Very well; you have my full permission.
Divert this soul from its primal source
And carry it, if you can seize it,
Down with you upon your course—
And stand ashamed when you must needs admit:
A good man with his groping intuitions
Still knows the path that's true and fit.

**MEPHISTOPHELES:** All right—but it won't last for long.
I'm not afraid my bet will turn out wrong.
And, if my aim prove true and strong,
Allow me to triumph wholeheartedly.
Dust shall he eat—and greedily—
Like my cousin the Snake renowned in tale and song.[4]

**LORD:** That too you are free to give a trial;
I have never hated the likes of you.
Of all the spirits of denial
The joker is the last that I eschew.
Man finds relaxation too attractive—
Too fond too soon of unconditional rest;
Which is why I am pleased to give him a companion
Who lures and thrusts and must, as devil, be active.
But ye, true sons of Heaven,[5] it is your duty
To take your joy in the living wealth of beauty.
The changing Essence which ever works and lives
Wall you around with love, serene, secure!
And that which floats in flickering appearance
Fix ye it firm in thoughts that must endure.

**CHOIR OF ANGELS:** Thine aspect cheers the Hosts of Heaven
Though what Thine essence none can say,
And all Thy loftiest creations
Keep the high state of their first day.
*(Heaven closes)*

**MEPHISTOPHELES** *(Alone)*: I like to see the Old One now and then
And try to keep relations on the level

---

[2]The name possibly derives from the Hebrew "Mephistoph," meaning "destroyer of the gods."

[3]Compare the exchange between God and Satan at the beginning of the Book of Job (see chapter 2).

[4]In Genesis 3.14, God condemns the serpent to go on its belly and eat dust for the rest of its days.

[5]The archangels.

It's really decent of so great a person
To talk so humanely even to the Devil.

**The First Part of the Tragedy**
**Night**

*(In a high-vaulted narrow Gothic room Faust, restless, in a chair at his desk)*

**FAUST:** Here stand I, ach, Philosophy
Behind me and Law and Medicine too
And, to my cost, Theology—[6]
All these I have sweated through and through
And now you see me a poor fool
As wise as when I entered school!
They call me Master, they call me Doctor,[7]
Ten years now I have dragged my college
Along by the nose through zig and zag
Through up and down and round and round
And this is all that I have found—
The impossibility of knowledge!
It is this that burns away my heart;
Of course I am cleverer than the quacks,
Than master and doctor, than clerk and priest,
I suffer no scruple or doubt in the least,
I have no qualms about devil or burning,
Which is just why all joy is torn from me,
I cannot presume to make use of my learning,
I cannot presume I could open my mind
To proselytize and improve mankind.

Besides, I have neither goods nor gold,
Neither reputation nor rank in the world;
No dog would choose to continue so!
Which is why I have given myself to Magic
To see if the Spirit may grant me to know
Through its force and its voice full many a secret,
May spare the sour sweat that I used to pour out
In talking of what I know nothing about,
May grant me to learn what it is that girds
The world together in its inmost being,
That the seeing its whole germination, the seeing
Its workings, may end my traffic in words.

O couldst thou, light of the full moon,
Look now thy last upon my pain,
Thou for whom I have sat belated
So many midnights here and waited
Till, over books and papers, thou
Didst shine, sad friend, upon my brow!
O could I but walk to and fro
On mountain heights in thy dear glow
Or float with spirits round mountain eyries
Or weave through fields thy glances glean
And freed from all miasmal theories
Bathe in thy dew and wash me clean![8]
Oh! Am I still stuck in this jail?
This God-damned dreary hole in the wall
Where even the lovely light of heaven
Breaks wanly through the painted panes!
Cooped up among these heaps of books
Gnawed by worms, coated with dust,
Round which to the top of the Gothic vault
A smoke-stained paper forms a crust.
Retorts and canisters lie pell-mell
And pyramids of instruments,
The junk of centuries, dense and mat—
Your world, man! World? They call it that!

And yet you ask why your poor heart
Cramped in your breast should feel such fear,
Why an unspecified misery
Should throw your life so out of gear?
Instead of the living natural world
For which God made all men his sons
You hold a reeking mouldering court
Among assorted skeletons.
Away! There is a world outside!
And this one book of mystic art
Which Nostradamus[9] wrote himself,
Is this not adequate guard and guide?
By this you can tell the course of the stars,
By this, once Nature gives the word,
The soul begins to stir and dawn,
A spirit by a spirit heard,
In vain your barren studies here
Construe the signs of sanctity.
You Spirits, you are hovering near;
If you can hear me, answer me!
*(He opens the book and perceives the sign of the Macrocosm)*[10]
Ha! What a river of wonder at this vision
Bursts upon all my senses in one flood!
And I feel young, the holy joy of life
Glows new, flows fresh, through nerve and blood!
Was it a god designed this hieroglyph to calm
The storm which but now raged inside me,
To pour upon my heart such balm,
And by some secret urge to guide me
Where all the powers of Nature stand unveiled around me?
Am I a God? It grows so light!
And through the clear-cut symbol on this page
My soul comes face to face with all creating Nature.
At last I understand the dictum of the sage:
"The spiritual world is always open,
Your mind is closed, your heart is dead;
Rise, young man, and plunge undaunted
Your earthly breast in the mourning red."
*(He contemplates the sign)*
Into one Whole how all things blend,
Function and live within each other!
Passing gold buckets to each other
How heavenly powers ascend, descend!

[6]Philosophy, law, medicine, and theology were the four programs of study in medieval universities.
[7]The two advanced degrees beyond the baccalaureate.
[8]Goethe's conception of nature as a source of sublime purification may be compared with similar ideas held by the nature poets and the transcendentalists discussed in chapter 27.
[9]Michel de Notredame or Nostradamus (1503–1566) was a French astrologer famous for his prophecies of future events.
[10]Signs of the universe, such as the pentagram, were especially popular among those who practiced magic and the occult arts.

The odor of grace upon their wings,
They thrust from heaven through earthly things
And as all sing so *the* All sings!
What a fine show! Aye, but only a show!
Infinite Nature, where can I tap thy veins?

Where are thy breasts, those well-springs of all life
On which hang heaven and earth,
Towards which my dry breast strains?
They well up, they give drink, but I feel drought and dearth.
*(He turns the pages and perceives the sign of the Earth Spirit)*[11]
How differently this new sign works upon me!
Thy sign, thou Spirit of the Earth, 'tis thine
And thou art nearer to me.
At once I feel my powers unfurled,
At once I grow as from new wine
And feel inspired to venture into the world,
To cope with the fortunes of earth benign or malign,
To enter the ring with the storm, to grapple and clinch,
To enter the jaws of the shipwreck and never flinch.
Over me comes a mist,
The moon muffles her light,
The lamp goes dark.
The air goes damp. Red beams flash
Around my head. There blows
A kind of a shudder down from the vault
And seizes on me.
It is thou must be hovering round me, come at my prayers!
Spirit, unveil thyself!
My heart, oh my heart, how it tears!
And how each and all of my senses
Seem burrowing upwards towards new light, new breath!
I feel my heart has surrendered, I have no more defences.
Come then! Come! Even if it prove my death!
*(He seizes the book and solemnly pronounces the sign of the Earth Spirit. There is a flash of red flame and the Spirit appears in it)*

**SPIRIT:** Who calls upon me?

**FAUST:** Appalling vision!

**SPIRIT:** You have long been sucking at my sphere,
Now by main force you have drawn me here
And now—

**FAUST:** No! Not to be endured!

**SPIRIT:** With prayers and with paintings you have procured
The sight of my face and the sound of my voice—
Now I am here. What a pitiable shivering
Seizes the Superman. Where is the call of your soul?
Where the breast which created a world in itself
And carried and fostered it, swelling up, joyfully quivering,
Raising itself to a level with Us, the Spirits?
Where are you, Faust, whose voice rang out to me,
Who with every nerve so thrust yourself upon me?
Are you the thing that at a whiff of my breath
Trembles throughout its living frame,
A poor worm crawling off, askance, askew?

**FAUST:** Shall I yield to Thee, Thou shape of flame?
I am Faust, I can hold my own with Thee.

**SPIRIT:** In the floods of life, in the storm of work,
In ebb and flow,
In warp and weft,
Cradle and grave,
An eternal sea,
A changing patchwork,
A glowing life,
At the whirring loom of Time I weave
The living clothes of the Deity.

**FAUST:** Thou who dost rove the wide world round,
Busy Spirit, how near I feel to Thee!

**SPIRIT:** You are like that Spirit which you can grasp,
Not me!
*(The Spirit vanishes)*

**FAUST:** Not Thee!
Whom then?
I who am Godhead's image,
Am I not even like Thee!
*(A knocking on the door)*
Death! I know who that is. My assistant!
So ends my happiest, fairest hour.
The crawling pedant must interrupt
My visions at their fullest flower!

*[Faust converses with his assistant Wagner on the fruitlessness of a life of study. When Wagner leaves, Faust prepares to commit suicide; but he is interrupted by the sounds of churchbells and choral music. Still brooding, he joins Wagner and the townspeople as they celebrate Easter Sunday. At the city gate, Faust encounters a black poodle, which he takes back with him to his studio. The dog is actually Mephistopheles, who soon makes his real self known to Faust.]*

*(The same room. Later)*

**FAUST:** Who's knocking? Come in! *Now* who wants to annoy me?

**MEPHISTOPHELES** *(outside door)*: It's I.

**FAUST:** Come in!

**MEPHISTOPHELES** *(outside door)*: You must say "Come in" three times.

**FAUST:** Come in then!

**MEPHISTOPHELES** *(entering)*: Thank you; you overjoy me.
We two, I hope, we shall be good friends;
To chase those megrims[12] of yours away
I am here like a fine young squire to-day,
In a suit of scarlet trimmed with gold
And a little cape of stiff brocade,
With a cock's feather in my hat
And at my side a long sharp blade,
And the most succinct advice I can give
Is that you dress up just like me,
So that uninhibited and free
You may find out what it means to live.

**FAUST:** The pain of earth's constricted life, I fancy,
Will pierce me still, whatever my attire;

[11]The Earth Spirit, here used to represent the active, sensual side of Faust's nature as opposed to the contemplative, spiritual side represented by the Macrocosm. Goethe suggested representing the *Erdgeist* on the stage by means of a magic lantern device that would magnify and project the head of Apollo or Zeus at giant proportions.

[12]Low or morbid spirits.

I am too old for mere amusement,
Too young to be without desire.
How can the world dispel my doubt?
You must do without, you must do without!
That is the everlasting song
Which rings in every ear, which rings,
And which to us our whole life long
Every hour hoarsely sings.
I wake in the morning only to feel appalled,
My eyes with bitter tears could run
To see the day which in its course
Will not fulfil a wish for me, not one;
The day which whittles away with obstinate carping
All pleasures—even those of anticipation,
Which makes a thousand grimaces to obstruct
My heart when it is stirring in creation.
And again, when night comes down, in anguish
I must stretch out upon my bed
And again no rest is granted me,
For wild dreams fill my mind with dread.
The God who dwells within my bosom
Can make my inmost soul react;
The God who sways my every power
Is powerless with external fact.
And so existence weighs upon my breast
And I long for death and life—life I detest.

**MEPHISTOPHELES:** Yet death is never a wholly welcome guest.

**FAUST:** O happy is he whom death in the dazzle of victory
Crowns with the bloody laurel in the battling swirl!
Or he whom after the mad and breakneck dance
He comes upon in the arms of a girl!
O to have sunk away, delighted, deleted,
Before the Spirit of the Earth,[13] before his might!

**MEPHISTOPHELES:** Yet I know someone who failed to drink
A brown juice on a certain night.[14]

**FAUST:** Your hobby is espionage—is it not?

**MEPHISTOPHELES:** Oh I'm not omniscient—but I know a lot.

**FAUST:** Whereas that tumult in my soul
Was stilled by sweet familiar chimes
Which cozened the child that yet was in me
With echoes of more happy times,
I now curse all things that encompass
The soul with lures and jugglery
And bind it in this dungeon of grief
With trickery and flattery.
Cursed in advance be the high opinion
That serves our spirit for a cloak!
Cursed be the dazzle of appearance
Which bows our senses to its yoke!
Cursed be the lying dreams of glory,
The illusion that our name survives!
Cursed be the flattering things we own,
Servants and ploughs, children and wives!
Cursed be Mammon[15] when with his treasures
He makes us play the adventurous man
Or when for our luxurious pleasures
He duly spreads the soft divan!
A curse on the balsam of the grape!
A curse on the love that rides for a fall!
A curse on hope! A curse on faith!
And a curse on patience most of all!
*(The invisible Spirits sing again)*

**SPIRITS:** Woe! Woe!
You have destroyed it,
The beautiful world;
By your violent hand
'Tis downward hurled!
A half-god has dashed it asunder!
From under
We bear off the rubble to nowhere
And ponder
Sadly the beauty departed.
Magnipotent
One among men,
Magnificent
Build it again,
Build it again in your breast!
Let a new course of life
Begin
With vision abounding
And new songs resounding
To welcome it in!

**MEPHISTOPHELES:** These are the juniors
Of my faction.
Hear how precociously they counsel
Pleasure and action.
Out and away
From your lonely day
Which dries your senses and your juices
Their melody seduces.
Stop playing with your grief which battens
Like a vulture on your life, your mind!
The worst of company would make you feel
That you are a man among mankind.
Not that it's really my proposition
To shove you among the common men;
Though I'm not one of the Upper Ten.
If you would like a coalition
With me for your career through life,
I am quite ready to fit in,
I'm yours before you can say knife.
I am your comrade;
If you so crave,
I am your servant, I am your slave.

**FAUST:** And what have I to undertake in return?

**MEPHISTOPHELES:** Oh it's early days to discuss what that is.

**FAUST:** No, no, the devil is an egoist
And ready to do nothing gratis
Which is to benefit a stranger.
Tell me your terms and don't prevaricate!
A servant like you in the house is a danger.

---

[13] The Earth Spirit of the previous passage.

[14] Mephistopheles alludes to Faust's contemplation of suicide by poison earlier in the drama.

[15] Riches or material wealth.

**MEPHISTOPHELES:** I will bind myself to your service in this world,
To be at your beck and never rest nor slack;
When we meet again on the other side,
In the same coin you shall pay me back.
**FAUST:** The other side gives me little trouble;
First batter this present world to rubble,
Then the other may rise—if that's the plan.
This earth is where my springs of joy have started.
And this sun shines on me when broken-hearted;
If I can first from them be parted,
*Then* let happen what will and can!
I wish to hear no more about it—
Whether there too men hate and love
Or whether in those spheres too, in the future,
There is a Below or an Above.
**MEPHISTOPHELES:** With such an outlook you can risk it.
Sign on the line! In these next days you will get
Ravishing samples of my arts;
I am giving you what never man saw yet.
**FAUST:** Poor devil, can *you* give anything ever?
Was a human spirit in its high endeavor
Even once understood by one of your breed?
Have you got food which fails to feed?
Or red gold which, never at rest,
Like mercury runs away through the hand?
A game at which one never wins?
A girl who, even when on my breast,
Pledges herself to my neighbor with her eyes?
The divine and lovely delight of honor
Which falls like a falling star and dies?
Show me the fruits which, before they are plucked, decay
And the trees which day after day renew their green!
**MEPHISTOPHELES:** Such a commission doesn't alarm me,
I have such treasures to purvey.
But, my good friend, the time draws on when we
Should be glad to feast at our ease on something good.
**FAUST:** If ever I stretch myself on a bed of ease,
Then I am finished! Is that understood?
If ever your flatteries can coax me
To be pleased with myself, if ever you cast
A spell of pleasure that can hoax me—
Then let *that* day be my last!
That's my wager![16]
**MEPHISTOPHELES:** Done!
**FAUST:** Let's shake!
If ever I say to the passing moment
"Linger for a while! Thou art so fair!"
Then you may cast me into fetters,
I will gladly perish then and there!
Then you may set the death-bell tolling,
Then from my service you are free,
The clock may stop, its hand may fall,
And that be the end of time for me!
**MEPHISTOPHELES:** Think what you're saying, we shall not forget it.
**FAUST:** And you are fully within your rights;
I have made no mad or outrageous claim.
If I stay as I am, I am a slave—
Whether yours or another's, it's all the same.
**MEPHISTOPHELES:** I shall this very day at the College Banquet
Enter your service with no more ado,
But just one point—As a life-and-death insurance
I must trouble you for a line or two.
**FAUST:** So you, you pedant, you too like things in writing?
Have you never known a man? Or a man's word? Never?
Is it not enough that my word of mouth
Puts all my days in bond for ever?
Does not the world rage on in all its streams
And shall a promise hamper *me*?
Yet this illusion reigns within our hearts
And from it who would be gladly free?
Happy the man who can inwardly keep his word;
Whatever the cost, he will not be loath to pay!
But a parchment, duly inscribed and sealed,
Is a bogey from which all wince away.
The word dies on the tip of the pen
And wax and leather lord it then.
What do you, evil spirit, require?
Bronze, marble, parchment, paper?
Quill or chisel or pencil of slate?
You may choose whichever you desire.
**MEPHISTOPHELES:** How can you so exaggerate
With such a hectic rhetoric?
Any little snippet is quite good—
And you sign it with one little drop of blood.
**FAUST:** If that is enough and is some use,
One may as well pander to your fad.
**MEPHISTOPHELES:** Blood is a very special juice.
**FAUST:** Only do not fear that I shall break this contract.
What I promise is nothing more
Than what all my powers are striving for.
I have puffed myself up too much, it is only
Your sort that really fits my case.
The great Earth Spirit has despised me
And Nature shuts the door in my face.
The thread of thought is snapped asunder.
I have long loathed knowledge in all its fashions.
In the depths of sensuality
Let us now quench our glowing passions!
And at once make ready every wonder
Of unpenetrated sorcery!
Let us cast ourselves into the torrent of time,
Into the whirl of eventfulness,
Where disappointment and success,
Pleasure and pain may chop and change
As chop and change they will and can;
It is restless action makes the man.
**MEPHISTOPHELES:** No limit is fixed for you, no bound;
If you'd like to nibble at everything
Or to seize upon something flying round—
Well, may you have a run for your money!
But seize your chance and don't be funny!

[16]The wager between Faust and Mephistopheles recalls that between God and Mephistopheles in the Prologue.

**FAUST:** I've told you, it is no question of happiness.
The most painful joy, enamored hate, enlivening
Disgust—I devote myself to all excess.
My breast, now cured of its appetite for knowledge,
From now is open to all and every smart,
And what is allotted to the whole of mankind
That will I sample in my inmost heart,
Grasping the highest and lowest with my spirit,
Piling men's weal and woe upon my neck,
To extend myself to embrace all human selves
And to founder in the end, like them, a wreck.
**MEPHISTOPHELES:** O believe *me*, who have been chewing
These iron rations many a thousand year,
No human being can digest
This stuff, from the cradle to the bier.
This universe—believe a devil—
Was made for no one but a god!
*He* exists in eternal light
But *us* he has brought into the darkness
While *your* sole portion is day and night.
**FAUST:** I will all the same!
**MEPHISTOPHELES:** That's very nice.
There's only one thing I find wrong;
Time is short, art is long.[17]
You could do with a little artistic advice.
Confederate with one of the poets
And let him flog his imagination
To heap all virtues on your head,
A head with such a reputation:
Lion's bravery,
Stag's velocity,
Fire of Italy,
Northern tenacity.
Let *him* find out the secret art
Of combining craft with a noble heart
And of being in love like a young man,
Hotly, but working to a plan.
Such a person—*I'd* like to meet him;
"Mr. Microcosm" is how I'd greet him.
**FAUST:** What am I then if fate must bar
My efforts to reach that crown of humanity
After which all my senses strive?
**MEPHISTOPHELES:** You are in the end . . . what you are.
You can put on full-bottomed wigs with a million locks,
You can put on stilts instead of your socks,
You remain for ever what you are.
**FAUST:** I feel my endeavours have not been worth a pin
When I raked together the treasures of the human mind,
If at the end I but sit down to find
No new force welling up within.
I have not a hair's breadth more of height,
I am no nearer the Infinite.
**MEPHISTOPHELES:** My very good sir, you look at things
Just in the way that people do;
We must be cleverer than that
Or the joys of life will escape from you.
Hell! You have surely hands and feet,
Also a head and you-know-what;
The pleasures I gather on the wing,
Are they less mine? Of course they're not!
Suppose I can afford six stallions,
I can add that horse-power to my score
And dash along and be a proper man
As if my legs were twenty-four.
So good-bye to thinking! On your toes!
The world's before us. Quick! Here goes!
I tell you, a chap who's intellectual
Is like a beast on a blasted heath
Driven in circles by a demon
While a fine green meadow lies round beneath.
**FAUST:** How do we start?
**MEPHISTOPHELES:** We just say go—and skip.
But please get ready for this pleasure trip.
*(Exit Faust)*
Only look down on knowledge and reason,
The highest gifts that men can prize,
Only allow the spirit of lies
To confirm you in magic and illusion,
And then I have you body and soul.
Fate has given this man a spirit
Which is always pressing onwards, beyond control,
And whose mad striving overleaps
All joys of the earth between pole and pole.
Him shall I drag through the wilds of life
And through the flats of meaninglessness,
I shall make him flounder and gape and stick
And to tease his insatiableness
Hang meat and drink in the air before his watering lips;
In vain he will pray to slake his inner thirst,
And even had he not sold himself to the devil
He would be equally accursed.
*(Re-enter Faust)*
**FAUST:** And now, where are we going?
**MEPHISTOPHELES:** Wherever you please.
The small world, then the great for us.
With what pleasure and what profit
You will roister through the syllabus!
**FAUST:** But I, with this long beard of mine,
I lack the easy social touch,
I know the experiment is doomed;
Out in the world I never could fit in much.
I feel so small in company
I'll be embarrassed constantly.
**MEPHISTOPHELES:** My friend, it will solve itself, any such misgiving;
Just trust yourself and you'll learn the art of living.
**FAUST:** Well, then, how do we leave home?
Where are your grooms? Your coach and horses?
**MEPHISTOPHELES:** We merely spread this mantle wide,
It will bear us off on airy courses.
But do not on this noble voyage
Cumber yourself with heavy baggage.
A little inflammable gas which I'll prepare
Will lift us quickly into the air.
If we travel light we shall cleave the sky like a knife.
Congratulations on your new course of life!

. . . . . . . . . . .

◆

[17]An adaptation of the famous Latin aphorism "Ars longa, vita brevis" ("Art is long-lasting, but life is short").

## *Romantic Love and Romantic Stereotypes*

Romantic love, the sentimental and all-consuming passion for spiritual as well as sexual union with the opposite sex, was a favorite theme of nineteenth-century writers, painters, and composers. Many artists perceived friendship, religious love, and sexual love as closely related expressions of an ecstatic harmony of souls. "In true complete love," wrote the French novelist Amantine Aurore Lucie Dupin, who used the pen name George Sand (1804–1876), "heart, mind and body meet in understanding and embrace." Less idealistically, romantics embraced love with self-indulgent abandon: "If I give myself up to love," declares one of Sand's characters, "I want it to wound me deeply, to electrify me, to break my heart or to exalt me. . . . What I want is to suffer, to go crazy." Passionate love, and especially unrequited or unfulfilled love, was the subject of numerous romantic literary works. To name but three: Goethe's *Sorrows of Young Werther* told the story of a lovesick hero whose passion for a married woman leads him to commit suicide—the book was so popular that it made suicide something of a nineteenth-century vogue; Hector Berlioz's *Symphonie fantastique* described the nineteenth-century composer's obsessive infatuation with a flamboyant actress (see chapter 29); and Richard Wagner's opera *Tristan and Isolde* dramatized the tragic fate of two legendary medieval lovers.

While male romantics generated an image of masculinity that emphasized self-invention, courage, and the quest for knowledge and power, they persisted in glorifying the female as chaste, passive, and submissive, or, on the other hand, characterizing her as dangerous and threatening. Romantic writers inherited the dual view of womankind that had prevailed since the Middle Ages: Like Eve, woman was the *femme fatale*, the seducer and destroyer of mankind; like Mary, however, woman was the source of salvation and the symbol of all that was pure and true. The Eve stereotype is readily apparent in such works as Prosper Mérimée's novel *Carmen* (on which the opera by Georges Bizet [1835–1875] was based), while the Mary stereotype is present in countless nineteenth-century stories, including *Faust* itself, where Gretchen is cast as the Eternal Female, the source of procreation and personal salvation. The following lines by the German poet Heinrich Heine (1797–1856), which were set to music by his contemporary Robert Schumann (1810–1856), typify the female as angelic, ethereal, and chaste—an object that thrilled and inspired the imaginations of many European romantics.

**READING 5.14**

### Heine's "You are Just Like a Flower"

You are just like a flower
So fair and chaste and dear;
Looking at you, sweet sadness
Invades my heart with fear.
I feel I should be folding
My hands upon your hair,
Praying that God may keep you
So dear and chaste and fair.

◆

The nineteenth century was the first great age of women writers. Examples include the English novelists George Eliot, a pseudonym for Mary Ann Evans (1819–1880); Jane Austen (1775–1817), whose novels on family life and love include *Emma, Sense and Sensibility* and *Pride and Prejudice*; Emily Brontë (1818–1848), author of the hypnotic novel *Wuthering Heights*; her sister Charlotte Brontë, author of *Jane Eyre* (hailed as a masterpiece only after her death); Mary Godwin Shelley, whose novel *Frankenstein* was mentioned earlier in this chapter; and the French novelist Germaine Necker, known as Madame de Staël (1766–1817). Some of these women struck a startling note of personal freedom in their lives. In their novels, however, they tended to perpetuate the romantic stereotype of the chaste and clinging female. Indeed, even the most free-thinking of nineteenth-century women novelists might portray her heroine as a creature who submitted to the will and values of the superior male. In general, the dominant and male-generated stereotype of the romantic hero influenced female literary characterization well into the mid-nineteenth century.

George Sand explored the popular stereotypes of womanhood from a variety of perspectives. She readily avowed that "Love's ideal is most certainly everlasting fidelity," and most of her more than eighty novels feature themes of romantic love and deep, undying friendship. But for some of her novels, she created heroines who freely exercised the right to love outside of marriage. These heroines did not, however, physically consummate their love, even when that love was reciprocal. Sand's heroines were very unlike Sand herself, whose numerous love affairs with leading romantic figures—including the poet Alfred de Musset, the novelist Prosper Mérimée, and the composer Frédéric Chopin—impassioned her life and work. When Sand's affair with Musset came to an unhappy end, she cut off her hair and sent it to him encased in a skull. Sand defied society not only by adopting a life of

**Figure 28.6** Eugène Delacroix, *Portrait of George Sand*, 1830. Musée Carnavalet, Paris. Photo: Musées de la Ville de Paris. © DACS 1997.

bohemianism and free love but also by her notorious habit of wearing men's clothes and smoking cigars (Figure **28.6**). The female counterpart of the Byronic hero, Sand confessed, "My emotions have always been stronger than the arguments of reason, and the restrictions I tried to impose on myself were to no avail."

Sand may have been expressing her own ambiguities concerning matters of love and marriage in her third novel, *Lélia* (1833), the pages of which are filled with musings on the meaning of "true love." At one point in her spiritual odyssey, the disenchanted Lélia openly ventures:

> As I continue to live, I cannot help realizing that youthful ideas about the exclusive passion of love and its eternal rights are false, even fatal. All theories ought to be allowed. I would give that of conjugal fidelity to exceptional souls. The majority have other needs, other strengths. To those others I would grant reciprocal freedom, tolerance, and renunciation of all jealous egotism. To others I would concede mystical ardors, fires brooded over in silence, a long and voluptuous reserve. Finally, to others I would admit the calm of angels, fraternal chastity, and an eternal virginity.—Are

> all souls alike? Do all men have the same abilities? Are not some born for the austerity of religious faith, others for voluptuousness, others for work and passionate struggle, and others, finally, for the vague reveries of the imagination? Nothing is more arbitrary than the understanding of *true love*. All loves are true, whether they be fiery or peaceful, sensual or ascetic, lasting or transient, whether they lead men to suicide or pleasure. The loves *of the mind* lead to actions just as noble as the loves *of the heart*. They have as much violence and power, if not as much duration.*

Sand's works provoke numerous ideas concerning the fragile relationship between men and women; they also provide a wealth of information about nineteenth-century European life and culture. A prolific writer, she left a body of work (much of which has still not been translated into English) that would fill at least 150 volumes, twenty-five of which, each a thousand pages long, would contain her correspondence with most of the leading artists and intellectuals of her day. In addition to her novels and letters, Sand also left an autobiography and dozens of essays and articles championing socialism, women, and the working classes. She summed up the nature of romantic creativity with these words: "The writer's trade is a violent, almost indestructible passion. Once it has entered a poor head, nothing can stop it . . . long live the artist's life! Our motto is freedom."

## *SUMMARY*

For nineteenth-century romantics, the hero was an expression of the expansive subjectivity of the individual. Characterized by superhuman ambition and talents, the romantic hero, whether a historical figure or a fictional personality, experienced life with self-destructive intensity. Napoleon Bonaparte's remarkable career became a model for heroic action propelled by unbounded imagination and ambition. Byron in England and Pushkin in Russia took Napoleon as their source of inspiration. The literary heroes Prometheus and Faust—figures symbolizing the quest to exceed the human limits of knowledge, experience, and power—also intrigued romantic writers. The fictional hero mirrored the romantic personality, a figure with whom many nineteenth-century artists identified. Mary Shelley, Byron, and other romantics found in Prometheus an apt metaphor for the creative and daring human spirit, while Goethe envisioned the legendary Faust as the quintessential romantic hero: a symbol of the ever-striving human will to master all forms of experience. In America, Douglass, champion of the abolitionist movement, serves as a prime example of the Promethean will to challenge inequity and defend the cause of human liberty.

Romantic love was a popular theme among nineteenth-century writers, many of whom tended to stereotype females as either angels or *femmes fatales*. With George Sand, however, the romantic heroine might be a self-directed creature whose passions incited her to contemplate (if not actually exercise) sexual freedom. If, to some extent, the literature of the early nineteenth century resembles a diary that tracks the moods and passions of the romantic personality, music and the visual arts—the focus of the next chapter—came even closer to capturing the spirit of the age.

*George Sand, *Lélia*, translated by Maria Espinosa. Bloomington, Ind.: Indiana University Press, 1978, 154–155.

### *SUGGESTIONS FOR READING*

Bergman-Carton, Janis. *The Woman of Ideas in French Art*. New Haven: Yale University Press, 1995.

Boyle, Nicholas. *Goethe: The Poetry of Desire*. New York: Oxford University Press, 1991.

Brown, David B. *Turner and Byron*. Seattle: University of Washington Press, 1993.

Brown, Jane K. *Goethe's Faust: The German Tragedy*. Ithaca, N.Y.: Cornell University Press, 1986.

Campbell, Joseph. *The Hero with a Thousand Faces*, rev. ed. Princeton, N.J.: Princeton University Press, 1980.

Gaull, Marilyn. *English Romanticism: The Human Context*. New York: Norton, 1988.

Newton, Eric. *The Romantic Rebellion*. New York: St. Martin's, 1963.

Pelles, Geraldine. *Art, Artists and Society: Origins of a Modern Dilemma*. Englewood Cliffs, N.J.: Prentice-Hall, 1963.

Praz, Mario. *The Romantic Agony*, translated by Angus Davidson. New York: Oxford University Press, 1950.

Watt, Ian. *Myths of Modern Individualism: Faust, Don Quixote, Don Juan, Robinson Crusoe*. New York: Cambridge University Press, 1996.

Wilson, James D. *The Romantic Heroic Idea*. Baton Rouge, La.: Louisiana State University, 1982.

# 29
# The Romantic Style in Art and Music

Romantic artists, like their literary counterparts, favored subjects that allowed them to explore their personal feelings and give free rein to the imagination. Nature and the natural landscape, the hero and heroism, and nationalist struggles for political independence—the very themes that captured the imagination of romantic writers—also inspired much of the art and music of the nineteenth century.

## *The Romantic Style in Painting*

Romantic artists abandoned the cool serenity and rationality of the neoclassical style in favor of emotion and spontaneity. Where neoclassicists sought symmetry and order, romantics favored irregularity and even irrationality. While neoclassical painters defined form by means of line (an artificial or "intellectual" boundary between the object and the space it occupied), romantics preferred to model form by way of color. While neoclassicists generally used shades of a single color for each individual object (coloring the red object red, for example), romantics might use touches of complementary colors to heighten the intensity of the painted object. And while neoclassical painters smoothed out brushstrokes to leave an even and polished surface finish, romantics often left their brushstrokes visible, as if to underline the immediacy of the creative act. Romantic artists often deliberately blurred details and exaggerated the sensuous aspects of texture and tone. Rejecting neoclassical propriety and decorum, they produced a style that made room for temperament, accident, and individual genius.

## *Heroic Themes in Art*

### Gros and the Glorification of the Hero

Among the principal themes of romantic art were those that glorified creative individualism, patriotism, and nationalism. Napoleon Bonaparte, the foremost living hero of the age and the symbol of French nationalism, was the favorite subject of many early nineteenth-century French painters. Napoleon's imperial status was celebrated in the official portraits executed by his "first painter," Jacques-Louis David (see Figure 28.1); but the heroic dimension of Napoleon's career was publicized by yet another member of his staff, Antoine-Jean Gros (1775–1835). Gros' representations of Napoleon's military campaigns became powerful vehicles of political propaganda.

Gros was a pupil of David, but, unlike David, Gros rejected the formal austerity of neoclassicism. In his monumental canvas, *Napoleon Visiting the Plague Victims at Jaffa* (Figure **29.1**), Gros converted a minor historical event—Napoleon's tour of his plague-ridden troops in Jaffa (in Palestine)—into a major allegorical drama. Gros cast Napoleon in the imposing guise of Christ healing the wounds of his followers and framed the hero beneath the arches of an exotic Islamic arcade. He enhanced the dramatic mood of the composition by means of atmospheric contrasts of light and dark and by vivid details that draw the eye from the foreground, filled with the bodies of the diseased and dying, deep into the background with its distant cityscape. Gros' imaginative composition and painterly technique anticipated the romantic style. In terms of content, Gros' *Plague Victims at Jaffa* manifested the romantic taste for themes of personal heroism, suffering, and death. When the painting was first exhibited in Paris, an awed public adorned it with palm branches and wreaths. But the inspiration for Gros' success was also the source of his undoing: After Napoleon was sent into exile, Gros' career declined, and he committed suicide by throwing himself into the River Seine.

### Romantic Heroism in Goya and Géricault

Throughout most of Western history, the heroic image in art was bound up with either classical lore or Christian legend. But with Gros, we see one of the first distinctive images of heroism based on contemporary events and political conditions. The Spanish master

**Figure 29.1** Antoine-Jean Gros, *Napoleon Visiting the Plague Victims at Jaffa*, 1804. Oil on canvas, 17 ft. 5 in. × 23 ft. 7 in. Louvre, Paris. Bridgeman Art Library, London.

Francisco Goya (1746–1828) helped to pioneer this phenomenon in nineteenth-century art. Having begun his career as a rococo-style tapestry designer, Goya came into prominence as court painter to the Spanish king Charles IV in Madrid. As court painter, Goya followed in the footsteps of Velásquez, despite the fact that he often brought unflattering realism to his portrait likenesses. During the latter half of his lifetime, and especially after the invasion of Spain by Napoleon's armies in 1808, Goya's art took a new turn. Horrified by the guerrilla violence of the Spanish occupation, he became a bitter social critic, producing some of the most memorable records of human warfare and savagery in the history of Western art.

*The Third of May, 1808: The Execution of the Defenders of Madrid* (Figure **29.2**) was Goya's response to the events following an uprising of Spanish citizens against the French army of occupation. In a punitive measure, the hostile French troops rounded up Spanish suspects in the streets of Madrid, transported them to the outskirts of the city, and brutally executed them. Goya recorded the macabre episode against a dark sky and an ominous urban skyline. In the foreground, an off-center lantern emits a triangular prism of light that illuminates the fate of the Spanish rebels: Some lie dead in pools of blood, while others cover their faces in fear and horror. Among the victims is the arresting figure of a young man, whose arms are flung upward in a final gesture of terror and defiance. Goya deliberately spotlights this wide-eyed and bewildered figure as he confronts imminent death. On the right, in the darkened shadows, the hulking executioners are lined up as anonymously as pieces of artillery. Goya composed the scene with an imaginative force that evoked strong feelings of sympathy and outrage. His emphatic contrasts of light and dark, his vivid use of color, and his willingness to alter details for the sake of emotional effect enhance the dramatic intensity of a contemporary political event.

An indictment of butchery in the name of war, *The Third of May, 1808* is itself restrained compared to "The Disasters of War," a series of etchings and **aquatints** that Goya produced in the years of the French occupation of Spain. The gruesome prints that make up "The Disasters of War" have their source in fact as well as in Goya's imagination. *Brave Deeds Against the Dead* (Figure **29.3**) is a shocking record of the inhuman cruelty of Napoleon's

**Figure 29.2** Francisco Goya, *The Third of May, 1808: The Execution of the Defenders of Madrid*, 1814. Oil on canvas, 8 ft. 6 in. × 10 ft. 4 in. Prado, Madrid.

**Figure 29.3** Francisco Goya, *Brave Deeds Against the Dead*, from the "Disasters of War" series, ca. 1814. Etching.

**Figure 29.4** Théodore Géricault, *The Raft of the "Medusa,"* 1818. Oil on canvas, 16 ft. 1 in. × 23 ft. 6 in. Louvre, Paris.

troops, as well as a reminder that the heroes of modern warfare are often its innocent victims.

Goya's contemporary, the French painter Théodore Géricault (1791–1824), further broadened the range of romantic subjects. Géricault found inspiration in the restless movements of untamed horses and the ravaged faces of the clinically insane, subjects uncommon in academic art which reflect the romantic fascination with the life that lay beyond the bounds of reason. The painting that brought Géricault instant fame, *The Raft of the "Medusa,"* immortalized a dramatic event that made headlines in Géricault's own time: the wreck of a government frigate called the "Medusa" and the ghastly fate of its survivors (Figure **29.4**). When the ship hit a reef 50 miles off the coast of West Africa, the inexperienced captain, a political appointee, tried ignobly to save himself and his crew, who filled the few available lifeboats. Over a hundred passengers piled onto a makeshift raft, which was to be towed by the lifeboats. Cruelly, the crew set the raft adrift. With almost no food and supplies, chances of survival were scant; after almost two weeks, in which most died and several resorted to cannibalism, the raft was sighted and fifteen survivors were rescued.

Géricault (a staunch opponent of the regime that appointed the captain of the "Medusa") was so fired by newspaper reports of the tragedy that he resolved to immortalize it. He interviewed the few survivors, made drawings of the mutilated corpses in the Paris morgue, and even had a model of the raft constructed in his studio. The result was enormous, both in size (the canvas measures 16 feet 1 inch × 23 feet 6 inches) and in dramatic impact. In the decade immediately preceding the invention of photography, Géricault provided the public with a powerful visual record of a sensational contemporary event. He organized his composition on the basis of a double triangle: One triangle, defined by the mast and left line, incorporates the bodies of the dying and the dead; the other consists of a mass of agitated figures culminating in the magnificently painted torso of a black man who signals the distant vessel that will make the rescue. Sharp diagonals, vivid contrasts of light and dark (reminiscent of Caravaggio), and muscular nudes (inspired by Michelangelo and Rubens) heighten the emotional impact of the piece. Géricault's *Raft* elevates ordinary men to the position of heroic combatants in the eternal struggle against the forces of nature. It eulogizes, moreover, the collective heroism of humble human beings confronting deadly danger, a motif equally popular in romantic literature—witness, for instance, Victor Hugo's *Les Misérables* (1862).

## Delacroix and the Imagery of Heroism

While Goya and Géricault democratized the image of the hero, Géricault's pupil and follower Eugène Delacroix (1798–1863) raised the hero to Byronic proportions. The most dazzling of nineteenth-century French romantic painters, Delacroix personified the romantic fascination with the sometimes terrible and violent aspects of contemporary life. A melancholic intellectual, he shared Byron's intense hatred of tyranny, his sense of alienation, his self-glorifying egotism, and his faith in the role of the imagination—features all readily discernible in the pages of his diary. In words whose passion recalls Byron, Wordsworth, and Goethe, Delacroix called the imagination "paramount" in the life of the artist. "Strange as it may seem," he observed in his diary, "the great majority of people are devoid of imagination. Not only do they lack the keen, penetrating imagination which would allow them to see objects in a vivid way—which would lead them, as it were, to the very root of things—but they are equally incapable of any clear understanding of works in which imagination predominates."*

Delacroix loved dramatic narrative; he favored sensuous and violent subjects drawn from contemporary life, popular literature, and ancient and medieval history. A six-month visit in 1832 to Morocco, neighbor of France's newly conquered colony of Algeria, was to have a lifelong impact on his interest in exotic subjects and his love of light and color. He depicted the harem women of Islamic Africa, recorded the poignant and shocking results of the Turkish massacres in Greece, brought to life Dante's *Inferno*, and made memorable illustrations for Goethe's *Faust* (see Figure 28.5). His paintings of human and animal combat, such as *Arabs Skirmishing in the Mountains* (Figure **29.5**), are filled with fierce vitality and passion. Such works are faithful to his declaration, "I have no love for reasonable painting."

* *The Journal of Eugène Delacroix*, translated by Lucy Norton. London: Phaidon Press, 1951, 137, 348–349).

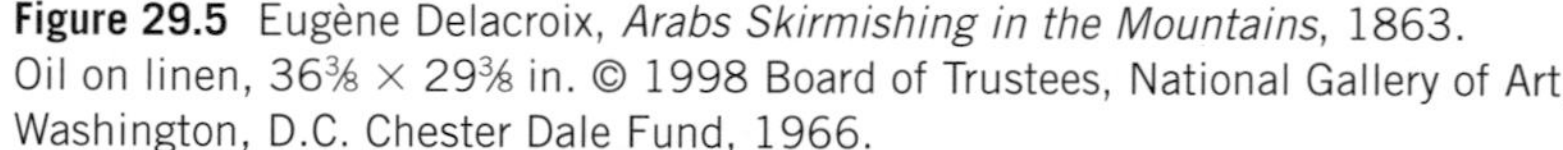

**Figure 29.5** Eugène Delacroix, *Arabs Skirmishing in the Mountains*, 1863. Oil on linen, $36\frac{3}{8} \times 29\frac{3}{8}$ in. © 1998 Board of Trustees, National Gallery of Art, Washington, D.C. Chester Dale Fund, 1966.

**Figure 29.6** (above) Eugène Delacroix, *Liberty Leading the People*, 1830. Oil on canvas, 8 ft. 6 in. × 10 ft. 7 in. Louvre, Paris. Photo: © R.M.N., Paris.

**Figure 29.7** Jacques-Louis David, *The Oath of the Horatii*, 1785. Oil on canvas, 10 ft. 10 in. × 14 ft. Louvre, Paris. Photo: © R.M.N., Paris.

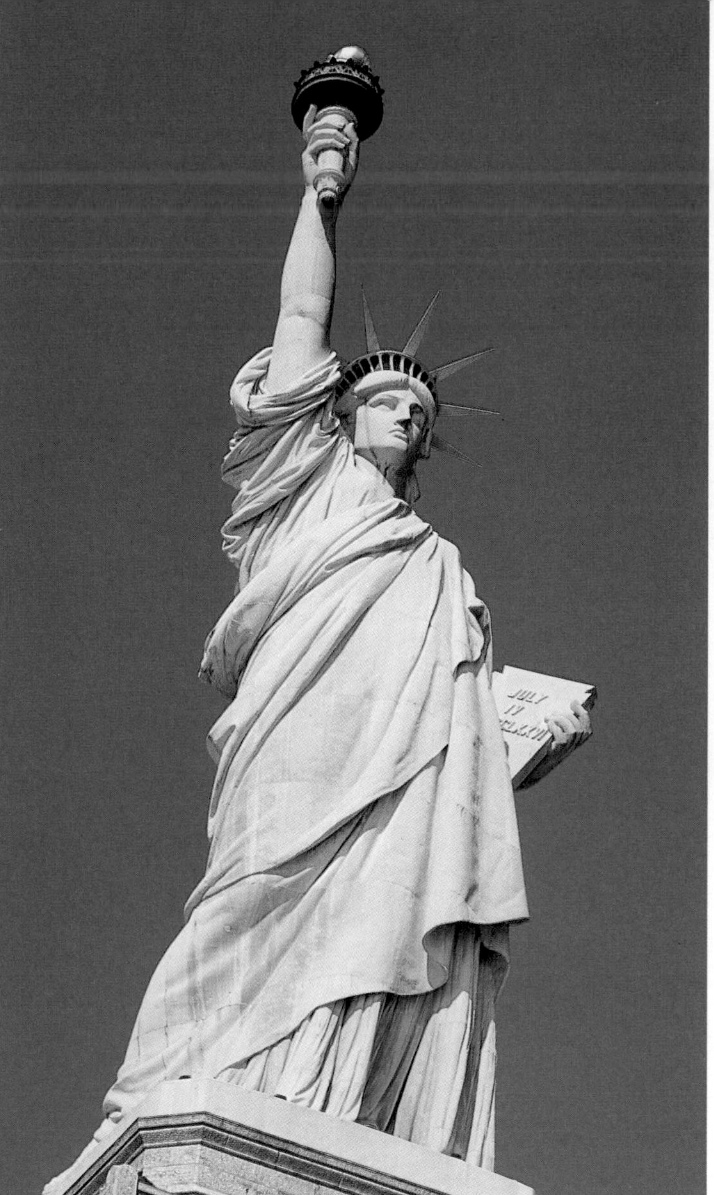

**Figure 29.8** Frédéric-Auguste Bartholdi, Statue of Liberty (Liberty Enlightening the World), Liberty Island (Bedloe's Island), New York, 1871–1884. Framework constructed by A. G. Eiffel. Copper sheets mounted on steel frame, height 152 ft. Photo: Mike Newton/Robert Harding Picture Library, London.

In his politically charged *Liberty Leading the People* (Figure **29.6**), Delacroix transformed a contemporary event (the Revolution of 1830) into a heroic allegory of the struggle for human freedom. When King Charles X dissolved the French legislature and took measures to repress voting rights and freedom of the press, liberal leaders, radicals, and journalists rose in rebellion. Delacroix translated this rebellion into a monumental painting that showed a handsome, bare-breasted female—the personification of Liberty—leading a group of French rebels through the narrow streets of Paris and over barricades strewn with corpses. A bayonet in one hand and the tricolor flag of France in the other, Liberty presses forward to challenge the forces of tyranny. She is champion of "the people": the middle class, as represented by the gentleman in a frock coat; the lower class, as symbolized by the scruffy youth carrying pistols; and racial minorities, as conceived in the black saber-bearer at the left. She is, moreover, France itself, the banner-bearer of the spirit of nationalism that infused nineteenth-century European history.

Delacroix's painting *Liberty Leading the People* is often compared with David's *Oath of the Horatii* (Figure **29.7**) because both paintings are clear calls to heroic action. But in conception and in style, the two paintings are totally different. While David looked to the Roman past for his theme, Delacroix drew on the issues of his time, allegorizing *real* events in order to increase their dramatic impact. And whereas David's appeal was essentially elitist, Delacroix celebrated the collective heroism of ordinary people. Yet Delacroix was never a slave to the facts: Although, for instance, the nudity of the fallen rebel in the left foreground (clearly related to the nudes of Géricault's *Raft)* had no basis in fact—it is uncommon to lose one's trousers in combat—the detail served to emphasize vulnerability and the imminence of death in battle. In his diary, Delacroix defended the artist's freedom to take liberties with form and content: "The most sublime effects of every master," he wrote, "are often the result of *pictorial licence*; for example, the lack of finish in Rembrandt's work, the exaggeration in Rubens. Mediocre painters never have sufficient daring, they never get beyond themselves." Stylistically, Delacroix's *Liberty* explodes with romantic passion. Surging rhythms link the smoke-filled background with the figures of the advancing rebels and the bodies of the fallen heroes heaped in the foreground. Gone are the cool restraints, the linear clarity, and the gridlike regularity of David's *Oath*. Gone also are the slick, finished surfaces. Delacroix's canvas resonates with dense textures and loose, rich brushstrokes. Color charges through the painting in a manner that recalls Rubens (see chapter 23), whose style Delacroix deeply admired.

Delacroix's *Liberty* instantly became a symbol of democratic aspirations. In 1884 France sent as a gift of friendship to the young American nation a monumental copper and cast-iron statue of an idealized female bearing a tablet and a flaming torch (Figure **29.8**). Designed by Frédéric-Auguste Bartholdi (1834–1904), the Statue of Liberty (Liberty Enlightening the World) is the "sister" of Delacroix's painted heroine; it has become a classic image of freedom for homeless and oppressed people everywhere.

**1836** Samuel Colt produces a six-cylinder revolver
**1841** the breech-loading rifle known as the "needlegun" is introduced
**1847** an Italian chemist develops explosive nitroglycerin

**Figure 29.9** François Rude, *La Marseillaise (The Departure of the Volunteers of 1792)*, 1833–1836. Stone, approx. 42 ft. × 26 ft. Arch of Triumph, Paris. Lauros-Giraudon, Paris.

### The Heroic Theme in Sculpture

In sculpture as in painting, heroic subjects served the cause of nationalism. *The Departure of the Volunteers of 1792* (Figure **29.9**) by François Rude (1784–1855) embodied the dynamic heroism of the Napoleonic Era. Installed at the foot of the Arch of Triumph (see chapter 26), which stands at the end of the Champs Elysées in Paris, the 42-foot-high stone sculpture commemorates the patriotism of a band of French volunteers—presumably the battalion of Marseilles, who marched to Paris in 1792 to defend the Republic. Young or old, nude or clothed in ancient or medieval garb (a device that augmented dramatic effect while universalizing the heroic theme), the spirited members of this small citizen army are led by the allegorical figure of Bellona, the Roman goddess of war. Like Delacroix's Liberty, Rude's classical goddess urges the patriots onward. The vitality of the piece is enhanced by deep undercutting, which results in dramatic contrasts of light and dark. In this richly textured work, Rude captured the revolutionary spirit and emotional fervor of the marching song of this battalion, *La Marseillaise*, which the French later adopted as their national anthem.

**Figure 29.10** Charles-Henri-Joseph Cordier, *African in Algerian Costume*, ca. 1856–1857. Bronze and onyx, 37¾ × 26 × 14 in. Musée d'Orsay, Paris. Photo: © R.M.N., Paris.

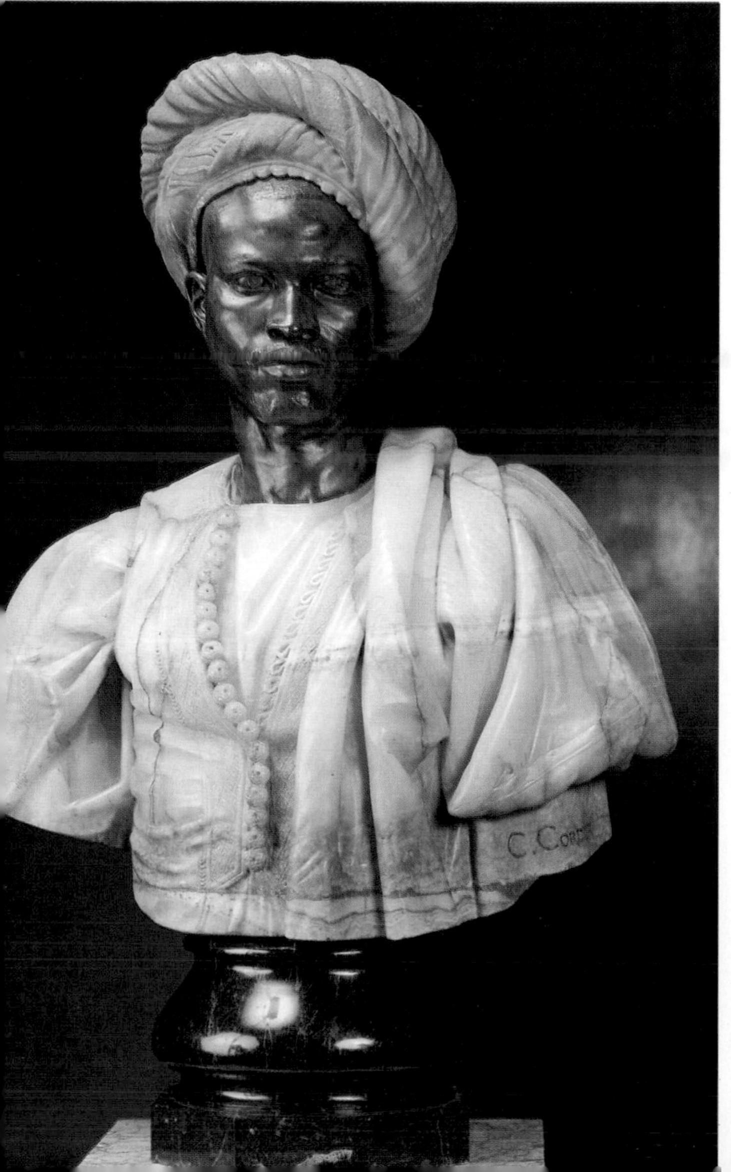


The spirit of nationalism prompted a passionate curiosity about other nations and ethnic groups. Just as Catlin looked to Native Americans as a source of colorful imagery, so European artists turned to the East and to Africa for exotic subjects. Napoleon's invasion of Egypt (1798–1801) had started a virtual craze for things North African, and these interests were further stimulated by the French presence in Algeria beginning in the 1830s. Charles-Henri-Joseph Cordier (1827–1905), a member of Rude's studio and a favorite exhibitor in the academic Salon of Paris, requested a governmental assignment in Africa in order to make a record of its peoples. The result of Cordier's ethnological studies was a series of twelve busts of Africans and Asians, executed by means of innovative polychrome techniques that combined bronze or colored marble with porphyry, jasper, and onyx from Algerian quarries (Figure **29.10**). Cordier's portrait heads reveal a sensitivity to individual personality and a commitment to capturing the dignity of his models. Rather than perceiving his subjects as exotic "others," he regarded them as racial types "at the point," as he explained, "of merging into one and the same people."

## *Trends in Mid-Nineteenth-Century Architecture*

### Neomedievalism in the West

Architects of the early to mid-nineteenth century regarded the past as a source of inspiration and moral instruction. Classical Greek and republican Roman buildings embodied the political and aesthetic ideals of nation-builders like Napoleon and Jefferson (see chapter 26); but the austere dignity of neoclassicism did not appeal to all tastes, nor did the romantic embrace of the past confine itself to Greco-Roman culture. More typical of the romantic imagination was a deep affection for the medieval world with its brooding castles and towering cathedrals. No less than neoclassicism, neomedievalism was the product of an energetic effort to revive the distinctive features of a nation's historical and cultural past, hence an expression of nationalism. In England, where the Christian heritage of the Middle Ages was closely associated with national identity, writers embraced the medieval past: Alfred Lord Tennyson (1802–1892), poet laureate of Great Britain, for instance, fused early British legend with the Christian

**Figure 29.11** Charles Barry and A. W. N. Pugin, Houses of Parliament, London, 1840–1860. Length 940 ft. Photo: A. F. Kersting, London.

mission in a cycle of Arthurian poems entitled *Idylls of the King*; while Sir Walter Scott immortalized medieval heroes and heroines in avidly read historical novels and romantic poems.

In architecture, the revival of the Gothic style was equally distinctive. The British Houses of Parliament, conceived by Charles Barry (1795–1860) and Augustus Welby Northmore Pugin (1812–1852) and begun in 1836, are among the most aesthetically successful large-scale neo-Gothic public buildings. The picturesque combination of spires and towers fronting on the River Thames in London was the product of Pugin's conviction that the Gothic style best expressed the dignity befitting the official architecture of a Christian nation (Figure **29.11**). Moreover, the Gothic style was symbolically appropriate for the building that epitomized the principles of parliamentary rule, pioneered in England with the signing of the Magna Carta in 1215. Pugin's affection for the neo-Gothic also reflected his own personal experience: His architectural conversion to the Gothic occurred almost simultaneously with his religious conversion to Roman Catholicism. For Pugin, Christian architecture, characterized by purity of structure and the meaningful application of details, was the visual correlation of the Catholic faith. The Houses of Parliament might be said to reflect the importance of medieval historical tradition—both religious and political—in shaping England's self-image.

Neomedievalism gave rise to a movement for the archeological restoration of churches and castles throughout Europe; but it also inspired some extraordinary new architectural activity in North America. College and university buildings (such as those at Harvard

**Figure 29.12** James Renwick and William Bodrigue, Saint Patrick's Cathedral, Fifth Avenue and 50th Street, New York, 1853–1858. World Wide Photo. © Museum of the City of New York.

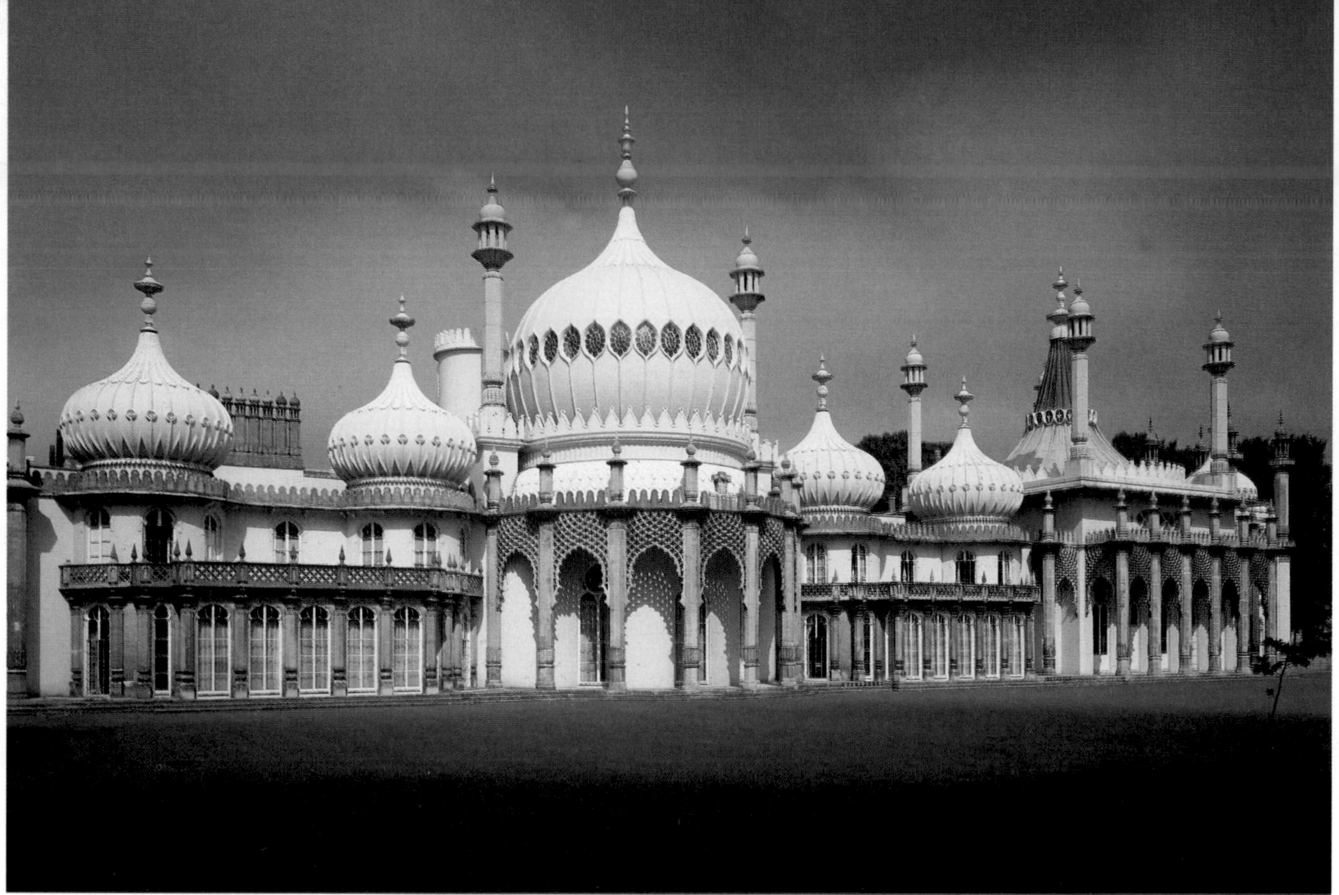

**Figure 29.13** John Nash, The Royal Pavilion, Brighton, from the northeast, 1815–1821. Photo: A. F. Kersting, London.

and Yale), museums (such as the Smithsonian in Washington, D.C.), and numerous churches and cathedrals became candidates for construction in the Romanesque or the Gothic style. One of the most elegant examples of the Gothic revival in the United States is Saint Patrick's Cathedral in New York City (Figure **29.12**), which (along with Grace Church in Manhattan and the Smithsonian) was designed by James Renwick (1818–1895)

### Exoticism in Western Architecture

While nineteenth-century architects embraced both the classical and medieval past, they also found inspiration in the "exotic" architecture of the East, and especially those parts of the world in which the European powers were building colonial empires. The most intriguing Western pastiche of non-Western styles is the Royal Pavilion at Brighton, which combines a fanciful assortment of Chinese, Indian, and Islamic motifs (Figure **29.13**). Designed by the English architect John Nash (1752–1835) between 1815 and 1821 as a seaside resort for the Prince Regent, Nash raised bulbous domes and slender minarets over a hidden frame of cast iron, the structural medium that would soon come to dominate modern architecture (see chapter 30). The bizarre fantasy of the interior decor, which includes water lily chandeliers and cast-iron palm trees with copper leaves, produced an eclectic style that was called in its own time "Indian Gothic."

## *The Romantic Style in Music*

"Music is the most romantic of all the arts—one might almost say, the only genuine romantic one—for its sole subject is the infinite." Thus wrote the German novelist and musician, E. T. A. Hoffmann (1776–1822). Like many romantic composers, Hoffmann believed that music held a privileged position in its capacity to express what he called "an inexpressible longing." For the romantics, music—the most abstract and elusive of the arts—was capable of freeing the intellect and speaking directly to the heart.

The nineteenth century produced an enormous amount of fine music in all genres—a phenomenon that is reflected in the fact that audiences today listen to more nineteenth-century music than to music of any other time period. The hallmark of romantic music is personalized expression, and this feature is as apparent in large orchestral works as it is in small, intimate pieces. Like romantic poets and painters, romantic composers modified classical "rules" in order to increase expressive effects. They abandoned the precise forms and clear contours of classical music in favor of expanded or loosened forms, singable melodies, and lively rhythms. Just as romantic painters exploited color to heighten emotional impact, so composers elevated tone color (the distinctive quality of musical sound made by a voice, a musical instrument, or a combination of instruments) to a status equal to melody, harmony, and rhythm.

During the romantic era the orchestra grew to grand proportions. Mid-nineteenth-century orchestras were often five times larger than those used by Haydn and Mozart. While the volume of sound expanded, the varieties of instrumental possibilities also grew larger, in part because of technical improvements made in the instruments themselves. For instance, brass instruments (such as the trumpet and the tuba) gained new pitches and a wider range with the addition of valves; and woodwind instruments (such as the flute and the clarinet) underwent structural changes that greatly facilitated fingering and tuning. Such mechanical improvements expanded the tonal potential of musical instruments and produced a virtual revolution in orchestral textures.

In terms of musical composition, the symphony and the concerto were the most important of the large forms; equally popular, however, were song forms, especially songs that dealt with themes of love and death or nature and nature's moods. Composers found inspiration in heroic subjects, in contemporary events, and in the legends and histories of their native lands. Like the romantic painters and writers, they favored exotic, faraway themes. Both in small musical forms and in large operatic compositions, they made every effort to achieve an ideal union of poetry and music. Finally, as if to draw attention to their own technical abilities, many romantic composers wrote music (usually for piano or violin) that only highly accomplished musicians like themselves could perform with facility.

## The Genius of Beethoven

The leading composer of the early nineteenth century and one of the greatest musicians of all time was the German-born Ludwig van Beethoven (1770–1827). Beethoven lived most of his life in Vienna, where he became acquainted with Mozart and studied briefly with Haydn. A skillful pianist, organist, and violinist, Beethoven composed works in almost every medium and form. His thirty-two piano sonatas tested the expressive potential of an instrument that—having acquired in the early nineteenth century an iron frame, two or three pedals, and thicker strings—was capable of extraordinary brilliance in tone and greater degrees of expressiveness, features that made the piano the most popular musical instrument of the nineteenth century.

Beethoven's greatest enterprise was his nine symphonies. These remarkable compositions generally adhered to the format of the classical symphony, but they moved beyond the boundaries of classical structure and were longer and more complex than any instrumental compositions written by Mozart or Haydn. Nevertheless, his indebtedness to classical composition makes him something of a bridge between the classical and romantic eras. By adding trombones and bass clarinet to the symphony orchestra and doubling the number of flutes, oboes, clarinets, and bassoons in his scoring, Beethoven vastly broadened the expressive range and dramatic power of orchestral sound. The expanded tone color and rich sonorities of Beethoven's symphonies are in part the product of such instruments as the piccolo, bass drum, and cymbals, all of which Beethoven added to the symphony orchestra.

Beethoven's genius lay in his introduction of a new rhythmic vitality that governed shifting patterns of grandeur and intimacy. In his use of musical **dynamics** (gradations of loudness and softness), Beethoven was more explicit and varied than his classical predecessors. Prior to 1812 Beethoven made use of only five terms to indicate the softness or loudness of piano performance; increasingly, however, he expanded this vocabulary with such words as *dolente* ("sorrowful") and *teneramente* ("tenderly") to indicate nuances. Like other romantic artists—Delacroix, in particular, comes to mind—Beethoven blurred the divisions between the structural units of a composition, exploiting textural contrasts for expressive effect. He often broke with classical form, adding, for example, a fifth movement to his Sixth (or "Pastoral") Symphony and embellishing the finale of his Ninth Symphony with a chorus and solo voices. Beethoven's daring use of dissonances, his sudden pauses and silences, and his brilliance of thematic and rhythmic invention reflect his preference for dramatic spontaneity over measured regularity. The powerful opening notes of the Fifth Symphony—a motif that Beethoven is said to have called "fate knocking at the door"—exemplify his affection for inventive repetitions and surging rhythms that propel the music toward a powerful climax.

Like Byron and Gros, Beethoven admired Napoleon as a popular hero and a champion of liberty. In 1799, he dedicated his Third Symphony to Napoleon, adding to the title page the subtitle "Eroica" ("Heroic"). When Napoleon crowned himself emperor in 1804, however, Beethoven angrily scratched out Napoleon's name, so that when the piece was published, it bore only a generalized dedication: "to the memory of a great man." Beethoven's Third Symphony is colossal in size and complexity. It follows the standard number and order of movements found in the classical symphony, but it is almost twice as long as a typical classical symphony of some twenty to twenty-five minutes. The first movement,♪ which one French critic called "the Grand Army of the soul," engages six rather than the traditional two themes dictated by sonata form. The movement begins with two commanding hammer strikes of sound and follows with a series of themes that feature

♪See Music Listening Selections at end of chapter.

Beethoven = Bigger & Better.

**Figure 29.14** *Beethoven Composing the "Pastoral" by a Brook*, from the Twenty-Second Almanac of the Zürich Musikgesellschaft for 1834: Biography of Ludwig van Beethoven. Colored lithograph, $5\frac{2}{5} \times 6\frac{1}{2}$ in. By permission of the Beethoven Haus, Bonn. H. C. Bodmer Collection.

the French horn, the symbol of the hero throughout the entire piece. The second movement is a somber and solemn funeral march. For the third movement, instead of the traditional minuet, Beethoven penned a vigorous *scherzo* (in Italian, "joke"), which replaced the elegance of a courtly dance with a melody that was fast and vigorous—a joke in that it was undanceable! The last movement, a victory finale, brings the themes of the first movement together with a long coda that again features the horn. It is worth noting that for the triumphant last movement of this stirring symphony, Beethoven included musical passages originally written for a ballet on the theme of Prometheus.

Difficult as it is to imagine, Beethoven wrote much of his greatest music when he was functionally deaf. From the age of twenty-nine, when he became aware of a progressive degeneration of his hearing, he labored against depression and despair. Temperamental and defiant, Beethoven scorned the patronage system that had weighed heavily upon both Mozart and Haydn, and sold his musical compositions as an independent artist. Unlike Haydn and Mozart, he declared contempt for the nobility and ignored their demands. In 1802 he confided to his family, "I am bound to be misunderstood; for me there can be no relaxation with my fellow men, no refined conversations, no mutual exchange of ideas. I must live alone like one who has been banished." In retreat from society, the alienated composer turned to nature (Figure **29.14**). In the woods outside of Vienna, Beethoven roamed with his musical sketchbook under one arm, often singing to himself in a loud voice. "Woods, trees and rock," he wrote in his diary, "give the response that man requires." Beethoven's discovery that nature mirrored his deepest emotions inspired his programmatic Sixth (or "Pastoral") Symphony of 1808, which he subtitled "A recollection of country life." Each of the five movements of the "Pastoral" is labeled with a specific reference to nature: "Awakening of happy feelings on arriving in the country"; "By the brook"; "Joyous gatherings of country folk"; "Storm"; and "Shepherd's Song, happy and thankful feelings after the storm." In the tradition of Vivaldi's *Four Seasons* (see chapter 22), Beethoven occasionally imitated the sounds of nature. For example, at the end of the second movement, flute, oboe, and clarinet join to create bird calls; and a quavering ***tremolo*** (the rapid repetition of a tone to produce a trembling effect) on the lower strings suggests the sounds of a murmuring brook.

## German Art Songs

The art songs of Beethoven's Austrian contemporary Franz Schubert (1797–1828) aptly reflect the nineteenth-century composer's ambition to unite poetry and music. Schubert is credited with originating the ***lied*** (German for "song," pl. *lieder*), an independent song for solo voice and piano. The *lied* is not a song in the traditional sense but, rather, a poem recreated in musical terms. Its lyric qualities, like those of simple folk songs, are generated by the poem itself. The *lieder* of Schubert, Robert Schumann (1810–1856), and Johannes Brahms (1833–1897), which set to music the poetry of Heine and Goethe, among others, are intimate evocations of personal feelings and moods. Such pieces recount tales of love and longing, describe nature and its moods (some forty songs are related to water or to fish), or lament the transience of human happiness.

Among Schubert's 1,000 or so works (which include 9 symphonies and numerous chamber pieces) are 600 *lieder*. The song "Gretchen am Spinnrade" ("Gretchen at the Spinning Wheel")♫ is based on a poem by Goethe which occurs near the end of Part I of *Faust*. In the piece, Gretchen laments the absence of her lover Faust and anticipates the sorrows that their love will bring. Repeated three times are the poignant lines with which the song opens: "My peace is gone, my heart is sore:/I shall find it never and never more." While the melody and tone color of the voice line convey the sadness expressed in the words of the poem, the lively piano line captures the rhythms of the spinning wheel.

## The Programmatic Symphonies of Berlioz

The French composer Hector Berlioz (1803–1869) began his first symphony in 1830. An imaginative combination of the story of Faust and Berlioz's own life, the *Symphonie fantastique* tells the dramatic tale of Berlioz's "interminable and inextinguishable passion"—as he described it—for the captivating Irish actress Harriet Smithson. Berlioz wrote the symphony in the first flush of his passion, when he was only twenty-seven years old. Following an intense courtship, he married Harriet, only to discover that he and the woman he idolized were dreadfully mismatched—the marriage turned Smithson into an alcoholic and Berlioz into an adulterer.

The *Symphonie fantastique* belongs to the genre known as **program music**, that is, instrumental music endowed with a specific literary or pictorial content indicated by the composer. Berlioz was not the first to write music that was programmatic: In *The Four Seasons*, Vivaldi had linked music to poetic phrases, as had Beethoven in his "Pastoral" Symphony. But Berlioz was the first to build an entire symphony around a set of musical motifs that told a story. The popularity of program music during the nineteenth century testifies to the powerful influence of literature upon the other arts. Berlioz, whose second symphony, *Harold in Italy*, was inspired by Byron's *Childe Harold* (see chapter 28), was not alone in his attraction to literary subjects. The Hungarian composer Franz Liszt (1811–1886) wrote symphonic poems based on the myth of Prometheus and Shakespeare's *Hamlet*. He also composed the *Faust Symphony*, which he dedicated to Berlioz. And the Russian composer Peter Ilich Tchaikovsky (1840–1893) wrote many programmatic pieces, including the tone poem *Romeo and Juliet*.

♫See Music Listening Selections at end of chapter.

**Figure 29.15** Gustave Doré, *Berlioz Conducting Massed Choirs*, nineteenth-century caricature. © The Bettmann Archive, New York.

In the *Symphonie fantastique*, Berlioz links a specific mood or event to a musical phrase, or *idée fixe* ("fixed idea"). This recurring musical motif, which Berlioz introduces within the first five minutes of the opening movement, becomes the means by which the composer binds together the individual parts of his dramatic narrative. Subtitled "Episode in the Life of an Artist," the *Symphonie fantastique* is an account of the young musician's opium-induced dream, in which, according to Berlioz's program notes, "the Beloved One takes the form of a melody in his mind, like a fixed idea which is ever returning and which he hears everywhere." Unified by the *idée fixe*, the symphony consists of a sequence of five parts, each distinguished by a particular mood: the lover's "reveries and passions"; a ball at which the hero meets his beloved; a stormy scene in the country; a "March to the Scaffold"𝄞 (marking the hero's dream of murdering his lover and his subsequent execution); and a final and feverishly orchestrated "Dream of a Witches' Sabbath" inspired by Goethe's *Faust*. (Berlioz's *Damnation of Faust*, a piece for soloists, chorus, and orchestra, likewise drew on Goethe's great drama.) The "plot" of the *Symphonie fantastique*, published along with the musical score, was (and usually still is) printed in program notes available to listeners. But the written narrative is *not* essential to the enjoyment of the music, for, as Berlioz himself explained, the music holds authority as absolute sound, above and beyond its programmatic associations.

𝄞See Music Listening Selections at end of chapter.

Berlioz, the spiritual heir to Beethoven, took liberties with traditional symphonic form. He composed the *Symphonie fantastique* in five movements instead of the usual four and combined instruments inventively so as to create unusual sets of sound. In the third movement, for example, a solo English horn and four kettledrums produce the effect of "distant thunder." He also expanded tone color, stretching the register of clarinets to screeching highs, for instance, and playing the strings of the violin with the wood of the bow instead of with the hair. Berlioz's favorite medium was the full symphony orchestra, which he enlarged to include 150 musicians. Called "the apostle of bigness," Berlioz conceived an *ideal* orchestra that consisted of over 400 musicians, including 242 string instruments, 30 pianos, 30 harps, and a chorus of 360 voices. The monumental proportions of Berlioz's orchestras drew spoofs in contemporary cartoons, such as that by the French illustrator Gustave Doré (Figure **29.15**). But Berlioz, who was also a talented writer and a music critic for Parisian newspapers, thumbed his nose at the critics in lively essays that defended his own musical philosophy.

## The Piano Music of Chopin

If the nineteenth century was the age of romantic individualism, it was also the age of the **virtuoso**. In music, this meant that composers wrote music that might be performed gracefully and accurately only by individuals with extraordinary technical skills. One such individual was the Polish-born composer Frédéric Chopin (1810–1849). At the age of seven, Chopin gave his first piano concert in Warsaw. Slight in build even as an adult, Chopin had small hands that nevertheless could reach like "the jaws of a snake" (as one of his peers observed) across the keys of the piano. After leaving Warsaw, Chopin became the acclaimed pianist of the Paris *salons* and a close friend of Delacroix (who painted the portrait in Figure **29.16**), Berlioz, and many of the leading novelists of his age, including George Sand (see chapter 28), with whom he had a stormy nine-year love affair.

In his brief lifetime—he died of tuberculosis at the age of thirty-nine—Chopin created an entirely personal musical idiom linked to the expressive potential of the modern piano. For the piano, Chopin wrote over two hundred pieces, most of which were small, intimate works, such as dances, *préludes* (short keyboard pieces in one movement), **nocturnes** (slow, songlike pieces), **impromptus** (short keyboard compositions that sound improvised), and *études* (instrumental studies designed to improve a player's technique). Chopin's Etude in G-flat Major, **Opus** 10, No. 5,𝄞 is a breathtaking piece that

𝄞See Music Listening Selections at end of chapter.

**Figure 29.16** Eugène Delacroix, *Frédéric Chopin*, 1838. Oil on canvas, 18 × 15 in. Louvre, Paris. Giraudon/Art Resource, New York.

challenges the performer to play very rapidly on the black keys, which are less than half the width of the white keys.

As with Delacroix's paintings, which though carefully contrived give the impression of spontaneity, so Chopin's music seems improvised—the impetuous record of fleeting feeling, rather than the studied product of diligent construction. The most engaging of his compositions are marked by fresh turns of harmony and free tempos and rhythms. Chopin might embellish a melodic line with unusual and flamboyant devices, such as a rolling **arpeggio** (the sounding of the notes of a chord in rapid succession). His *préludes* provide bold contrasts of calm meditation and bravura, while his nocturnes—like the romantic landscapes of Friedrich and Corot (see Figures 27.9 and 27.10)—are often dreamy and wistful. Of his dance forms, the polonaise and the mazurka preserve the robustness of the folk tunes of his native Poland, while the waltz mirrors the romantic taste for a new type of dance, more sensuous and physically expressive than the courtly and formal minuet. Considered vulgar and lewd when it was introduced in the late eighteenth century, the waltz, with its freedom of movement and intoxicating rhythms, became the most popular of all nineteenth-century dances.

## *The Romantic Ballet*

The theatrical art form known as "ballet" reached immense popularity in the Age of Romanticism. While the great ballets of Tchaikovsky—*Swan Lake, The Nutcracker*, and *Sleeping Beauty*—brought fame to Russia at the end of the century, it was in nineteenth-century Paris that romantic ballet was born. By the year 1800, ballet had moved from the court to the theater, where it was enjoyed as a middle-class entertainment. Magnificent theaters, such as the Paris Opéra (Figure **29.17**),

**Figure 29.17** J. L. Charles Garnier, the facade of the Opéra, Paris, 1860–1875. Giraudon, Paris.

**Figure 29.18** J. L. Charles Garnier, the Grand Staircase in the Opéra, Paris, 1862–1875. Engraving from Charles Garnier, *Le Nouvel Opéra de Paris*, 1880, Vol. 2, plate 8.

**Figure 29.19** Jean-Baptiste Carpeaux, *The Dance*, 1867–1869. Stone. Created for the facade of the Opéra, Paris, now in Musée de l'Opéra, Paris. Giraudon/Art Resource, New York.

completed in 1875 by J. L. Charles Garnier (1825–1878), became showplaces for public entertainment. The neobaroque facade of the opera house reflects Garnier's awareness that Greek architects had painted parts of their buildings; but the glory of the structure is its interior, which takes as its focus a sumptuous grand staircase (Figure **29.18**). Luxuriously appointed, and illuminated by means of the latest technological invention, gaslight, the Paris Opéra became the model for public theaters throughout Europe. For the facade, Jean-Baptiste Carpeaux (1827–1875) created a 15-foot-high sculpture whose exuberant rhythms capture the spirit of the dance as the physical expression of human joy (Figure **29.19**).

The ballets performed on the stage of the Paris Opéra launched a Golden Age in European dance. In Paris in 1832, the Italian-born **prima ballerina** (the first, or leading, female dancer in a ballet company) Maria Taglioni (1804–1884) perfected the art of dancing *sur les points* ("on the toes") (Figure **29.20**). Taglioni's performance in the ballet *La Sylphide* (choreographed by her father) was hailed as nothing less than virtuoso. Clothed in a diaphanous dress with a fitted bodice and a bell-shaped skirt (the prototype of the tutu), Taglioni performed perfect **arabesques**—a ballet position in which the dancer stands on one leg with the other extended in back and one or both arms held to create the longest line possible from one extremity to the other. She also astonished audiences by crossing the stage in three magnificent, floating leaps. While faithful to the exact steps of the classical ballet, Taglioni brought to formal dance the new, more sensuous spirit of nineteenth-century romanticism.

Popular legends and fairy tales inspired many of the ballets of the romantic era, including *La Sylphide, Giselle,* and the more widely known *Swan Lake* and *Sleeping Beauty,* composed by Tchaikovsky. The central figure of each ballet is usually some version of the angelic female—a fictional creature drawn from fable, fairy tale, and fantasy. The sylph in *La Sylphide* was a mythical nature deity who was thought to inhabit the air, as, for instance, nymphs were thought to inhabit the woodlands. In *La Sylphide,* a sylph enchants the hero and lures him away from his bride-to-be. Pursued by the hero, she nevertheless evades his grasp and dies—the victim of a witch's malevolence—before their love is

**Figure 29.20** Maria Taglioni in her London debut of 1830. Bibliothèque Nationale, Paris.

consummated. The heroine of *La Sylphide* (and other romantic ballets) along with the prima ballerina who assumed that role were symbols of the elusive ideals of love and beauty eulogized by such romantic poets as Byron and Keats (see chapters 27 and 28). She conformed as well to the stereotype of the pure and virtuous female found in the pages of Sand's romantic novels. The traditional equation of beauty and innocence in the person of the idealized female is well illustrated in the comments of one French critic, who described "the aerial and virginal grace of Taglioni," and exulted, "She flies like a spirit in the midst of transparent clouds of white muslin—she resembles a happy angel." Clearly, the nineteenth-century ballerina was the romantic realization of the Eternal Female, a figure that fits the stereotype of the angelic woman.

# *Romantic Opera*

## Verdi and Italian Grand Opera

Romantic opera, designed to appeal to a growing middle-class audience, came into existence after 1820. The culmination of baroque theatricality, romantic opera was grand both in size and in spirit. It was a flamboyant spectacle that united all aspects of theatrical production—music, dance, stage sets, and costumes. While Paris was the operatic capital of Europe in the first half of the nineteenth century, Italy ultimately took the lead in seducing the public with hundreds of wonderfully tuneful and melodramatic romantic operas.

The leading Italian composer of the romantic era was Giuseppe Verdi (1813–1901). In Verdi's twenty-six operas, including *Rigoletto* (1851), *La Traviata* (1853), and *Otello* (1887), the long, unbroken Italian operatic tradition that began with Monteverdi (see chapter 20) came to its peak. Reflecting on his gift for capturing high drama in music, Verdi exclaimed, "Success is impossible for me if I cannot write as my heart dictates." The heroines of Verdi's operas, also creatures of the heart, usually die for love. Perhaps the most famous of Verdi's operas is *Aida*, which was commissioned in 1870 by the Turkish viceroy of Egypt to mark the opening of the Suez Canal. *Aida* made a nationalistic plea for unity against foreign domination—one critic called the opera "agitator's music." Indeed, the aria "O patria mia" ("O my country") is an expression of Verdi's ardent love for the newly unified Italy. But *Aida* is also the passionate love story of an Egyptian prince and an Ethiopian princess held as a captive slave. Verdi's stirring arias, vigorous choruses, and richly colored orchestral passages can be enjoyed by listening alone, but the dramatic force of this opera can only be appreciated by witnessing first-hand a theatrical performance—especially one that engages such traditional paraphernalia as horses, chariots, and, of course, elephants.

## Wagner and the Birth of Music-Drama

In Germany, the master of grand opera and one of the most formidable composers of the century was Richard Wagner (1813–1883). The stepson of a gifted actor, Wagner spent much of his childhood composing poems and plays and setting them to music. This union of music and literature culminated in the birth of what Wagner called ***music-drama***, a unique synthesis of sound and story. Wagner drew on romantic themes from German history and legend. He wrote his own librettos and composed scores that brought to life the events and personalities featured in his stories. His aim, as he himself explained, was "to force the listener, for the first time in the history of opera, to take an interest in a poetic idea, by making him follow all its developments" as dramatized simultaneously in sound and story.

Of Wagner's nine principal operas, his greatest is a monumental, fifteen-hour cycle of four music-dramas collectively titled *Der Ring des Nibelungen* (*The Ring of the Nibelung*; Figure 29.21). Based on Norse and Germanic mythology, *The Ring* involves the quest for a magical but

**Figure 29.21** New York Metropolitan Opera production of Wagner's *The Rhinegold* from *The Ring of the Nibelung*. 

accursed golden ring, the power of which would provide its possessor with the potential to control the universe. Out of a struggle between the gods of Valhalla and a race of giants emerges the hero, Siegfried, whose valorous deeds secure the ring for his lover Brünnhilde. In the end Siegfried loses both his love and his life, and Valhalla crumbles in flames, destroying the gods and eliciting the birth of a new order. Like Goethe, whose *Faust* was a lifetime effort and a tribute to his nation's past, Wagner toiled on the monumental *Ring* for over twenty-five years, from 1848 to 1874.

Awesome in imaginative scope, *The Ring* brings to life some of the hero myths that shaped the Western, and especially Germanic, literary tradition. Equally imaginative is the music, which matches its poetry in scope and drama. According to Wagner, heroic music was made possible only by a heroic orchestra—his totaled 115 pieces, including 64 strings. Unlike Verdi, whose operas generally reflect nineteenth-century musical practice, Wagner's music-dramas anticipate some of the more radical experiments of the twentieth century, including the dissolution of classical tonality (see chapter 32). In fact, Wagner's music-dramas shattered traditional Western operatic techniques. Whereas composers normally divided the dramatic action into recitatives, arias, choruses, and instrumental passages, with the vocal line predominating, the mature Wagner gives the entire dramatic action to the orchestra, which engulfs the listener in a maelstrom of uninterrupted melody. In Wagner's operas, the vocal line is blended with a continuous orchestral line. Character and events emerge with clarity, however, owing to Wagner's use of ***leitmotifs*** (an anglicized German word for "leading motifs"), short musical phrases that—like Berlioz's *idées fixes*—designate a particular person, thing, or idea in the story. *The Ring*, which features a total of twenty *leitmotifs*, is a complex web of dramatic and musical themes. "Every bar of dramatic music," Wagner proclaimed, "is justified only by the fact that it explains something in the action or in the character of the actor." The artist's mission, insisted Wagner, is to communicate "the necessary spontaneous emotional mood"; and in his expressive union of poetry and music, Wagner fulfilled that mission.

## *SUMMARY*

In both form and content, romantic art ignited the imagination. Romantic artists generally elevated the heart over the mind and the emotions over the intellect. They favored subjects that gave free rein to the imagination, to the mysteries of the spirit, and to the cult of the ego. Increasingly independent of the official sources of patronage, they regarded themselves as the heroes of their age and often turned their works into autobiographical expressions of their own ideas, dreams, and feelings.

Romantic artists favored heroic themes and personalities, especially those that illustrated the struggle for political independence. Gros, Géricault, Goya, and Delacroix stretched the bounds of traditional subject matter to include controversial contemporary events, exotic subjects, and medieval legends. Delacroix's *Liberty Leading the People* (Figure 29.6) and Rude's *Departure of the Volunteers of 1792* (Figure 29.9) are quintessential examples of the spirit of nationalism that swept through nineteenth-century Europe. The search for national identity is also evident in the Gothic revival in Western architecture. Neomedievalism challenged neoclassicism in paying homage to Europe's historic past. As the romantics preferred themes exalting spontaneous emotion over poised objectivity, they launched a style that exalted freedom in composition and technique. Romantic painters, for instance, rejected neoclassical rules of balance and clarity in composition and tended to model forms by means of bold color and vigorous brushwork.

Romantic composers, like other romantic artists, found inspiration in heroic and nationalistic themes, as well as in nature's moods and the vagaries of human love. In their desire to express strong personal emotions, they often abandoned classical models and stretched musical forms to fit their feelings. The enlargement of the symphony orchestra in size and expressive range is apparent in the works of Beethoven, Berlioz, and Wagner. Berlioz's *idée fixe* and Wagner's *leitmotif* tied sound to story, evidence of the romantic search for an ideal union of poetry and music. Lyrical melodies and tone color became as important to romantic music as the free use of form and color were to romantic painters. Schubert united poetry and music in the intimate form of the *lied*, while Chopin captured a vast range of moods and emotions in virtuoso piano pieces.

Two of the most popular forms of musical expression in the nineteenth century were ballet and opera. Romantic ballet, which featured themes drawn from fantasy and legend, flowered in France and, later, in Russia. Grand opera was brought to its peak in Italy by Verdi and in Germany by Wagner, both of whom exploited nationalistic themes. The fact that so much nineteenth-century art, music, and dance is still enjoyed today reflects the strength of romanticism both as a style and as an attitude of mind.

## GLOSSARY

**aquatint** a type of print produced by an engraving method similar to etching but involving finely granulated tonal areas rather than line alone

**arabesque** in ballet, a position in which the dancer stands on one leg with the other extended in back and one or both arms held to create the longest line possible from one extremity of the body to the other

**arpeggio** the sounding of the notes of a chord in rapid succession

**dynamics** the gradations of loudness or softness with which music is performed

***étude*** (French, "study") an instrumental study designed to improve a player's performance technique

***idée fixe*** (French "fixed idea") a term used by Berlioz for a recurring theme in his symphonic works

**impromptu** (French, "improvised") a short keyboard composition that sounds as if it were improvised

***leitmotif*** (German, "leading motif") a short musical theme that designates a person, object, place, or idea and that reappears throughout a musical composition

***lied*** (German, "song," pl. *lieder*) an independent song for solo voice and piano; also known as "art song"

**music-drama** a unique synthesis of sound and story in which both are developed simultaneously and continuously; a term used to describe Wagner's later operas

**nocturne** a slow, songlike piece, usually written for piano; the melody is played by the right hand, and a steady, soft accompaniment is played by the left

**opus** (Latin, "work") a musical composition; followed by a number, it designates either the chronological place of a musical composition in the composer's total musical output or the order of its publication; often abbreviated "op."

**prima ballerina** the first, or leading, female dancer in a ballet company

**program music** instrumental music endowed with specific literary or pictorial content that is indicated by the composer

***scherzo*** (Italian, "joke") in Beethoven's music, a sprightly, lively movement

***tremolo*** in music, the rapid repetition of a single pitch or two pitches alternately, producing a trembling effect

**virtuoso** one who exhibits great technical ability, especially in musical performance; also used to describe a musical composition demanding (or a performance demonstrating) great technical skill

## SUGGESTIONS FOR READING


Boime, Albert. *Hollow Icons: The Politics of Sculpture in Nineteenth-Century France.* Kent, Ohio: Kent State University Press, 1987.

Clark, Kenneth. *The Romantic Rebellion: Romantic Versus Classic Art.* New York: Harper, 1986.

Conrad, Peter. *Romantic Opera and Literary Form.* Berkeley, Calif.: University of California Press, 1977.

Einstein, Alfred. *Music in the Romantic Era.* New York: Norton, 1947.

Friedlander, Walter. *David to Delacroix*, translated by Robert Goldwater. Cambridge, Mass.: Harvard University Press, 1952.

Hannoosh, Michele. *Painting and the Journal of Eugène Delacroix.* Princeton, N.J.: Princeton University Press, 1996.

Kerman, Joseph, and Alan Tyson. *The New Grove Beethoven.* London: Macmillan, 1983.

Longyear, Rey. *Nineteenth-Century Romanticism in Music.* Englewood Cliffs, N.J.: Prentice-Hall, 1973.

Migel, Parmenia. *The Ballerinas: From the Court of Louis XIV to Pavlova.* New York: Macmillan, 1972.

Plantinga, Leon. *Romantic Music.* New York: Norton, 1982.

Rosen, Charles. *The Romantic Generation.* Cambridge, Mass.: Harvard University Press, 1995.

Vaughan, William. *Romantic Art.* London: Thames and Hudson, 1978.

Weber, William. *Music and the Middle Classes: The Social Structure of Concert Life in London, Paris and Vienna.* New York: Holmes Meier, 1975.


## MUSIC LISTENING SELECTIONS

**Cassette II Selection 11** Beethoven, Symphony No. 3 in E-flat Major, "The Eroica," first movement, 1803–1804.

**Cassette II Selection 12** Schubert, "Gretchen am Spinnrade," 1814.

**Cassette II Selection 13** Berlioz, *Symphonie fantastique*, Op. 14, "March to the Scaffold," fourth movement, 1830.

**Cassette II Selection 14** Chopin, Etude in G-flat Major, Op. 10, No. 5, 1833.

# PART II

# REALISM AND THE MODERNIST TURN

While romanticism dominated the art and culture of the West until almost the last decade of the nineteenth century, the *realist* point of view began to take shape as early as the 1850s. As a style, *realism* called for an objective and unidealized assessment of everyday life. The new style emerged partly in response to the social and economic consequences of industrialism and partly as an expression of discontent with the contemporary political and economic climate. As a cultural movement, realism reflected popular demands for greater access to material wealth and a denunciation of the sentimental and nostalgic view of the past. Reformers weighed the benefits of industrialization against the human costs of modern technology. Realist artists exhibited a profound sense of social consciousness and a commitment to contemporary problems of class and gender. Unlike the romantics, who felt alienated from society and often sought to escape the oppressive materialism of the modern world, realists saw themselves as men and women "of their time."

The second half of the nineteenth century saw the modernization of Russia, the unification of both Italy and Germany, and the extension of Western economic control and political authority in Africa, Latin America, and Asia. The rush for territory and empire brought the West into a position of dominion over most of the less industrialized parts of the world. As Western nations scrambled for colonial influence, they assumed an ever-growing lead in technology and the arts. In the last quarter of the century, France emerged as the center of Western artistic productivity. Paris became a melting pot for artists and writers, many of whom turned their backs on both romanticism and realism. London and Paris hosted World's Fairs that brought the cultures of the non-Western world to the eyes of astonished Westerners. On the eve of the modern era, European culture experienced what Friedrich Nietzsche called "a chaos, a nihilistic sigh, an utter bewilderment, an instinct of weariness." Philosophers, poets, artists, and composers became preoccupied with fixing sensation and with trying to capture the fleeting world of experience. Some embraced non-Western styles and explored alternatives to traditional Western beliefs and customs. Amidst a prevailing mood of skepticism, artists expressed new concerns with art as a language of form and feeling rather than as a vehicle for moral or religious truths.

Chapter 30, "Industry, Empire, and the Realist Style," examines the move away from romanticism that took place during the second half of the nineteenth century. It deals with some of the emerging political and social ideologies of the age: imperialism, colonialism, liberalism, socialism, communism, and feminism. It examines the rise of photography and of the skyscraper as emblems of a new Western vision. Finally, it traces the shift from romanticism to realism in the writings of Dickens, Dostoevsky, Kate Chopin, Flaubert, and Ibsen; the paintings of Courbet and Manet; and the music of Puccini.

The final chapter, "The Move Toward Modernism," explores the developments of the last two decades of the nineteenth century. Nietzsche and Bergson anticipated the coming modernism in visionary analyses of nature and humankind. As the new technologies of electric light, synthetic paints, and stop-action photography emerged, symbolists and impressionists undertook to capture by way of language, painting, or music the fleeting sensations of nature. Asian, African, and Oceanic art and culture had a visible impact on the work of late nineteeth-century artists, inspiring the efforts of *art nouveau* designers and the bold styles of the post-impressionists van Gogh and Gauguin. Seurat and Cézanne worked to reorder nature in canvases that tested the expressive potential of form and color. These reassessments of prevailing nineteenth-century styles bring us to the threshold of the twentieth century.

(opposite) Winslow Homer, detail of *The Gulf Stream*, 1899. Oil on canvas, full image 28⅛ × 49⅛ in. The Metropolitan Museum of Art, New York. Catharine Lorillard Wolfe Collection. Catharine Lorillard Wolfe Fund, 1906 (06.1234). 

# 30

# Industry, Empire, and the Realist Style

Nations have long drawn their strength and identity from their economic and military superiority over other nations. In the decades following the American and French revolutions, nationalism and the quest for national identity spurred movements for popular sovereignty in the West. But a more aggressive form of nationalism marked the late nineteenth century. Fueled by advancing industrialism, Western nations not only continued to compete among themselves for economic and political preeminence, but they also sought control of markets throughout the world. The combined effects of nationalism, industrialism, and the consequent phenomenon of European and American colonialism influenced the direction of modern Western history and that of the world beyond the West as well.

It was in this climate that the realist style emerged. Realists challenged the acute subjectivity, exoticism, and escapism that typified romanticism. In the spirit of science and technology—enterprises that placed great value on the physical world—realists called for fidelity to nature and an unidealized assessment of contemporary life. Finally, they insisted on a clear-eyed attention to social problems, especially those related to the advance of nationalism and industrial progress.

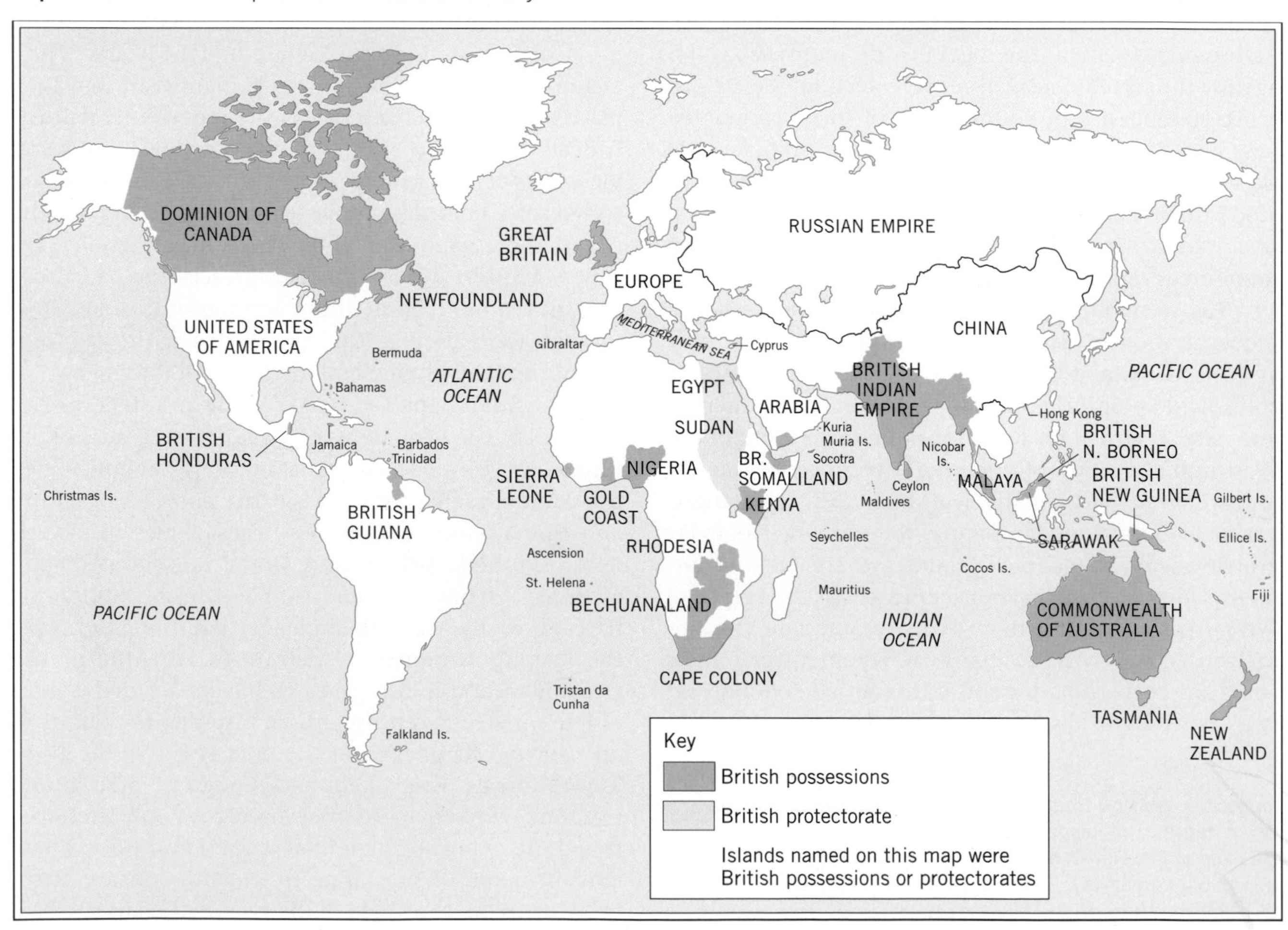


**Map 30.1** The British Empire in the Nineteenth Century.

# *The Global Dominion of the West*

## Advancing Industrialism

Industrialism provided the economic and military basis for the West's rise to a position of dominance over the rest of the world. This process is well illustrated in the history of the railroad, the most important technological phenomenon of the early nineteenth century and one made possible by the combined technologies of steam power, coal, and iron. The first all-iron rails were forged in England in 1767, but it was not until 1804 that the English built their first steam railway locomotive, and several more decades until "iron horses" became a major mode of transportation. By 1830, thousands of miles of railroad track linked England's major cities. The drive to build national railways spread throughout much of Europe and North America. By 1850, 23,000 miles of railway track crisscrossed Europe, linking the sources of raw materials to factories and markets. In the coal mining region of the Ruhr Valley in Northern Germany and across the vast continent of North America, railroads facilitated economic and political expansion. As Western nations colonized other parts of the globe, they took with them the railroad and other agents of industrialism.

By 1880, Western technology included the internal combustion engine, the telegraph, the telephone, the camera, and—perhaps most significant for the everyday life of human beings—electricity. Processed steel, aluminum, the steam turbine, and the pneumatic tire—all products of the 1880s—further altered the texture of life in the industrialized world. These devices, along with more lethal instruments of war such as the fully automatic "machine gun," gave Europe clear advantage over other parts of the globe and facilitated Western imperialism in less industrially developed areas. In the enterprise of empire-building, the industrialized nations of Great Britain, France, Belgium, Germany, Italy, and the United States took the lead.

## Colonialism

The history of European expansion into Asia, Africa, and other parts of the globe dates back at least to the Age of the Renaissance. Between approximately 1500 and 1800, Europeans established trading outposts in Africa, China, and India. But not until after 1800, in the wake of the Industrial Revolution, did European imperialism transform the territories of foreign powers into outright colonial possessions. Driven by the need for raw materials and markets for their manufactured goods, and aided immeasurably by their advanced military technology, the industrial nations quickly colonized vast parts of Asia, Africa, and Latin America. So massive was this effort that, by the end of the nineteenth century, the West had established economic, political, and cultural dominance over much of the world.

European imperialists defended the economic exploitation of weaker countries with the view, inspired by social Darwinism, that in politics, as in nature, the strongest or "most fit" prevailed in the "struggle for survival." Since Caucasians had proved themselves the "most fit," they argued, it was the white population's "burden" to care for, protect, and rule over the "less fit" nonwhite peoples of the earth. Britain, the leader in European industrialization, spearheaded the thrust of colonization. The self-appointed mission of Western rule in less technologically developed countries was best expressed in a poem by one of the most popular British writers of his time, Rudyard Kipling (1864–1936). Three verses of his poem "The White Man's Burden" sum up two of the key imperialist notions: racial superiority and the spirit of paternal and heroic deliverance.

**1844** Samuel Morse (American) transmits the first telegraph message
**1866** the first successful transatlantic telegraph cable is laid
**1869** the first American transcontinental railroad is completed
**1875** Alexander Graham Bell (Scottish) produces the first functional telephone in America

### READING 5.15

### From Kipling's "The White Man's Burden"

Take up the White Man's burden—
  Send forth the best ye breed—
Go bind your sons to exile
  To serve your captive's need;
To wait in heavy harness,
  On fluttered folk and wide—
Your new-caught, sullen peoples,
  Half-devil and half-child.

. . . . . . . . . . .

Take up the White Man's Burden—
  Ye dare not stoop to less—
Nor call too loud on Freedom
  To cloak your weariness;
By all ye cry or whisper,
  By all ye leave to do,
The silent, sullen peoples
  Shall weigh your Gods and you.

Take up the White Man's burden—
  Have done with childish days—
The lightly proffered laurel,
  The easy, ungrudged praise.
Comes now, to search your manhood
  Through all the thankless years,
Cold, edged with dear-bought wisdom,
  The judgment of your peers!

◆

Kipling dedicated "The White Man's Burden" to the United States to commemorate the American annexation of the Philippines in 1899, but the pattern for colonialism had been cut many decades earlier by his native Britain. The first major landmass to be subjugated by Britain was India, which officially fell to British rule in 1858. In less than a century, the British had established control over so much territory across the globe that they could legitimately claim "the sun never set" on the British Empire (Map **30.1**). While British policy in India moved from commerce to conquest and rule, France, Belgium, and Germany seized most of Africa. European nations controlled only ten percent of Africa in 1880; but by 1900 all of Africa save Ethiopia and Liberia had been carved up by European powers who introduced new models of political and economic authority, often with little regard for native populations. A century-long series of brutal wars with the Asante Empire in West Africa left the British in control of Africa's Gold Coast, while the conquest of the Sudan in 1898 saw eleven thousand Muslims killed by British machine guns (the British themselves lost twenty-eight men). Profit-seeking European companies leased large tracts of African land from which native goods such as rubber, diamonds, and gold might be extracted; and increasingly Africans were forced to work on white-owned plantations and mines. The seeds of racism and mutual contempt were sown in this troubled era, an era that predictably spawned modern liberation movements, such as those calling for Pan-Islamic opposition to colonialism (see chapter 36).

By the mid-nineteenth century, the United States (itself a colony of Britain until 1776) joined the scramble for economic control. America forced Japan to open its doors to Western trade in 1853. This event, which marked the end of Japan's seclusion, ushered in the overthrow of the Tokugawa regime (see chapter 23) and marked the beginning of Japanese modernization under Meiji rule (1858–1912). In the Western hemisphere, the United States established its own overseas empire. North Americans used the phrase "manifest destiny" to describe and justify a policy of unlimited expansion into the American West, Mexico, and elsewhere. The end result was the United States' acquisition of more than half of Mexico, the control of the Philippines and Cuba, and a dominant position in the economies of the politically unstable nations of Latin America. Although Westerners rationalized their militant expansionism by contending that they were "civilizing" the backward peoples of the globe, in fact their diplomatic policies contributed to undermining cultural traditions, to humiliating and often enfeebling the civilizations they dominated, and to creating conditions of economic dependency that would last well into the twentieth century (see chapter 36).

## China and the West

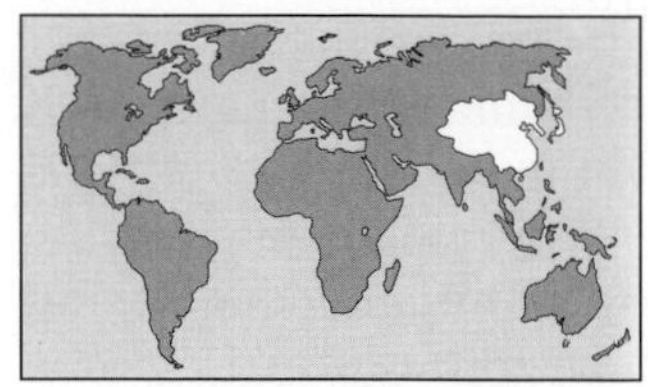

The nineteenth century marked the end of China's long history as an independent civilization. The European powers, along with Russia and Japan, carved out trade concessions in China. Subsequent trade policies, which took advantage of China's traditionally negative view of profit-taking, delayed any potential Chinese initiative toward industrialization. More devastating still was the triangular trade pattern in opium and tea between India, China, and Britain. Established by Britain in the early nineteenth century, the policy was based on the need to stem the tide of British gold and silver that flowed to China to buy tea, a favorite British beverage. The Chinese had used narcotic opium for centuries, but as a result of Britain's new trade policies, large quantities of the drug—harvested in India—were exported directly to China. In exchange, the Chinese shipped tea to Britain. As opium addiction became an increasingly severe social problem (and following the opium-related death of the Chinese emperor's son), the Chinese made every effort to restrict the importation of the drug and to stem the activities of opium smugglers (Figure **30.1**). British merchants refused to cooperate. The result was a series of wars between Britain and China (the Opium Wars, 1839–1850) that brought China to its knees. In 1839, just prior to the first of these wars, the Chinese Commissioner Lin Zexu (1785–1850) sent a detailed communication to the British queen pleading for Britain's assistance in ending opium smuggling and trade. Whether or not Queen Victoria ever read Lin's letter is unknown, but the document remains a literary monument to the futile efforts of a great Asian civilization to achieve peace through diplomacy in the age of imperialism.

### READING 5.16

### From Lin Zexu's *Letter of Advice to Queen Victoria*

A communication: magnificently our great Emperor soothes and pacifies China and the foreign countries, regarding all with the same kindness. If there is profit, then he shares it with the peoples of the world; if there is harm, then he removes it on behalf of the world. This is because he takes the mind of heaven and earth as his mind.

The kings of your honorable country by a tradition handed down from generation to generation have always been noted for their politeness and submissiveness. We have read your successive tributary memorials saying, "In general our countrymen who go to trade in China have always received His Majesty the Emperor's gracious treatment and equal justice," and so on. Privately we are delighted with the way in which the honorable rulers of your country deeply understand the grand principles and are grateful for the Celestial grace. For this reason the Celestial Court in soothing those from afar has redoubled its polite and kind treatment. The profit from trade has been enjoyed by them continuously for two hundred years. This is the source from which your country has become known for its wealth.

But after a long period of commercial intercourse, there appear among the crowd of barbarians both good persons and bad, unevenly. Consequently there are those who smuggle opium to seduce the Chinese people and so cause the spread of the poison to all provinces. Such persons who only care to profit themselves, and disregard their harm to others, are not tolerated by the laws of heaven and are unanimously hated by human beings. His Majesty the Emperor, upon hearing of this, is in a towering rage. He has especially sent me, his commissioner, to come to Kwangtung, and together with the governor-general and governor jointly to investigate and settle this matter. . . .

We find that your country is [some 20,000 miles] from China. Yet there are barbarian ships that strive to come here for trade for the purpose of making a great profit. The wealth of China is used to profit the barbarians. That is to say, the great profit made by barbarians is all taken from the rightful share of China. By what right do they then in return use the poisonous drug to injure the Chinese people? Even though the barbarians may not necessarily intend to do us harm, yet in coveting profit to an extreme, they have no regard for injuring others. Let us ask, where is your conscience? I have heard that the smoking of opium is very strictly forbidden by your country; that is because the harm caused by opium is clearly understood. Since it is not permitted to do harm to your own country, then even less should you let it be passed on to the harm of other countries—how much less to China! Of all that China exports to foreign countries, there is not a single thing which is not beneficial to people: they are of benefit when eaten, or of benefit when used, or of benefit when resold: all are beneficial. Is there a single article from China which has done any harm to foreign countries? Take tea and rhubarb, for example; the foreign countries cannot get along for a single day without them. If China cuts off these benefits with no sympathy for those who are to suffer, then what can the barbarians rely upon to keep themselves alive? Moreover the [textiles] of foreign countries cannot be woven unless they obtain Chinese silk. If China, again, cuts off this beneficial export, what profit can the barbarians expect to make? As for other foodstuffs, beginning with candy, ginger, cinnamon, and so forth, and articles for use, beginning with silk, satin, chinaware, and so on, all the things that must be had by foreign countries are innumerable. On the other hand, articles coming from the outside to China can only be used as toys. We can take them or get along without them. Since they are not needed by China, what difficulty would there be if we closed the frontier and stopped the trade? Nevertheless our Celestial Court lets tea, silk, and other goods be shipped without limit and circulated everywhere without begrudging it in the slightest. This is for no other reason but to share the benefit with the people of the whole world.

The goods from China carried away by your country not only supply your own consumption and use, but also can be divided up and sold to other countries, producing a triple profit. Even if you do not sell opium, you still have this threefold profit. How can you bear to go further, selling products injurious to others in order to fulfil your insatiable desire?

Suppose there were people from another country who carried opium for sale to England and seduced your people into buying and smoking it; certainly your honorable ruler would deeply hate it and be bitterly aroused. We have heard

**Figure 30.1** *Westerners Through Chinese Eyes*. Sketch from a Shanghai picture magazine, *Dian-shi-zhai-hua-bao*, founded in 1884. The inscription reads: "Opium coming to China has become an evil beyond control. If it is not Heaven's will to stop it, there is no other way to save the situation. Heretofore it has been said that only we Chinese are opium smokers. Not so. A French addict in the prime of life, traveling with his wife, an English friend, and a French servant, lay down to smoke in a Singapore hotel but next morning became ill and died—the doctor said from smoking too much. How can one not be afraid!"

heretofore that your honorable ruler is kind and benevolent. Naturally you would not wish to give unto others what you yourself do not want. We have also heard that the ships coming to Canton have all had regulations promulgated and given to them in which it is stated that it is not permitted to carry contraband goods. This indicates that the administrative orders of your honorable rule have been originally strict and clear. Only because the trading ships are numerous, heretofore perhaps they have not been examined with care. Now after this communication has been dispatched and you have clearly understood the strictness of the prohibitory laws of the Celestial Court, certainly you will not let your subjects dare again to violate the law. . . .

Now we have set up regulations governing the Chinese people. He who sells opium shall receive the death penalty and he who smokes it also the death penalty. Now consider this: if the barbarians do not bring opium, then how can the Chinese people resell it, and how can they smoke it? The fact is that the wicked barbarians beguile the Chinese people into a death trap. How then can we grant life only to these barbarians? He who takes the life of even one person still has to atone for it with his own life; yet is the harm done by opium limited to the taking of one life only? Therefore in the new regulations, in regard to those barbarians who bring opium to China, the penalty is fixed at decapitation or strangulation. This is what is called getting rid of a harmful thing on behalf of mankind. . . .

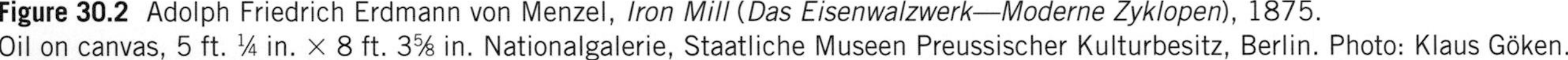

To the European mind, the benefits of Western science, technology, and religion far outweighed the negative impact of colonialism. But the "gift" of progress proved destructive to its recipients. No dramatically new developments took place in the arts of China (nor, for that matter, in India or Africa) during the nineteenth century; in general, there was a marked decline in productivity and originality. The full consequences of Western colonialism in Asia and elsewhere, however, would not become clear until the twentieth century (see chapter 34).

## Social and Economic Realities

In global terms, advancing industrialization polarized the nations of the world into the technologically advanced—the "haves"—and the technologically backward—the "have-nots." But industrialization had an equally profound impact within the industrialized nations themselves: It changed the nature and character of human work, altered relationships between human beings, and affected the natural environment. Prior to 1800 the practice of accumulating capital for industrial production and commercial profit played only a limited

**Figure 30.2** Adolph Friedrich Erdmann von Menzel, *Iron Mill* (*Das Eisenwalzwerk—Moderne Zyklopen*), 1875. Oil on canvas, 5 ft. ¼ in. × 8 ft. 3⅝ in. Nationalgalerie, Staatliche Museen Preussischer Kulturbesitz, Berlin. Photo: Klaus Göken.

**Figure 30.3** Käthe Kollwitz, *March of the Weavers*, from "The Weavers Cycle," 1897. Etching, 8⅜ × 11⅝ in. The University of Michigan Museum of Art, 1956/1.21.

role in European societies. But after 1800, industrial production, enhanced by advances in machine technology, came to be controlled by a relatively small group of middle class **entrepreneurs** (those who organize, manage, and assume the risks of a business) and by an even smaller number of **capitalists** (those who provide investment capital). Industrialization created wealth, but that wealth was concentrated in the hands of a small minority of the population. The vast majority of men and women lived hard lives supported by meager wages—the only thing they had to sell was their labor. Factory laborers, including women and children, worked under dirty and dangerous conditions for long hours—sometimes up to sixteen hours per day (Figure 30.2). Mass production brought more (and cheaper) goods to more people more rapidly, ultimately raising the standard of living for industrialized nations. But European industrialism and the unequal distribution of wealth contributed to a dramatic gap between capitalist entrepreneurs—the "haves" of society—and the working classes—the "have-nots." In 1846, the British statesman Benjamin Disraeli (1804–1881) described England under the rule of Queen Victoria (1819–1901) as two nations: the nation of the poor and the nation of the rich.

Beginning in 1848, the lower classes protested against these conditions with sporadic urban revolts. Economic unrest prevailed not only in the cities but in rural areas as well, where agricultural laborers were often treated like slaves—in America, until after the Civil War (1861–1865), most of those who worked the great Southern plantations were, in fact, African-American slaves. Between 1855 and 1861, there were almost five hundred peasant uprisings across Europe (Figure 30.3). Reform, however, was slow in coming. Outside of England—in Germany, for instance—trade unions and social legislation to benefit the working classes did not appear until 1880 or later, while in Russia economic reform would require nothing less than a full-scale revolution.

**1839** Charles Goodyear (American) produces industrial-strength rubber
**1846** Elias Howe (American) patents an interlocking-stitch sewing machine
**1866** the first dynamo, capable of generating massive quantities of electricity, is produced
**1876** Nikolaus Otto (German) produces a workable internal-combustion engine

## Nineteenth-Century Social Theory

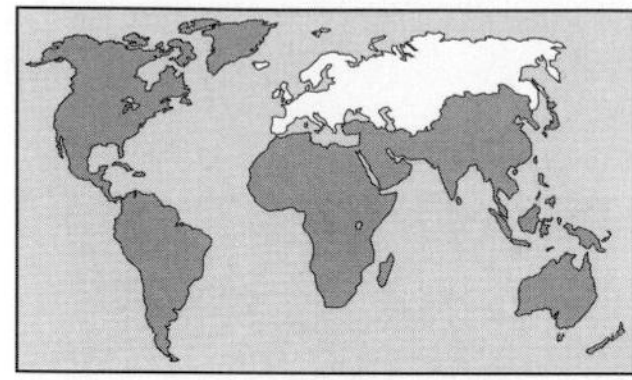

Among nineteenth-century European intellectuals there developed a serious debate over how to address the social results of industrial capitalism. Matters of social reform were central to the development of nineteenth-century ideologies, or doctrines, that dictated specific policies of political and economic action. Traditional *conservatives* stressed the importance of maintaining order and perpetuating conventional power structures and religious authority. *Liberals,* on the other hand, whose ideas were rooted in Enlightenment theories of human progress and perfectibility (see chapter 24), supported gradual reform through enlightened legal systems, constitutional guarantees, and a generally equitable distribution of material benefits. The British liberal Jeremy Bentham (1748–1832) advanced the doctrine of *utilitarianism,* which held that governments should work to secure "the greatest happiness for the greatest number of people"; while Bentham's student, John Stuart Mill (1806–1873), expounded the ideology of social liberalism. Mill emphasized freedom of thought over equality and personal happiness. He held that individuals must be free to direct their own lives, but, recognizing the disadvantages that might result from free competition, he argued that the state must protect its weaker members by acting to regulate the economy where private initiative failed to do so. Mill feared that the general will—the will of unenlightened, propertyless masses—might itself prove tyrannical and oppressive. He concluded, therefore, in his classic statement of the liberal creed, *On Liberty* (1859), that "as soon as any part of a person's conduct affects prejudicially the interests of others, society has jurisdiction over it." For Mill, as for most nineteenth-century liberals, governments had to intervene to safeguard and protect the wider interests of society.

Such theories met with strenuous opposition from European *socialists.* For the latter, neither conservatism nor liberalism responded adequately to current social and economic inequities. Socialists attacked capitalism as unjust; they called for the common ownership and administration of the means of production and distribution in the interest of a public good. Society, according to the socialists, should operate entirely in the interest of the needs of the people, communally and cooperatively, rather than competitively. Such utopian socialists as Pierre Joseph Proudhon (1809–1865) envisioned a society free of state control, while the more extreme *anarchists* favored the complete dissolution of the state and the elimination of the force of law.

### The Radical Views of Marx and Engels

The German theorist Karl Marx (1818–1883) agreed with the socialists that bourgeois capitalism corrupted humanity, but his theory of social reform was an even more radical version of socialism, for it preached violent revolution that would both destroy the old order and usher in a new society. Marx began his career by taking a degree in philosophy at the University of Berlin. Moving to Paris, he became a lifelong friend of the social scientist and journalist Friedrich Engels (1820–1895). Marx and Engels shared a similar critical attitude toward the effects of European industrial capitalism. By 1848 they completed the *Communist Manifesto,* a short treatise published as the platform of a workers' association called the Communist League. The *Manifesto,* which still remains the "guidebook" of Marxist socialism, demanded the "forcible overthrow of all existing social conditions" and the liberation of the **proletariat**, or working class. Marx offered an even more detailed criticism of the free enterprise system in *Das Kapital,* a work on which he toiled for thirty years.

The *Communist Manifesto* is a condemnation of the effects of capitalism on the individual and society at large. The first section of the treatise (part of which is included in Reading 5.17) defends the claim that "the history of all hitherto existing society is the history of class struggles." The authors argue that capitalism concentrates wealth in the hands of the few, providing great luxuries for some, while creating an oppressed and impoverished proletariat. The psychological effects of such circumstances, they contend, are devastating: Bourgeois capitalism alienates workers from their own productive efforts and robs individuals of their basic humanity. Finally, the authors call for violent revolution by which workers will seize the instruments of capitalistic production and abolish private ownership.

The social theories of Marx and Engels had enormous practical and theoretical influence. They not only supplied a justification for lower-class revolt, but they brought attention to the role of economics in the larger life of a society. Marx described human behavior and human history in exclusively materialistic terms, arguing that the conditions under which one earned a living determined all other aspects of life: social, political, and cultural. A student of the Hegelian dialectic (see chapter 27), Marx viewed history as a struggle between "haves" (thesis) and "have-nots" (antithesis) that would resolve in the synthesis of a classless society. From Hegel, Marx derived the utopian idea of the perfectibility of the state. The end product of dialectical change, argued Marx, was a society free of class antagonisms and the ultimate dissolution of the state itself.

Although Marx and Engels failed to anticipate capitalism's potential to spread rather than to limit wealth, their manifesto gave sharp focus to prevailing class differences and to the actual condition of the European economy of their time. And despite the fact that Marx and Engels did not provide any explanation of *how* their classless society might function, their call to revolution would be heeded in the decades to come. Oddly enough, Communist revolutions would occur in some of the least industrialized countries of the world, such as Russia and China, rather than in the most industrialized countries, as Marx and Engels expected. Elsewhere, Communists would operate largely through *nonrevolutionary* vehicles, such as labor unions and political organizations, to initiate better working conditions, higher wages, and greater social equality. But the anti-Communist revolutions and the collapse of the Communist government in the Soviet Union in the late twentieth century reveal mounting frustration with the failure of most Communist regimes to raise economic standards among the masses.

## READING 5.17

## From Marx's and Engels' *Communist Manifesto*

**I Bourgeois and Proletarians**[1]

The history of all hitherto existing society is the history of class struggles.

Freeman and slave, patrician and plebeian, lord and serf, guild-master[2] and journeyman, in a word, oppressor and oppressed, stood in constant opposition to one another, carried on an uninterrupted, now hidden, now open fight, a fight that each time ended either in a revolutionary reconstitution of society at large or in the common ruin of the contending classes.

In the earlier epochs of history we find almost everywhere a complicated arrangement of society into various orders, a manifold gradation of social rank. In ancient Rome we have patricians, knights, plebeians, slaves; in the Middle Ages, feudal lords, vassals, guild-masters, journeymen, apprentices, serfs; in almost all of these classes, again, subordinate gradations.

The modern bourgeois society that has sprouted from the ruins of feudal society has not done away with class antagonisms. It has but established new classes, new conditions of oppression, new forms of struggle in place of the old ones.

Our epoch, the epoch of the bourgeoisie, possesses, however, this distinctive feature: it has simplified the class antagonisms. Society as a whole is splitting up more and more into two great hostile camps, into two great classes directly facing each other: Bourgeoisie and Proletariat.

From the serfs of the Middle Ages sprang the chartered burghers of the earliest towns. From these burgesses the first elements of the bourgeoisie were developed.

The discovery of America, the rounding of the Cape, opened up fresh ground for the rising bourgeoisie. The East Indian and Chinese markets, the colonization of America, trade with the colonies, the increase in the means of exchange and in commodities generally, gave to commerce, to navigation, to industry, an impulse never before known, and thereby, to the revolutionary element in the tottering feudal society, a rapid development.

The feudal system of industry, under which industrial production was monopolized by closed guilds, now no longer sufficed for the growing wants of the new markets. The manufacturing system took its place. The guild-masters were pushed on one side by the manufacturing middle class; division of labor between the different corporate guilds vanished in the face of division of labor in each single workshop.

Meantime the markets kept ever growing, the demand ever rising. Even manufacture no longer sufficed. Thereupon, steam and machinery revolutionized industrial production. The place of manufacture was taken by the giant, Modern Industry, the place of the industrial middle class by industrial millionaires—the leaders of whole industrial armies, the modern bourgeois.

Modern industry has established the world market, for which the discovery of America paved the way. This market has given an immense development to commerce, to navigation, to communication by land. This development has, in its turn, reacted on the extension of industry; and in proportion as industry, commerce, navigation, railways extended, in the same proportion the bourgeoisie developed, increased its capital, and pushed into the background every class handed down from the Middle Ages.

We see, therefore, how the modern bourgeoisie is itself the product of a long course of development, of a series of revolutions in the modes of production and of exchange.

Each step in the development of the bourgeoisie was accompanied by a corresponding political advance of that class. An oppressed class under the sway of the feudal nobility, an armed and self-governing association in the medieval commune,[3] here independent urban republic (as in Italy and Germany), there taxable "third estate" of the monarchy (as in France), afterward, in the period of manufacture proper, serving either the semi-feudal or the absolute monarchy as a counterpoise against the nobility, and, in fact, cornerstone of the great monarchies in general, the bourgeoisie has at last, since the establishment of Modern Industry and of the world market, conquered for itself, in the modern representative State, exclusive political sway. The executive of the modern State is but a committee for managing the common affairs of the whole bourgeoisie.

The bourgeoisie, historically, has played a most revolutionary part.

[1]By bourgeoisie is meant the class of modern capitalists, owners of the means of social production and employers of wage labor. By proletariat, the class of modern wage-laborers who, having no means of production of their own, are reduced to selling their labor power in order to live. [1888.]

[2]Guild-master, that is, a full member of a guild, a master within, not a head of a guild. [1888.]

[3]"Commune" was the name taken in France by the nascent towns even before they had conquered from their feudal lords and masters local self-government and political rights as the "Third Estate." Generally speaking, for the economic development of the bourgeoisie, England is here taken as the typical country; for its political development, France. [1888.]

The bourgeoisie, wherever it has got the upper hand, has put an end to all feudal, patriarchal, idyllic relations. It has pitilessly torn asunder the motley feudal ties that bound man to his "natural superiors," and has left remaining no other nexus between man and man than naked self-interest, than callous "cash payment." It has drowned the most heavenly ecstasies of religious fervor, of chivalrous enthusiasm, of philistine sentimentalism, in the icy water of egotistical calculation. It has resolved personal worth into exchange value, and in place of the numberless indefeasible chartered freedoms has set up that single, unconscionable freedom—Free Trade. In one word, for exploitation, veiled by religious and political illusions, it has substituted naked, shameless, direct, brutal exploitation.

The bourgeoisie has stripped of its halo every occupation hitherto honored and looked up to with reverent awe. It has converted the physician, the lawyer, the priest, the poet, the man of science, into its paid wage-laborers.

The bourgeoisie has torn away from the family its sentimental veil, and has reduced the family relation to a mere money relation. . . .

The bourgeoisie, by the rapid improvement of all instruments of production, by the immensely facilitated means of communication, draws all, even the most barbarian, nations into civilization. The cheap prices of its commodities are the heavy artillery with which it batters down all Chinese walls, with which it forces the barbarians' intensely obstinate hatred of foreigners to capitulate. It compels all nations, on pain of extinction, to adopt the bourgeois mode of production; it compels them to introduce what it calls civilization into their midst, i.e., to become bourgeois themselves. In a word, it creates a world after its own image.

The bourgeoisie has subjected the country to the rule of the towns. It has created enormous cities, has greatly increased the urban population as compared with the rural, and has thus rescued a considerable part of the population from the idiocy of rural life. Just as it has made the country dependent on the towns, so it has made barbarian and semi-barbarian countries dependent on the civilized ones, nations of peasants on nations of bourgeois, the East on the West.

The bourgeoisie keeps doing away more and more with the scattered state of the population, of the means of production, and of property. It has agglomerated population, centralized means of production, and has concentrated property in a few hands. The necessary consequence of this was political centralization. Independent or but loosely connected provinces with separate interests, laws, governments and systems of taxation became lumped together into one nation, with one government, one code of laws, one national class interest, one frontier and one customs tariff.

The bourgeoisie during its rule of scarce one hundred years has created more massive and more colossal productive forces than have all preceding generations together. Subjection of nature's forces to man, machinery, application of chemistry to industry and agriculture, steam navigation, railways, electric telegraphs, clearing of whole continents for cultivation, canalization of rivers, whole populations conjured out of the ground—what earlier century had even a presentiment that such productive forces slumbered in the lap of social labor? . . .

But not only has the bourgeoisie forged the weapons that bring death to itself; it has also called into existence the men who are to wield those weapons—the modern working class, the proletarians.

In proportion as the bourgeoisie, i.e., capital, is developed, in the same proportion is the proletariat, the modern working class, developed—a class of laborers who live only as long as they find work, and who find work only as long as their labor increases capital. These laborers, who must sell themselves piecemeal, are a commodity like every other article of commerce, and are consequently exposed to all the vicissitudes of competition, to all the fluctuations of the market.

Owing to the extensive use of machinery and to division of labor, the work of the proletarians has lost all individual character and, consequently, all charm for the workman. He becomes an appendage of the machine, and it is only the most simple, most monotonous, and most easily acquired knack that is required of him. . . .

Modern industry has converted the little workshop of the patriarchal master into the great factory of the industrial capitalist. Masses of laborers, crowded into the factory, are organized like soldiers. As privates of the industrial army they are placed under the command of a perfect hierarchy of officers and sergeants. Not only are they slaves of the bourgeois class and of the bourgeois State; they are daily and hourly enslaved by the machine, by the overseer and, above all, by the individual bourgeois manufacturer himself. The more openly this despotism proclaims gain to be its end and aim, the more petty, the more hateful and the more embittering it is.

The less the skill and exertion of strength implied in manual labor, in other words, the more modern industry becomes developed, the more is the labor of men superseded by that of women. Differences of age and sex no longer have any distinctive social validity for the working class. All are instruments of labor, more or less expensive to use, according to their age and sex.

No sooner is the exploitation of the laborer by the manufacturer so far at an end that he receives his wages in cash, than he is set upon by the other portions of the bourgeoisie, the landlord, and shopkeeper, the pawnkeeper, etc. . . .

**II Proletarians and Communists**

. . . The Communist revolution is the most radical rupture with traditional property relations; no wonder that its development involves the most radical rupture with traditional ideas.

But let us have done with the bourgeois objections to Communism.

We have seen above that the first step in the revolution by the working class is to raise the proletariat to the position of ruling class, to win the battle of democracy.

The proletariat will use its political supremacy to wrest, by degrees, all capital from the bourgeoisie, to centralize all instruments of production in the hands of the State, i.e., of the proletariat organized as the ruling class; and to increase the total of productive forces as rapidly as possible. . . .

**III Position of the Communists**

. . . The Communists disdain to conceal their views and aims. They openly declare that their ends can be attained only by the forcible overthrow of all existing social conditions. Let the ruling classes tremble at a Communistic revolution. The proletarians have nothing to lose but their chains. They have a world to win.

WORKING MEN OF ALL COUNTRIES, UNITE!

◆

## Mill and Women's Rights

While Marx and Engels criticized a society that made middle-class women "mere instrument[s] of production," Mill (see p. 78) described women of all classes as the unwilling subjects of more powerful males. In the eloquent treatise entitled *The Subjection of Women* (1869), Mill condemned the legal subordination of one sex to the other as objectively "wrong in itself, and . . . one of the chief hindrances to human improvement." Mill's optimism concerning the unbounded potential for social change—a hallmark of liberalism—may have been shortsighted, for women would not obtain voting rights in Britain until 1928. Nevertheless, the first women's college—Mount Holyoke—was founded at South Hadley, Massachusetts, in 1836; and in 1848, at Seneca Falls in upstate New York, American feminists, led by Elizabeth Cady Stanton (1815–1902) and Susan B. Anthony (1820–1906), issued the first of many declarations that demanded female equality in all areas of life. The rights of women had been an issue addressed in the literature of feminists from Christine de Pisan to Condorcet and Mary Wollstonecraft, but nowhere was the plight of women more eloquently treated than in Mill's essay. Mill compared the subjection of women to that of other subject classes in the history of culture. But his most original contribution was his analysis of the male/female relationship and his explanation of how that relationship differed from that of master and slave.

### READING 5.18

### From Mill's *The Subjection of Women*

All causes, social and natural, combine to make it unlikely that women should be collectively rebellious to the power of men. They are so far in a position different from all other subject classes that their masters require something more from them than actual service. Men do not want solely the obedience of women, they want their sentiments. All men, except the most brutish, desire to have, in the woman most nearly connected with them, not a forced slave but a willing one, not a slave merely, but a favorite. They have therefore put everything in practice to enslave their minds. The masters of all other slaves rely, for maintaining obedience, on fear, either fear of themselves, or religious fears. The masters of women wanted more than simple obedience, and they turned the whole force of education to effect their purpose. All women are brought up from the very earliest years in the belief that their ideal of character is the very opposite to that of men; not self-will and government by self-control, but submission and yielding to the control of others. All the moralities tell them that it is the duty of women and all the current sentimentalities that it is their nature to live for others, to make complete abnegation of themselves, and to have no life but in their affections. And by their affections are meant the only ones they are allowed to have—those to the men with whom they are connected, or to the children who constitute an additional and indefeasible tie between them and a man. When we put together three things—first, the natural attraction between opposite sexes; secondly, the wife's entire dependence on the husband, every privilege or pleasure she has being either his gift, or depending entirely on his will; and lastly, that the principal object of human pursuit, consideration, and all objects of social ambition can in general be sought or obtained by her only through him, it would be a miracle if the object of being attractive to men had not become the polar star of feminine education and formation of character. And this great means of influence over the minds of women having been acquired, an instinct of selfishness made men avail themselves of it to the utmost as a means of holding women in subjection, by representing to them meekness, submissiveness, and resignation of all individual will into the hands of a man, as an essential part of sexual attractiveness. . . .

The preceding considerations are amply sufficient to show that custom, however universal it may be, affords in this case no presumption and ought not to create any prejudice in favor of the arrangements which place women in social and political subjection to men. But I may go further, and maintain that the course of history, and the tendencies of progressive human society afford not only no presumption in favor of this system of inequality of rights, but a strong one against it; and that, so far as the whole course of human improvement up to this time, the whole stream of modern tendencies warrants any inference on the subject, it is that this relic of the past is discordant with the future and must necessarily disappear.

For, what is the peculiar character of the modern world—the difference which chiefly distinguishes modern institutions, modern social ideas, modern life itself, from those of times long past? It is, that human beings are no longer born to their place in life and chained down by an inexorable bond to the place they are born to, but are free to employ their faculties and such favorable chances as offer, to achieve the lot which may appear to them most desirable. Human society of old was constituted on a very different principle. All were born to a fixed social position and were mostly kept in it by law or interdicted from any means by which they could emerge from it. As some men are born white and others black, so some were born slaves and others freemen and citizens; some were born patricians, others plebeians; some were born feudal nobles, others commoners. . . .

The old theory was that the least possible should be left to the choice of the individual agent; that all he had to do should, as far as practicable, be laid down for him

> by superior wisdom. Left to himself he was sure to go wrong. The modern conviction, the fruit of a thousand years of experience, is that things in which the individual is the person directly interested never go right but as they are left to his own discretion; and that any regulation of them by authority, except to protect the rights of others, is sure to be mischievous. . . .

◆

### The New Historicism

While issues of class and gender preoccupied some of the finest minds of the nineteenth century, so too did matters surrounding the interpretation of the historical past. For many centuries, history was regarded as a branch of literature rather than a social science. The romantic histories, such as those of Thomas Carlyle (see chapter 25), served to emphasize the role of great men in shaping the destinies of nations. At the same time, the spirit of high patriotism inspired nineteenth-century historians such as Thomas Babington Macaulay in England and Fustel de Coulanges in France to write nationalistic histories that brought attention to the greatness of their own people and culture.

Patriotism, however, also led historians to renew their efforts to retrieve the evidence of the past. Scholars compiled vast collections of primary source materials; and, enamoured of the new, positivist zeal for objective measurement and recording, they tried to apply scientific methods to the writing of history. The result was an effort to recreate history "as it actually was," a movement later called *historicism*. Led by the German historian Leopold von Ranke (1795–1886), historians made every attempt to produce historical works that depended on the objective interpretation of eyewitness reports and authentic documents. Von Ranke himself produced sixty volumes on modern European history which rested on the critical study of sources that he had gleaned from various archives. This method of writing history still dominates modern-day historiography.

The new historicism that scholars brought to the critical study of religious history stirred great controversy and challenged the compatibility of science and religion. Rejecting all forms of supernaturalism, some nineteenth-century scholars disputed the literal interpretation of the Bible, especially where its contents conflicted with scientific evidence (as in the case of the Virgin Birth). Since the facts of Jesus' life were so few, some also questioned the historicity of Jesus (whether or not he had ever actually lived), while still others—such as the eminent French scholar Ernest Renan, author of the *Life of Jesus* (1863)—questioned his divinity. Renan and his followers offered a rationalist reconstruction of religious history which worked to separate personal belief and moral conduct from conventional religious history and dogma. At the same time, as universal education spread throughout the literate world and Church and state moved further apart, education and teaching became increasingly secularized.

## *Realism in Literature*

### The Novels of Dickens and Twain

Inequities of class and gender had existed throughout the course of history, but in an age that pitted the progressive effects of industrial capitalism against the realities of poverty and inequality, social criticism was inevitable. Nineteenth-century writers pointed to these conditions and described them with unembellished objectivity. This unblinking attention to contemporary life and experience was the basis for the style known as *literary realism*.

More than any other genre, the nineteenth-century novel—by its capacity to detail characters and conditions—best fulfilled the realist credo of depicting life with complete candor. In contrast with romanticism, which embraced heroic and exotic subjects, realism portrayed men and women in actual, everyday, and often demoralizing situations. It examined the social consequences of middle-class materialism, the plight of the working class, and the subjugation of women, among other matters. While realism did not totally displace romanticism as the dominant literary mode of the nineteenth century, it often appeared alongside the romantic—indeed, romantic and sentimental elements might be found in generally realistic narratives. Such was the case in the novels of Charles Dickens (1812–1870) in England and Mark Twain, a pseudonym of Samuel Longhorne Clemens (1835–1910), in America. Twain's writings, including his greatest achievement, *The Adventures of Huckleberry Finn* (1885), reveal a blend of humor and irony that is not generally characteristic of Dickens. But both writers employ a masterful use of dialect, sensitivity to pictorial detail, and a humanitarian sympathy in their descriptions of nineteenth-century life in specific locales—for Twain, the rural farmlands along the Mississippi River, and for Dickens, the streets of England's industrial cities.

Dickens, the most popular English novelist of his time, came from a poor family who provided him with little formal education. His early experiences supplied some of the themes for his most famous novels: *Oliver Twist* (1838) vividly portrays the slums, orphanages, and boarding schools of London; *Nicholas Nickleby* (1839) is a bitter indictment of England's brutal rural schools; and *David Copperfield* (1850) condemns debtors' prisons and the conditions that produced them. Dickens' novels are frequently theatrical, his characters may be drawn to the point of caricature, and his themes often suggest a sentimental faith in kindness and good cheer as the best antidotes to the bitterness of contemporary life. But, as the following excerpt illustrates, Dickens' grasp of realistic detail was acute, and his portrayal of physical ugliness was unflinching. In this passage from *The Old Curiosity Shop* (1841), Dickens painted an unforgettable picture of the horrifying urban conditions that gave rise to the despair of the laboring classes and inspired their cries for social reform. Dickens' description of the English milltown of Birmingham, as first viewed by the novel's heroine, little Nell, and her grandfather, finds striking parallels in nineteenth-century visual representations of Europe's laboring poor; it also calls to mind the popular conceptions of Hell found in medieval art and literature (see chapter 12).

### READING 5.19

### From Dickens' *Old Curiosity Shop*

. . . A long suburb of red-brick houses—some with patches of garden-ground, where coal-dust and factory smoke darkened the shrinking leaves and coarse, rank flowers; and where the struggling vegetation sickened and sank under the hot breath of kiln and furnace, making them by its presence seem yet more blighting and unwholesome than in the town itself—a long, flat, straggling suburb passed, they came by slow degrees upon a cheerless region, where not a blade of grass was seen to grow; where not a bud put forth its promise in the spring; where nothing green could live but on the surface of the stagnant pools, which here and there lay idly sweltering by the black roadside.

Advancing more and more into the shadow of this mournful place, its dark depressing influence stole upon their spirits, and filled them with a dismal gloom. On every side, as far as the eye could see into the heavy distance, tall chimneys, crowding on each other, and presenting that endless repetition of the same dull, ugly form, which in the horror of oppressive dreams, poured out their plague of smoke, obscured the light, and made foul the melancholy air. On mounds of ashes by the wayside, sheltered only by a few rough boards, or rotten pent-house roofs, strange engines spun and writhed like tortured creatures; clanking their iron chains, shrieking in their rapid whirl from time to time as though in torment unendurable, and making the ground tremble with their agonies. Dismantled houses here and there appeared, tottering to the earth, propped up by fragments of others that had fallen down, unroofed, windowless, blackened, desolate, but yet inhabited. Men, women, children, wan in their looks and ragged in attire, tended the engines, fed their tributary fires, begged upon the road, or scowled half naked from the doorless houses. Then came more of the wrathful monsters, whose like they almost seemed to be in their wildness and their untamed air, screeching and turning round and round again; and still, before, behind, and to the right and left, was the same interminable perspective of brick towers, never ceasing in their black vomit, blasting all things living or inanimate, shutting out the face of day, and closing in on all these horrors with a dense dark cloud.

But night-time in this dreadful spot!—night, when the smoke was changed to fire; when every chimney spirited up its flame; and places, that had been dark vaults all day, now shone red-hot, with figures moving to and fro within their blazing jaws, and calling to one another with hoarse cries—night, when the noise of every strange machine was aggravated by the darkness; when the people near them looked wilder and more savage; when bands of unemployed laborers paraded in the roads, or clustered by torch-light round their leaders, who told them in stern language of their wrongs, and urged them on to frightful cries and threats; when maddened men, armed with sword and firebrand, spurning the tears and prayers of women who would restrain them, rushed forth on errands of terror and destruction, to work no ruin half so surely as their own—night, when carts came rumbling by, filled with rude coffins (for contagious disease and death had been busy with the living crops); when orphans cried, and distracted women shrieked and followed in their wake—night, when some called for bread, and some for drink to drown their cares; and some with tears, and some with staggering feet, and some with bloodshot eyes, went brooding home—night, which, unlike the night that Heaven sends on earth, brought with it no peace, nor quiet, nor signs of blessed sleep—who shall tell the terrors of the night to that young wandering child! . . .

◆

## Russian Realism: Dostoevsky and Tolstoy

Even more pessimistic than Dickens, and more profoundly analytic of the universal human condition, were the Russian novelists Fyodor Dostoevsky (1821–1881) and Leo Tolstoy (1828–1910). Both men were born and bred in wealth, but both turned against upper-class Russian society and sympathized with the plight of the lower classes. Tolstoy ultimately renounced his wealth and property and went to live and work among the peasants. Tolstoy's historical novel *War and Peace* (1869), often hailed as the greatest example of realistic Russian fiction, traces the progress of five families whose destinies unroll against the background of Napoleon's invasion of Russia in 1812. In this sprawling narrative, as in many of his other novels, Tolstoy exposes the privileged position of the nobility and the cruel exploitation of the great masses of Russian people.

Dostoevsky's novels, on the other hand, generally address philosophical and psychological issues. The characters in Dostoevsky's novels are often victims of a dual plight: poverty and conscience. Their energies are foiled by the struggle to resolve their own contradictory passions. The novels *Crime and Punishment* (1866), *The Possessed* (1871), and *The Brothers Karamazov* (1880) feature protagonists whose irrational behavior and its psychological consequences form the central theme of the novel. In *Crime and Punishment,* Raskolnikov, a young, poor student, murders an old woman and her younger sister; his crime goes undetected. Thereafter, he struggles with guilt—the self-punishment for his criminal act. He also struggles with the problems arising from one's freedom to commit evil. In the following excerpt, the protagonist addresses the moral question of whether extraordinary individuals, by dint of their uniqueness, have the right to commit immoral acts. The conversation, which takes place between Raskolnikov and his friends, is spurred by an article on crime that Raskolnikov had published in a journal shortly after dropping out of university. This excerpt is typical of Dostoevsky's fondness for developing character through monologue and dialogue, rather than through descriptive detail. Dostoevsky's realism (and his genius) lies in the way in which he forces the reader to understand the character as that character tries to understand himself.

## READING 5.20

## From Dostoevsky's *Crime and Punishment*

". . . the 'extraordinary' man has the right . . . I don't mean a formal, official right, but he has the right in himself, to permit his conscience to overstep . . . certain obstacles, but only in the event that his ideas (which may sometimes be salutary for all mankind) require it for their fulfilment. You are pleased to say that my article is not clear; I am ready to elucidate it for you, as far as possible. Perhaps I am not mistaken in supposing that is what you want. Well, then. In my opinion, if the discoveries of Kepler and Newton, by some combination of circumstances, could not have become known to the world in any other way than by sacrificing the lives of one, or ten, or a hundred or more people, who might have hampered or in some way been obstacles in the path of those discoveries, then Newton would have had the right, or might even have been under an obligation . . . to *remove* those ten or a hundred people, so that his discoveries might be revealed to all mankind. It does not follow from this, of course, that Newton had the right to kill any Tom, Dick, or Harry he fancied, or go out stealing from market-stalls every day. I remember further that in my article I developed the idea that all the . . . well, for example, the law-givers and regulators of human society, beginning with the most ancient, and going on to Lycurgus, Solon, Mahomet, Napoleon and so on, were without exception transgressors,[1] by the very fact that in making a new law they *ipso facto* broke an old one, handed down from their fathers and held sacred by society; and, of course, they did not stop short of shedding blood, provided only that the blood (however innocent and however heroically shed in defence of the ancient law) was shed to their advantage. It is remarkable that the greater part of these benefactors and law-givers of humanity were particularly blood-thirsty. In a word, I deduce that all of them, not only the great ones, but also those who diverge ever so slightly from the beaten track, those, that is, who are just barely capable of saying something new, must, by their nature, inevitably be criminals—in a greater or less degree, naturally. Otherwise they would find it too hard to leave their rut, and they cannot, of course, consent to remain in the rut, again by the very fact of their nature; and in my opinion they ought not to consent. In short, you see that up to this point there is nothing specially new here. It has all been printed, and read, a thousand times before. As for my division of people into ordinary and extraordinary, that I agree was a little arbitrary, but I do not insist on exact figures. Only I do believe in the main principle of my idea. That consists in people being, by the law of nature, divided *in general* into two categories: into a lower (of ordinary people), that is, into material serving only for the reproduction of its own kind, and into people properly speaking, that is, those who have the gift or talent of saying *something new* in their sphere. There are endless subdivisions, of course, but the distinctive characteristics of the two categories are fairly well marked: the first group, that is the material, are, generally speaking, by nature staid and conservative, they live in obedience and like it. In my opinion they ought to obey because that is their destiny, and there is nothing at all degrading to them in it. The second group are all law-breakers and transgressors, or are inclined that way, in the measure of their capacities. The aims of these people are, of course, relative and very diverse; for the most part they require, in widely different contexts, the destruction of what exists in the name of better things. But if it is necessary for one of them, for the fulfilment of his ideas, to march over corpses, or wade through blood, then in my opinion he may in all conscience authorize himself to wade through blood—in proportion, however, to his idea and the degree of its importance—mark that. It is in that sense only that I speak in my article of their right to commit crime. (You will remember that we really began with the question of legality.) There is, however, not much cause for alarm: the masses hardly ever recognize this right of theirs, and behead or hang them (more or less), and in this way, quite properly, fulfil their conservative function, although in following generations these same masses put their former victims on a pedestal and worship them (more or less). The first category are always the masters of the present, but the second are the lords of the future. The first preserve the world and increase and multiply; the second move the world and guide it to its goal. Both have an absolutely equal right to exist. In short, for me all men have completely equivalent rights, and—*vive la guerre éternelle*—until we have built the New Jerusalem, of course!"[2]

[1]Raskolnikov's views are similar to those expressed by Napoleon III in his book *Life of Julius Caesar*. The newspaper *Golos* (*Voice*) had recently summarized the English *Saturday Review*'s analysis of Napoleon's ideas about the right of exceptional individuals (such as Lycurgus, Mahomet, and Napoleon I) to transgress laws and even to shed blood. The book appeared in Paris in March 1865; the Russian translation in April! [Lycurgus: the founder of the military regime of ancient Sparta; Mahomet: Muhammad, the prophet of Allah and founder of the religion Islam; Solon: statesman and reformer in sixth-century-B.C.E. Athens.]

[2]New Jerusalem, symbolic of the ideal order, after the end of time, is a Heaven on Earth, a new paradise. See the description in Revelation 21 (the Apocalypse). The French phrase means, "Long live perpetual war."

"You do believe in the New Jerusalem, then?"

"Yes, I do," answered Raskolnikov firmly; he said this with his eyes fixed on one spot on the carpet, as they had been all through his long tirade.

"A-and you believe in God? Forgive me for being so inquisitive."

"Yes, I do," repeated Raskolnikov, raising his eyes to Porfiry.

"A-a-and do you believe in the raising of Lazarus?"

"Y-yes. Why are you asking all this?"

"You believe in it literally?"

"Yes."

"Ah . . . I was curious to know. Forgive me. But, returning to the previous subject—they are not always put to death. Some, on the contrary . . ."

"Triumph during their lifetime? Oh, yes, some achieve their ends while they still live, and then . . ."

"They begin to mete out capital punishment themselves?"

"If necessary, and, you know, it is most usually so. Your observation is very keen-witted."

"Thank you. But tell me: how do you distinguish these extraordinary people from the ordinary? Do signs and portents appear when they are born? I mean to say that we could do with rather greater accuracy here, with, so to speak, rather more outward signs: please excuse the natural anxiety of a practical and well-meaning man, but couldn't there be, for example, some special clothing, couldn't they carry some kind of brand or something? . . . Because, you will agree, if there should be some sort of mix-up, and somebody from one category imagined that he belonged to the other and began 'to remove all obstacles,' as you so happily put it, then really . . ."

"Oh, that very frequently happens! This observation of yours is even more penetrating than the last."

"Thank you."

"Not at all. But you must please realize that the mistake is possible only among the first group, that is, the 'ordinary' people (as I have called them, perhaps not altogether happily). In spite of their inborn inclination to obey, quite a number of them, by some freak of nature such as is not impossible even among cows, like to fancy that they are progressives, 'destroyers,' and propagators of the 'new world,' and all this quite sincerely. At the same time, they really take no heed of *new people*; they even despise them, as reactionary and incapable of elevated thinking. But, in my opinion, they cannot constitute a real danger, and you really have nothing to worry about, because they never go far. They might sometimes be scourged for their zealotry, to remind them of their place; there is no need even for anyone to carry out the punishment: they will do it themselves, because they are very well conducted: some of them do one another this service, and others do it for themselves with their own hands . . . And they impose on themselves various public penances besides—the result is beautifully edifying, and in short, you have nothing to worry about . . . This is a law of nature."

"Well, at least you have allayed my anxieties on that score a little; but here is another worry: please tell me, are there many of these people who have the right to destroy others, of these 'extraordinary' people? I am, of course, prepared to bow down before them, but all the same you will agree that it would be terrible if there were very many of them, eh?"

"Oh, don't let that trouble you either," went on Raskolnikov in the same tone. "Generally speaking, there are extremely few people, strangely few, born, who have a new idea, or are even capable of saying anything at all *new*. One thing only is clear, that the ordering of human births, all these categories and subdivisions, must be very carefully and exactly regulated by some law of nature. This law is, of course, unknown at present, but I believe that it exists, and consequently that it may be known. The great mass of men, the common stuff of humanity, exist on the earth only in order that at last, by some endeavour, some process, that remains as yet mysterious, some happy conjunction of race and breeding, there should struggle into life a being, one in a thousand, capable, in however small a degree, of standing on his own feet. Perhaps one in ten thousand (I am speaking approximately, by way of illustration) is born with a slightly greater degree of independence, and one in a hundred thousand with even more. One genius may emerge among millions, and a really great genius, perhaps, as the crowning point of many thousands of millions of men. In short, I have not been able to look into the retort whence all this proceeds. But a definite law there must be, and is; it cannot be a matter of chance. . . ."

◆

## The Literary Heroines of Flaubert and Chopin

Nineteenth-century novelists shared a special interest in examining conflicts between social conventions and personal values, especially as they affected the everyday lives of women. Gustave Flaubert's *Madame Bovary* (1857), Tolstoy's *Anna Karenina* (1877), and Kate Chopin's *The Awakening* (1899) are representative of the nineteenth-century writer's concern with the tragic consequences following from the defiance of established social and moral codes by passionate female figures. The heroines in these novels do not create the world in their own image; rather, the world—or more specifically, the social and economic environment—molds them and governs their destinies. Flaubert (1821–1880), whom critics have called "the inventor of the modern novel," stripped his novels of sentimentality and of all preconceived notions of behavior. He aimed at a precise description of not only the stuff of the physical world but also the motivations of his characters.

In *Madame Bovary* (1857), his most famous novel, Flaubert tells the story of a middle-class woman who desperately seeks to escape the boredom of her mundane existence. Educated in the convent and married to a dull, small-town physician, Emma Bovary tries to live out the fantasies that fill the pages of her favorite romance novels, but her efforts to do so prove disastrous and lead to her ultimate destruction. Flaubert reconstructs with a minimum of interpretation the details of Emma's provincial surroundings and her bleak marriage. A meticulous observer, he sought *le mot juste* ("the precise word") to describe each concrete object and each psychological state—a practice that often prevented him from writing more than one or two pages of prose per week. Since the novel achieves its full effect through the gradual development of plot and character, no brief excerpt can possibly do it justice. Nevertheless, the following excerpt, which describes the deterioration of the adulterous affair between Emma Bovary and the young clerk Léon, illustrates Flaubert's ability to characterize places and persons by means of the fastidious selection and accumulation of descriptive details.

## READING 5.21

## From Flaubert's *Madame Bovary*

In the end Léon had promised never to see Emma again; and he reproached himself for not having kept his word, especially considering all the trouble and reproaches she still probably held in store for him—not to mention the jokes his fellow clerks cracked every morning around the stove. Besides, he was about to be promoted to head clerk: this was the time to turn over a new leaf. So he gave up playing the flute and said good-bye to exalted sentiments and romantic dreams. There isn't a bourgeois alive who in the ferment of his youth, if only for a day or for a minute, hasn't thought himself capable of boundless passions and noble exploits. The sorriest little woman-chaser has dreamed of Oriental queens; in a corner of every notary's heart lie the moldy remains of a poet.

These days it only bored him when Emma suddenly burst out sobbing on his breast: like people who can stand only a certain amount of music, he was drowsy and apathetic amidst the shrillness of her love; his heart had grown deaf to its subtler overtones.

By now they knew each other too well: no longer did they experience, in their mutual possession, that wonder that multiplies the joy a hundredfold. She was as surfeited with him as he was tired of her. Adultery, Emma was discovering, could be as banal as marriage.

But what way out was there? She felt humiliated by the degradation of such pleasures; but to no avail: she continued to cling to them, out of habit or out of depravity; and every day she pursued them more desperately, destroying all possible happiness by her excessive demands. She blamed Léon for her disappointed hopes, as though he had betrayed her; and she even longed for a catastrophe that would bring about their separation, since she hadn't the courage to bring it about herself.

Still, she continued to write him loving letters, faithful to the idea that a woman must always write to her lover.

But as her pen flew over the paper she was aware of the presence of another man, a phantom embodying her most ardent memories, the most beautiful things she had read and her strongest desires. In the end he became so real and accessible that she tingled with excitement, unable though she was to picture him clearly, so hidden was he, godlike, under his manifold attributes. He dwelt in that enchanted realm where silken ladders swing from balconies moon-bright and flower-scented. She felt him near her: he was coming—coming to ravish her entirely in a kiss. And the next moment she would drop back to earth, shattered; for these rapturous love-dreams drained her more than the greatest orgies.

◆

Almost immediately after *Madame Bovary* appeared (in the form of six installments in the *Revue de Paris*), the novel was denounced as an offense against public and religious morals, and Flaubert, as well as the publisher and the printer of the *Revue*, was brought to trial before a criminal court. All three men were ultimately acquitted, but not before an eloquent lawyer had defended all the passages (including those in Reading 5.21) that had been condemned as wanton and immoral.

A similar situation befell the American writer Kate Chopin (1851–1904), whose novel *The Awakening* was banned in her native city of St. Louis shortly after its publication in 1899. The novel, a frank examination of female sexual passion and marital infidelity, violated the tastes of the society in which Chopin had been reared and to which she returned in 1883. Unlike Flaubert, whose novels convey the staleness and inescapability of French provincial life, many of Chopin's stories deliberately ignore the specifics of time and place. Others are set in Louisiana, where Chopin lived for twelve years with her husband and six children. Chopin was successful in selling her Louisiana dialect stories, many of which explore matters of class, race, and gender within the world of Creole society, but her novels fell into obscurity soon after her death: *The Awakening*, whose heroine defies convention by committing adultery, did not receive positive critical attention until the 1950s.

While Chopin absorbed the realist strategies and social concerns of Flaubert, she brought to her prose a unique sensitivity to the nuances of human (and especially female) behavior—a challenge to popular romantic female stereotypes (see chapter 28). Her work also reveals a remarkable talent for narrating a story with jewel-like precision. Chopin's taut descriptive style reaches unparalleled heights in the short prose piece known as "The Story of an Hour." Here, the protagonist's brief taste of liberation takes on an ironic fatal turn.

## READING 5.22

# Kate Chopin's "The Story of an Hour" ("The Dream of an Hour")

Knowing that Mrs. Mallard was afflicted with a heart trouble, great care was taken to break to her as gently as possible the news of her husband's death.

It was her sister Josephine who told her, in broken sentences: veiled hints that revealed in half concealing. Her husband's friend Richards was there, too, near her. It was he who had been in the newspaper office when intelligence of the railroad disaster was received, with Brently Mallard's name leading the list of "killed." He had only taken time to assure himself of its truth by a second telegram, and had hastened to forestall any less careful, less tender friend in bearing the sad message.

She did not hear the story as many women have heard the same, with a paralysed inability to accept its significance. She wept at once, with a sudden, wild abandonment, in her sister's arms. When the storm of grief had spent itself she went away to her room alone. She would have no one follow her.

There stood, facing the open window, a comfortable, roomy armchair. Into this she sank, pressed down by a physical exhaustion that haunted her body and seemed to reach into her soul.

She could see in the open square before her house the tops of trees that were all aquiver with the new spring life. The delicious breath of rain was in the air. In the street below a peddler was crying his wares. The notes of a distant song which some one was singing reached her faintly, and countless sparrows were twittering in the eaves.

There were patches of blue sky showing here and there through the clouds that had met and piled one above the other in the west facing her window.

She sat with her head thrown back upon the cushion of the chair, quite motionless, except when a sob came into her throat and shook her, as a child who has cried itself to sleep continues to sob in its dreams.

She was young, with a fair, calm face, whose lines bespoke repression and even a certain strength. But now there was a dull stare in her eyes, whose gaze was fixed away off yonder on one of those patches of blue sky. It was not a glance of reflection, but rather a suspension of intelligent thought.

There was something coming to her and she was waiting for it, fearfully. What was it? She did not know; it was too subtle and elusive to name. But she felt it, creeping out of the sky, reaching toward her through the sounds, the scents, the color that filled the air.

Now her bosom rose and fell tumultuously. She was beginning to recognize this thing that was approaching to possess her, and she was striving to beat it back with her will—as powerless as her white slender hands would have been.

When she abandoned herself a little whispered word escaped her slight parted lips. She said it over and over under her breath: "free, free, free!" The vacant stare and the look of terror that had followed it went from her eyes. They stayed keen and bright. Her pulses beat fast, and the coursing blood warmed and relaxed every inch of her body.

She did not stop to ask if it were not a monstrous joy that held her. A clear and exalted perception enabled her to dismiss the suggestion as trivial.

She knew that she would weep again when she saw the kind, tender hands folded in death: fixed and grey and dead. But she saw beyond that bitter moment a long procession of years to come that would belong to her absolutely. And she opened and spread her arms out to them in welcome.

There would be no one to live for her during those coming years; she would live for herself. There would be no powerful will bending hers in that blind persistence with which men and women believe they have a right to impose a private will upon a fellow-creature. A kind intention or a cruel intention made the act seem no less a crime as she looked upon it in that brief moment of illumination.

And yet she loved him—sometimes. Often she had not. What did it matter! What could love, the unsolved mystery, count for in the face of this possession of self-assertion which she suddenly recognized as the strongest impulse of her being!

"Free! Body and soul free!" she kept whispering.

Josephine was kneeling before the keyhole, imploring for admission. "Louise, open the door! I beg: open the door—you will make yourself ill. What are you doing, Louise? For heaven's sake open the door."

"Go away. I'm not making myself ill." No: she was drinking in a very elixir of life through that open window.

Her fancy was running riot along those days ahead of her. Spring days, and summer days, and all sorts of days that would be her own. She breathed a quick prayer that life might be long. It was only yesterday she had thought with a shudder that life might be long.

She arose at length and opened the door to her sister's importunities. There was a feverish triumph in her eyes, and she carried herself unwittingly like a goddess of Victory. She clasped her sister's wrist, and together they descended the stairs. Richards stood waiting for them at the bottom.

Some one was opening the front door with a latchkey. It was Brently Mallard who entered, a little travel-stained, composedly carrying his grip-sack and umbrella. He had been far from the scene of accident, and did not even know there had been one. He stood amazed at Josephine's piercing cry; at Richards' quick motion to screen him from the view of his wife.

But Richards was too late.

When the doctors came they said she had died of heart disease—of joy that kills.

◆

## Zola and the Naturalistic Novel

Kate Chopin's contemporary Emile Zola (1840–1902) initiated a variant form of literary realism known as *naturalism*. Somewhat like realism, naturalist fiction was based on the premise that life should be represented objectively and without embellishment or idealization. But naturalists differed from realists in taking a deterministic approach that showed human beings as products of environmental or hereditary factors over which they had little or no control. Just as Marx held that economic life shaped all aspects of culture, so naturalists believed that material and social elements determined human conduct. In his passion to describe the world with absolute fidelity, Zola amassed notebooks of information on a wide variety of subjects, including coal mining, the railroads, the stock market, and the science of surgery. Zola treated the novel as an exact study of commonplace, material existence. He presented a slice of life that showed how social and material circumstances influenced human behavior. Zola's subjects were as brutally uncompromising as his style. *The Grog Shop* (1877) offered a terrifying picture of the effects of alcoholism on industrial workers; *Germinal* (1885) exposed the bitter lives of French coal miners; and his most scandalous novel, *Nana* (1880), was a scathing portrayal of a beautiful but unscrupulous prostitute.

Strong elements of naturalism are found in the novels of many late nineteenth-century writers in both Europe and America. Thomas Hardy (1840–1928) in England, and Stephen Crane (1871–1900), Jack London (1876–1916), and Theodore Dreiser (1871–1945) in America are the most notable of the English-language literary naturalists.

## The Plays of Ibsen

The Norwegian dramatist Henrik Ibsen (1828–1906) brought to the late nineteenth-century stage concerns similar to those that appeared in the novels of the European and American realists. A moralist and a student of human behavior, Ibsen rebelled against the artificial social conventions that led people to pursue self-deluding and hypocritical lives. Ibsen was deeply concerned with contemporary issues and social problems. He shocked the public by writing prose dramas that addressed such controversial subjects as insanity, incest, and venereal disease. At the same time, he explored universal themes of conflict between the individual and society, between love and duty, and between husband and wife.

In 1879, Ibsen wrote the classic drama of female liberation, *A Doll's House*. The play traces the awakening of a middle-class woman to the meaninglessness of her role as "a doll-wife" living in "a doll's house." Threatened by blackmail over a debt she incurred years earlier, Nora Helmer looks to her priggish, egotistical husband Torvald for protection. When he fails to provide that protection, Nora realizes the frailty of her dependent lifestyle. She comes to recognize that her first obligation is to herself and to her dignity as a reasonable human being. Nora's revelation brings to life, in the forceful language of everyday speech, the psychological tension between male and female that Mill had analyzed only ten years earlier in his treatise on the subjection of women. Ibsen does not resolve the question of whether a woman's duties to husband and children come before her duty to herself; yet, as is suggested in the following exchange between Nora and Torvald (excerpted from the last scene of *A Doll's House*), Nora's self-discovery precipitates the end of her marriage. Nora shuts the door on the illusions of the past as emphatically as Ibsen—a half-century after Goethe's *Faust*—may be said to have turned his back on the world of romantic idealism.

### READING 5.23

### From Ibsen's *A Doll's House*

**Act III, Final Scene**

*[Late at night in the Helmers' living room. Instead of retiring, Nora suddenly appears in street clothes.]*

**HELMER:** . . . What's all this? I thought you were going to bed. You've changed your dress?

**NORA:** Yes, Torvald; I've changed my dress.

**HELMER:** But what for? At this hour?

**NORA:** I shan't sleep tonight.

**HELMER:** But, Nora dear—

**NORA** *[looking at her watch]*: It's not so very late—Sit down, Torvald; we have a lot to talk about.

*[She sits at one side of the table.]*

**HELMER:** Nora—what does this mean? Why that stern expression?

**NORA:** Sit down. It'll take some time. I have a lot to say to you.

*[Helmer sits at the other side of the table.]*

**HELMER:** You frighten me, Nora. I don't understand you.

**NORA:** No, that's just it. You don't understand me; and I have never understood you either—until tonight. No, don't interrupt me. Just listen to what I have to say. This is to be a final settlement, Torvald.

**HELMER:** How do you mean?

**NORA** *[after a short silence]*: Doesn't anything special strike you as we sit here like this?

**HELMER:** I don't think so—why?

**NORA:** It doesn't occur to you, does it, that though we've been married for eight years, this is the first time that we two—man and wife—have sat down for a serious talk?

**HELMER:** What do you mean by serious?

**NORA:** During eight whole years, no—more than that—ever since the first day we met—we have never exchanged so much as one serious word about serious things.

**HELMER:** Why should I perpetually burden you with all my cares and problems? How could you possibly help me to solve them?

**NORA:** I'm not talking about cares and problems. I'm simply saying we've never once sat down seriously and tried to get to the bottom of anything.

**HELMER:** But, Nora, darling—why should you be concerned with serious thoughts?

**NORA:** That's the whole point! You've never understood me—A great injustice has been done me, Torvald; first by Father, and then by you.

**HELMER:** What a thing to say! No two people on earth could ever have loved you more than we have!

**NORA** *[shaking her head]*: You never loved me. You just thought it was fun to be in love with me.

**HELMER:** This is fantastic!

**NORA:** Perhaps. But it's true all the same. While I was still at home I used to hear Father airing his opinions and they became my opinions; or if I didn't happen to agree, I kept it to myself—he would have been displeased otherwise. He used to call me his doll-baby, and played with me as I played with my dolls. Then I came to live in your house—

**HELMER:** What an expression to use about our marriage!

**NORA** *[undisturbed]*: I mean—from Father's hands I passed into yours. You arranged everything according to your tastes, and I acquired the same tastes, or I pretended to—I'm not sure which—a little of both, perhaps. Looking back on it all, it seems to me I've lived here like a beggar, from hand to mouth. I've lived by performing tricks for you, Torvald. But that's the way you wanted it. You and Father have done me a great wrong. You've prevented me from becoming a real person.

**HELMER:** Nora, how can you be so ungrateful and unreasonable! Haven't you been happy here?

**NORA:** No, never. I thought I was; but I wasn't really.

**HELMER:** Not—not happy!

**NORA:** No, only merry. You've always been so kind to me. But our home has never been anything but a playroom. I've been your doll-wife, just as at home I was Papa's doll-child. And the children, in turn, have been my dolls. I thought it fun when you played games with me, just as they thought it fun when I played games with them. And that's been our marriage, Torvald.

**HELMER:** There may be a grain of truth in what you say, even though it is distorted and exaggerated. From now on things will be different. Play-time is over now; tomorrow lessons begin!

**NORA:** Whose lessons? Mine, or the children's?

**HELMER:** Both, if you wish it, Nora, dear.

**NORA:** Torvald, I'm afraid you're not the man to teach me to be a real wife to you.

**HELMER:** How can you say that?

**NORA:** And I'm certainly not fit to teach the children.

**HELMER:** Nora!

**NORA:** Didn't you just say, a moment ago, you didn't dare trust them to me?

**HELMER:** That was in the excitement of the moment! You mustn't take it so seriously!

**NORA:** But you were quite right, Torvald. That job is beyond me; there's another job I must do first: I must try and educate myself. You could never help me to do that; I must do it quite alone. So, you see—that's why I'm going to leave you.

**HELMER:** *[jumping up]*: What did you say—?

**NORA:** I shall never get to know myself—I shall never learn to face reality—unless I stand alone. So I can't stay with you any longer.

**HELMER:** Nora! Nora!

**NORA:** I am going at once. I'm sure Kristine will let me stay with her tonight—

**HELMER:** But, Nora—this is madness! I shan't allow you to do this. I shall forbid it!

**NORA:** You no longer have the power to forbid me anything. I'll only take a few things with me—those that belong to me. I shall never again accept anything from you.

**HELMER:** Have you lost your senses?

**NORA:** Tomorrow I'll go home—to what *was* my home, I mean. It might be easier for me there, to find something to do.

**HELMER:** You talk like an ignorant child, Nora—!

**NORA:** Yes. That's just why I must educate myself.

**HELMER:** To leave your home—to leave your husband, and your children! What do you suppose people would say to that?

**NORA:** It makes no difference. This is something I *must* do.

**HELMER:** It's inconceivable! Don't you realize you'd be betraying your most sacred duty?

**NORA:** What do you consider that to be?

**HELMER:** Your duty towards your husband and your children—I surely don't have to tell you that!

**NORA:** I've another duty just as sacred.

**HELMER:** Nonsense! What duty do you mean?

**NORA:** My duty towards myself.

**HELMER:** Remember—before all else you are a wife and mother.

**NORA:** I don't believe that any more. I believe that before all else I am a human being, just as you are—or at least that I should try and become one. I know that most people would agree with you, Torvald—and that's what they say in books. But I can no longer be satisfied with what most people say—or what they write in books. I must think things out for myself—get clear about them.

**HELMER:** Surely your position in your home is clear enough? Have you no sense of religion? Isn't that an infallible guide to you?

**NORA:** But don't you see, Torvald—I don't really know what religion is.

**HELMER:** Nora! How *can* you!

**NORA:** All I know about it is what Pastor Hansen told me when I was confirmed. He taught me what he thought religion was—said it was *this* and *that*. As soon as I get away by myself, I shall have to look into that matter too, try and decide whether what he taught me was right—or whether it's right for *me*, at least.

**HELMER:** A nice way for a young woman to talk! It's unheard of! If religion means nothing to you, I'll appeal to your conscience; you must have some sense of ethics, I suppose? Answer me! Or have you none?

**NORA:** It's hard for me to answer you, Torvald. I don't think I know—all these things bewilder me. But I *do* know that I think quite differently from you about them.

I've discovered that the law, for instance, is quite different from what I had imagined; but I find it hard to believe it can be right. It seems it's criminal for a woman to try and spare her old, sick, father, or save her husband's life! I can't agree with that.

**HELMER:** You talk like a child. You have no understanding of the society we live in.

**NORA:** No, I haven't. But I'm going to try and learn. I want to find out which of us is right—society or I.

**HELMER:** You are ill, Nora; you have a touch of fever; you're quite beside yourself.

**NORA:** I've never felt so sure—so clear-headed—as I do tonight.

**HELMER:** "Sure and clear-headed" enough to leave your husband and your children?

**NORA:** Yes.

**HELMER:** Then there is only one explanation possible.

**NORA:** What?

**HELMER:** You don't love me any more.

**NORA:** No; that is just it.

**HELMER:** Nora!—What are you saying!

**NORA:** It makes me so unhappy, Torvald; for you've always been so kind to me. But I can't help it. I don't love you any more.

**HELMER** *[mastering himself with difficulty]*: You feel "sure and clear-headed" about this too?

**NORA:** Yes, utterly sure. That's why I can't stay here any longer. . . .

◆

# *Realism in the Visual Arts*

## The Birth of Photography

One of the most significant factors in the development of the realist mentality was the birth of photography. While a painting or an engraving might bring to life the content of the artist's imagination, a photograph offered an authentic record of a moment vanished in time. Photography, literally "writing with light," had its beginnings in 1839, when the French inventor Louis-J.-M. Daguerre (1787–1851) successfully exposed a light-sensitive metal plate and fixed the image with common chemicals. Gradual improvements in camera lenses and in the chemicals used to develop the visible image hastened the rise of photography as a popular device for recording the physical world with unprecedented accuracy.

**1839** L.-J.-M. Daguerre (French) perfects the first practicable photographic process
**1860** production begins on the first Winchester repeating rifle (in America)
**1866** explosive dynamite is first produced in Sweden
**1888** George Eastman (American) perfects the "Kodak" box camera

Photography presented an obvious challenge to the authority of the artist, who, throughout history, had assumed the role of nature's imitator. But artists were slow to realize the long-range impact of photography—that is, the camera's potential to liberate artists from reproducing the physical "look" of nature. Critics proclaimed that photographs, as authentic facsimiles of the physical world, should serve artists as aids to achieving greater realism in canvas painting; and many artists did indeed use photographs as factual resources for their compositions. Nevertheless, by mid-century, both Europeans and Americans were using the camera for a wide variety of purposes: They made topographical studies of geographic sites, recorded architectural monuments, and produced thousands of portrait images. Some photographers, such as the British pioneer Julia Margaret Cameron (1815–1879), used the camera to recreate the style of romantic painting. Imitating the effects of the artist's paintbrush, Cameron's soft-focus portraits are romantic in spirit and sentiment (Figure **30.5**). Others used the camera to establish themselves as masters of unvarnished realism. The French master Gaspart-Félix Tournachon, known as Nadar (1820–1910), made vivid portrait studies of such celebrities as George Sand,

**Figure 30.4** Thomas Annan, *Close No. 37 High Street*, ca. 1868. Harry Ransom Humanities Research Center, The University of Texas at Austin. Gernsheim Collection.

**Figure 30.5** Julia Margaret Cameron, *Whisper of the Muse (G. F. Watts and Children)*, ca. 1865. Photograph. The Royal Photographic Society, Bath.

Berlioz, and Sarah Bernhardt. Nadar was the first to experiment with aerial photography (see Figure 30.11). He also introduced the use of electric light in a series of extraordinary photographs documenting the sewers and catacombs beneath the city of Paris.

Inevitably, nineteenth-century photographs served as social documents: The black-and-white images of poverty-stricken families and ramshackle tenements produced by Thomas Annan (1829–1887), for instance, record with gritty realism the notorious slums of nineteenth-century Glasgow, Scotland (Figure **30.4**). Such photographs could easily illustrate the novels of Charles Dickens. In a similar vein, the documentary photographs of the American Civil War (1861–1865)

**Figure 30.6** Mathew B. Brady or staff, *Dead Confederate Soldier with Gun, Petersburg, Virginia*, 1865. Photograph. The Library of Congress, Washington, D.C.

produced by Mathew B. Brady (1823–1896) and his staff testify to the importance of the photographer as a chronicler of human life. Brady's thirty-five hundred Civil War photographs include mundane scenes of barracks and munitions as well as unflinching views of human carnage (Figure **30.6**).

## Courbet and French Realist Painting

In painting no less than in literature and photography, realism came to challenge the romantic style. The realist preference for concrete, matter-of-fact depictions of everyday life provided a sober alternative to both the remote, exotic, and heroic imagery of the romantics and the noble and elevated themes of the neoclassicists. Obedient to the credo that artists must confront the experiences and appearances of their own time, realist painters abandoned the nostalgic landscapes and heroic themes of romantic art in favor of compositions depicting the consequences of industrialism (see Figure 30.2) and the lives of ordinary men and women.

The leading realist of nineteenth-century French painting was Gustave Courbet (1819–1877). A farmer's son, Courbet was a self-taught artist, an outspoken socialist, and a staunch defender of the realist cause. "A painter," he protested, "should paint only what he can see." Indeed, most of Courbet's works—portraits, landscapes, and contemporary scenes—remain true to the tangible facts of his immediate vision. With the challenge "Show me an angel and I'll paint one," he taunted both the romantics and the neoclassicists. Not angels but ordinary individuals in their actual settings and circumstances interested Courbet.

In *The Stone-Breakers*, Courbet depicted two rural laborers performing the most menial of physical tasks (Figure **30.7**). The painting, which Courbet's friend

**Figure 30.7** Gustave Courbet, *The Stone-Breakers*, 1849. Oil on canvas, 5 ft. 3 in. × 8 ft. 6 in. Formerly Gemäldegalerie, Dresden (destroyed 1945).

**Figure 30.8** Jean-François Millet, *The Gleaners*, ca. 1857. Black conté crayon on paper, approx. $6\frac{7}{8} \times 10\frac{3}{8}$ in. The Baltimore Museum of Art. The George A. Lucas Collection (BMA 1996.53.18686).

**Figure 30.9** Gustave Courbet, *Burial at Ornans*, 1849–1850. Oil on canvas, 10 ft. 3 in. × 21 ft. 9 in. Louvre, Paris. Photo: © R.M.N., Paris.

Proudhon called "the first socialist picture," outraged the critics because its subject matter was mundane and its figures were crude, ragged, and totally unidealized. Moreover, the figures were positioned with their backs turned toward the viewer, thus violating, by nineteenth-century standards, the rules of propriety and decorum enshrined in French academic art (see chapter 23). But despite such "violations" Courbet's painting appealed to the masses. In a country whose population was still two-thirds rural and largely poor, the stolid dignity of hard labor was a popular subject—so popular, in fact, that it was often romanticized. A comparison of *The Stone-Breakers* with a study by Jean-François Millet (1814–1875) for his painting *The Gleaners* (Figure **30.8**) illustrates the difference between Courbet's undiluted realism and Millet's romanticized realism. Millet's workers are as ordinary and anonymous as Courbet's, but they are also dignified and graceful, betraying a distant kinship with Raphael's heroic figures (see chapter 17). Whereas Courbet's workers seem trapped behind the narrow roadside bank, Millet's dominate a broad and ennobling vista. And while Courbet's scene has the "random" and accidental look of a snapshot, Millet's composition—in which the contours of haystacks and wagon subtly echo the curved backs of the laborers—observes the traditional academic precepts of balance and formal design. Millet removed nature's "flaws" and imposed the imagination upon the immediate evidence of the senses. His romanticized views of the laboring classes became some of the best-loved images of the nineteenth century (and were later sold in popular engraved versions). Courbet, however, remained brutally loyal to nature and the mundane world; he knew that the carefree peasant was an idyllic stereotype that existed not in real life, but rather in the urban imagination. He surely would have agreed with his British contemporary, the novelist George Eliot (Mary Ann Evans), that "no one who is well acquainted with the English peasantry can pronounce them merry."

Courbet's most daring effort to record ordinary life in an unembellished manner was his monumental *Burial at Ornans* (Figure **30.9**). The huge canvas (over 10 × 21 feet) consists of fifty-two life-sized figures disposed around the edges of a freshly-dug grave. Western representations of Christian burial traditionally emphasized the ritual or theatrical aspects of death and disposal, but in this painting Courbet minimizes any display of pomp and ceremony. The kneeling gravedigger and the attendant dog are as important to the pictorial statement as are the priest and his retinue. And the mourners, including some of Courbet's most homely subjects, play a more prominent role in the composition than the deceased, whose body is nowhere in view. With the objectivity of a camera eye, Courbet banished from his canvas all sentimentality and artifice.

**1798** Aloys Senefelder (Bavarian) develops lithography
**1822** William Church (American) patents an automatic typesetting machine
**1844** wood-pulp production provides cheap paper for newspapers and periodicals

## Social Realism in the Art of Daumier

The French artist Honoré Daumier (1808–1879) left the world a detailed record of the social life of his time. He had no formal academic education, but his earliest training was in **lithography**—a printmaking process created by drawing on a stone plate (Figure 30.10). Lithography, a product of nineteenth-century print technology, was a cheap and popular means of providing illustrations for newspapers, magazines, and books. Daumier produced over four thousand lithographs, often turning out two to three per week for distribution by various Paris newspapers and journals. For his subject matter, Daumier turned directly to the world around him: the streets of Paris, the theater, the law courts. The advancing (and often jarring) technology of modern life attracted Daumier's interest: pioneer experiments in aerial photography (Figure 30.11), the telegraph, the sewing machine, the repeating rifle, the railroad, and urban renewal projects that included widening the streets of Paris. But Daumier did not simply depict the facts of modern life; he frequently ridiculed them. Skeptical as to whether new technology and social progress could radically alter the human condition, he drew attention to characteristic human weaknesses, from the hypocrisy of lawyers and the pretensions of the *nouveaux riches* to the pompous and all too familiar complacency of self-serving officials (Figure 30.12). The ancestors of modern-day political cartoons, Daumier's lithographs often depend on gesture and caricature to convey his bitter opposition to monarchy, political corruption, and profiteering. Such criticism did not go unnoticed: Following the publication of his 1831 lithograph, which depicted the French king Louis Philippe as an obese Gargantua atop a commode/throne from which he defecated bags of gold, Daumier spent six months in jail.

**Figure 30.11** Honoré Daumier, *Nadar Raising Photography to the Heights of Art*, 1862. Lithograph. The balloonist, photographer, draftsman, and journalist Gaspard-Félix Tournachon, called Nadar, took his first photograph from a balloon. Historical Pictures Service, Chicago.

**Figure 30.10** Lithography is a method of making prints from a flat surface; it is also called planography. An image is first drawn or painted with an oil-based lithographic crayon or pencil on a smooth limestone surface. The surface is wiped with water, which will not stick to the applied areas of greasy lithographic ink because oil and water do not mix. The greasy areas resist the water and are thus exposed. The surface is then rolled with printing ink, which adheres only to the parts drawn in the oil-based medium. Dampened paper is placed over the stone, and a special flatbed press rubs the back of the paper, transferring the work from the stone to the covering sheet.

Primarily a graphic artist, Daumier completed fewer than three hundred paintings. In *The Third-Class Carriage*, he captured on canvas the shabby monotony of nineteenth-century lower-class railway travel (Figure 30.13). The part of the European train in which tickets were the least expensive was also, of course, the least comfortable: It lacked glass windows (hence was subject to more than average amounts of smoke, cinders, and clatter) and was equipped with hard wooden benches rather than cushioned seats. Three generations of poor folk—an elderly woman, a younger woman, and her children—occupy the foreground of Daumier's painting. Their lumpish bodies suggest weariness and futility, yet they convey a humble dignity reminiscent of Rembrandt's figures (see chapter 21). Dark and loosely sketched oil glazes underscore the mood of cheerless resignation. Daumier produced a forthright image of common humanity in a contemporary urban setting.

**Figure 30.12** Honoré Daumier, *Le Ventre Législatif* (*The Legislative Belly*), 1834. Lithograph, 11 × 17 in. Arizona State University Art Collections, Arizona State University, Tempe, Arizona. Gift of Oliver B. James.

**Figure 30.13** Honoré Daumier, *The Third-Class Carriage*, ca. 1862. Oil on canvas, 25¾ × 35½ in. The Metropolitan Museum of Art, New York. H. O. Havemeyer Collection. Bequest of Mrs. H. O. Havemeyer, 1929 (29.100.129). Photograph by Malcolm Varon. © 1986 The Metropolitan Museum of Art.

## The Scandalous Realism of Manet

Realism in the paintings of Edouard Manet (1832–1883) presented an unsettling challenge to tradition. Manet was an admirer of the art of the old masters, especially Velásquez, but he was equally enthralled by the life of his own time—by Parisians and their middle-class pleasures. No less than Flaubert or Ibsen, Manet shocked the public by recasting traditional subjects in modern guise. In a large canvas of 1863 entitled *Déjeuner sur l'herbe* (*Luncheon on the Grass*), he depicted a nude woman calmly enjoying a picnic lunch with two fully clothed men, while a second, partially clothed woman bathes in a nearby stream (Figure **30.14**).

When submitted to the Paris Salon of 1863, *Déjeuner* was rejected by the jury of the Royal Academy. Nevertheless, that same year it was displayed at the Salon des Refusés ("the Salon of the Rejected Painters"), a landmark exhibition authorized by the French head of state in response to public agitation against the tyranny of the Academy. No sooner was Manet's painting hung, however, than visitors tried to poke holes in the canvas and critics began to attack its coarse "improprieties"; *Déjeuner sur l'herbe* was pronounced scandalous.

While Manet's subject matter—the nude in a landscape—was quite traditional (see, for instance, *Pastoral Concert,* Figure **30.15**) and some of his motifs were borrowed from a sixteenth-century engraving of a Raphael tapestry (Figure **30.16**), the figures in *Déjeuner* were neither classical nor historical. They represent neither woodland nymphs nor Olympian gods and goddesses, but blatantly contemporary people—specifically, Manet's favorite female model, Victorine Meurent (in the nude), and his future brother-in-law (the reclining male figure).

**Figure 30.14** Edouard Manet, *Déjeuner sur l'herbe*, 1863. Oil on canvas, 7 ft. × 8 ft. 10 in. Musée d'Orsay, Paris. Photo: © R.M.N., Paris.

**Figure 30.15** Titian (begun by Giorgione), *Pastoral Concert*, ca. 1505. Oil on canvas, 3 ft. 7¼ in. × 4 ft. 6¼ in. Louvre, Paris. Photo: © R.M.N., Paris.

**Figure 30.16** Marcantonio Raimondi, detail from *The Judgment of Paris*, ca. 1520. Engraving after Raphael tapestry. Giraudon/Art Resource, New York.

Female nudity had been acceptable in European art since the early Renaissance, as long as it was cast in terms of myth or allegory, but in a contemporary setting—one that eliminated the barrier between fantasy and ordinary life—such nudity was considered indecent. By denying his audience the traditional conventions by which to view the painting, Manet created a work of art that—as with *Madame Bovary*—implied the degeneracy of French society. Like Flaubert, who cultivated authenticity of detail and an impersonal narrative style, Manet took a neutral stance, one that presented the facts with cool objectivity. Critics also attacked Manet's inelegant style: One wrote, "The nude does not have a good figure, and one cannot imagine anything uglier than the man stretched out beside her, who has not even thought of removing, out of doors, his horrible padded cap."

In a second painting completed in 1863, *Olympia*, Manet again "debased" a traditional subject—the reclining nude (Figure 30.17). The short, stocky Olympia (Victorine again) stares at the viewer boldly and with none of the subtle allure of a Titian Venus or an Ingres Odalisque. Her satin slippers, the enticing black ribbon at her throat, and other details in the painting distinguish her as a courtesan—a high-class

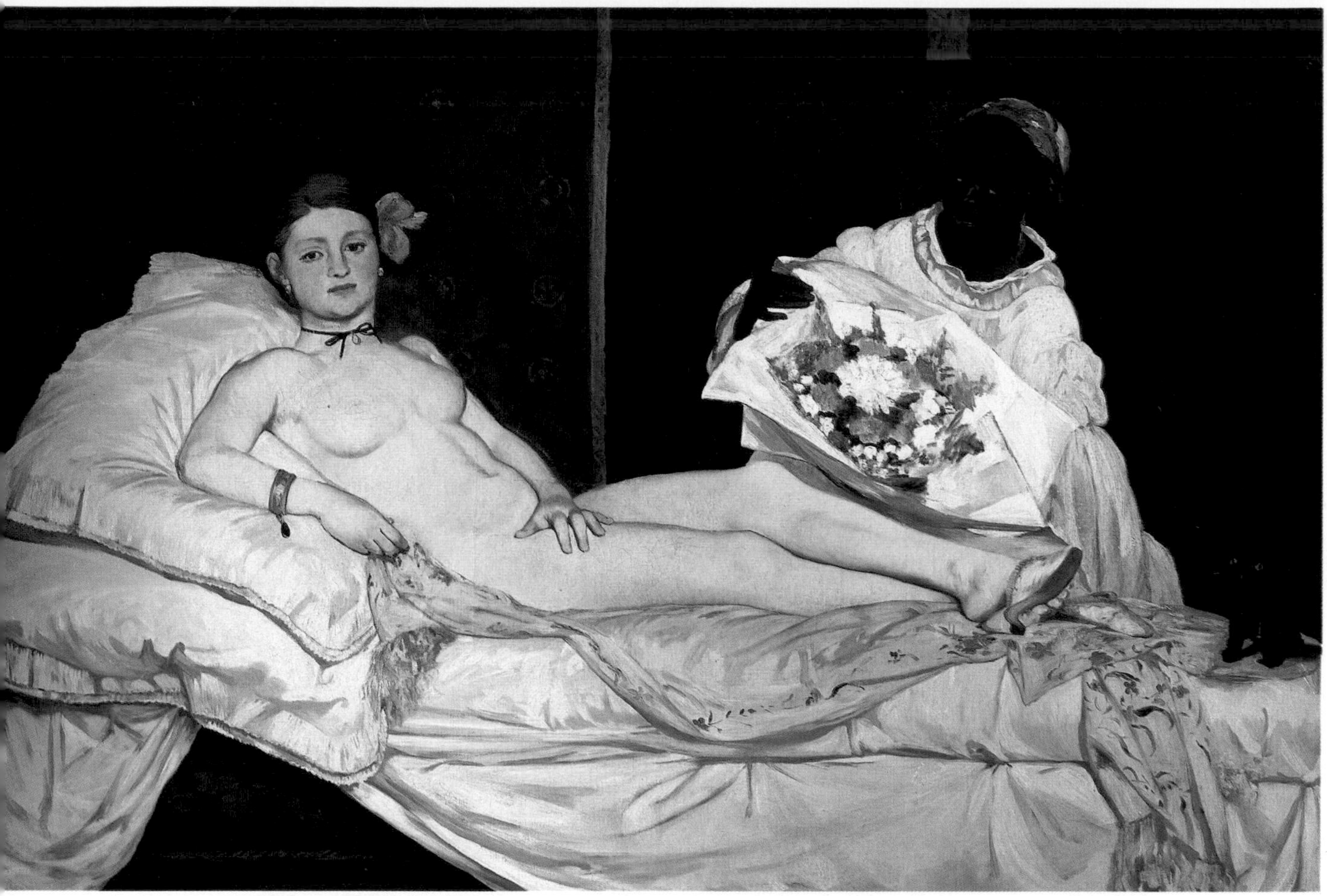

**Figure 30.17** Edouard Manet, *Olympia*, 1863. Oil on canvas, 4 ft. 3¼ in. × 6 ft. 2¾ in. Musée d'Orsay, Paris. Photo: © R.M.N., Paris.

prostitute. Manet's urban contemporaries were not blind to this fact, but the critics were unsparingly brutal. One journalist called Olympia "a sort of female gorilla" and warned, "Truly, young girls and women about to become mothers would do well, if they are wise, to run away from this spectacle." Like Flaubert's *Madame Bovary* or Zola's *Nana*, Manet's *Olympia* desentimentalized the image of the female. By deflating the ideal and rendering reality in commonplace terms, Manet not only offended public taste, he implicitly challenged the traditional view of art as the bearer of noble themes.

Manet further defied tradition by employing new painting techniques. Imitating current photographic practice, he bathed his figures in bright light and, using a minimum of shading, flattened them so that they resembled the figures in Japanese prints (see Figure 31.11). Even Manet's friends were critical: Courbet mockingly compared Olympia to the Queen of Spades in a deck of playing cards. Manet's practice of eliminating halftones and laying on fresh, opaque colors (instead of building up form by means of thin, transparent glazes) anticipated impressionism, a style he embraced later in his career.

## Realism in American Painting

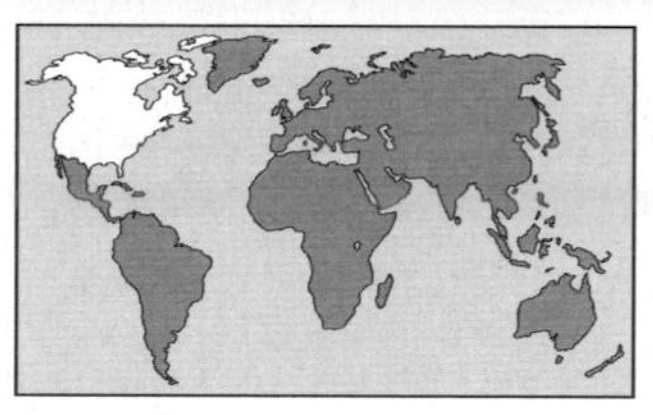

Although most American artists received their training in European art schools, their taste for realism seems to have sprung from a native affection for the factual and the material aspects of their immediate surroundings. In the late nineteenth century, an era of gross materialism known as the Gilded Age, America produced an extraordinary number of first-rate realist painters. These individuals explored a wide variety of subjects, from still life and portraiture to landscape and genre painting. Like such literary giants as Mark Twain, American realist painters fused keen observation with remarkable descriptive skills. One of the most talented of the American realists was William M. Harnett (1848–1892), a still-life painter and a master of *trompe l'oeil* ("fool the eye") illusionism. Working in the tradition of the Dutch still-life masters, Harnett recorded mundane objects with such hair-fine precision that

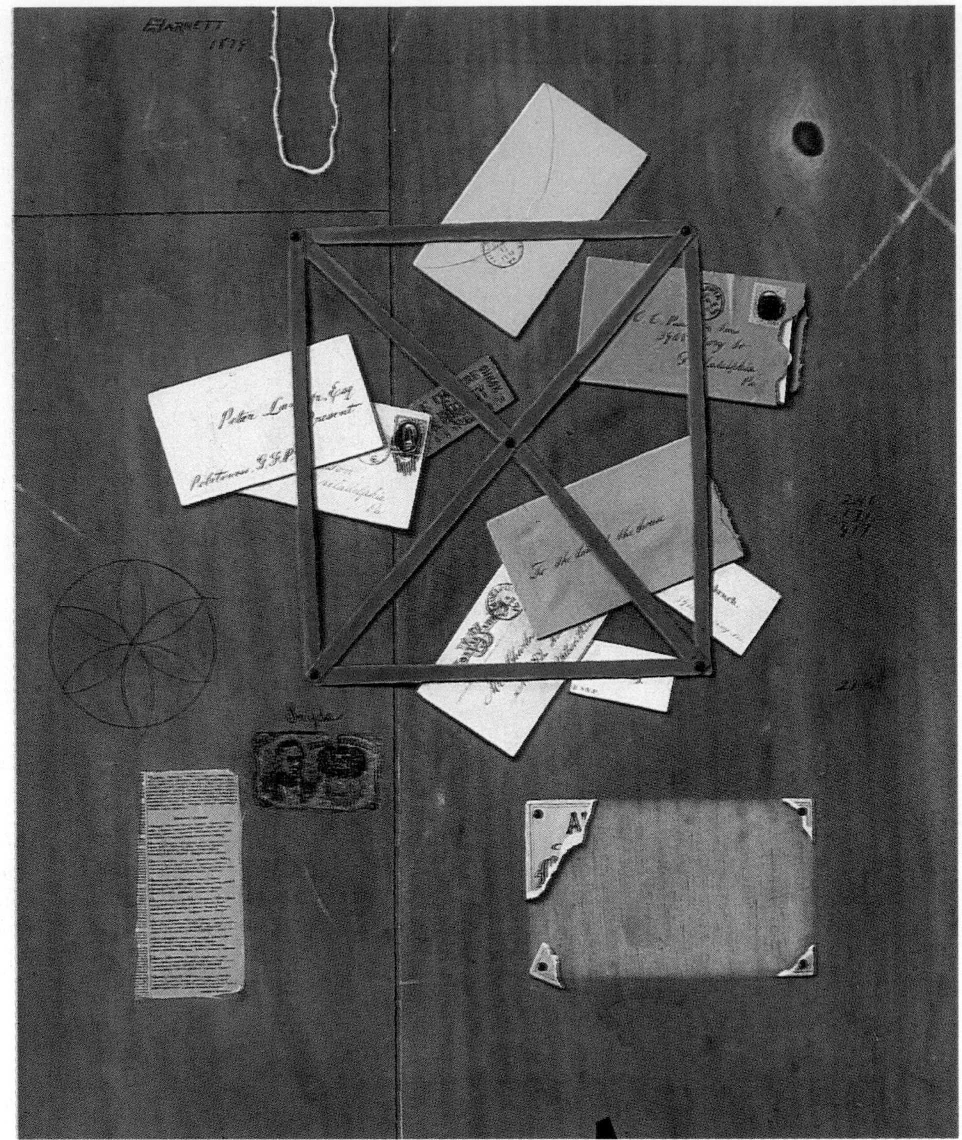

**Figure 30.18** William Michael Harnett, *The Artist's Letter Rack*, 1879. Oil on canvas, 30 × 25 in. The Metropolitan Museum of Art, New York. Morris K. Jesup Fund, 1966 (66.13). © 1981 The Metropolitan Museum of Art.

some of them—letters, newspaper clippings, and calling cards—seem to be pasted on the canvas (Figure **30.18**).

In the genre of portraiture, the Philadelphia artist Thomas Eakins (1844–1916) mastered the art of producing uncompromising likenesses such as that of the poet Walt Whitman (see Figure 27.11). Like most nineteenth-century American artists, Eakins received his training in European art schools, but he ultimately emerged as a painter of the American scene and as an influential art instructor. At the Pennsylvania Academy of Fine Arts, he received criticism for his insistence on working from nude models and was forced to resign for removing the loincloth of a male model in a class that included female students. Eakins was among the first artists to choose subjects from the world of sports, such as boxing and boating, while his fascination with scientific anatomy—he dissected cadavers at Jefferson Medical College in Philadelphia—led him to produce some unorthodox representations of medical training and practice. One of his most notable canvases, *The Agnew Clinic* (Figure **30.19**), is a dispassionate view of a hospital amphitheater in which a doctor lectures to students on the subject of a surgical procedure. Eakins, a photographer of some note, often used the camera to collect visual data for his compositions. He never romanticized his subjects, and while he owed much to Rembrandt and Velásquez—*The Agnew Clinic* surely looks back to Rembrandt's *Anatomy Lesson* (Figure **30.20**)—his works communicate a fresh and stubbornly precise record of the natural world.

If American realists were keenly aware of the new art of photography, they were also indebted to the

**Figure 30.19** (above) Thomas Eakins, *The Agnew Clinic*, 1889. Oil on canvas, 6 ft. 2½ in. × 10 ft. 10½ in. University of Pennsylvania School of Medicine.

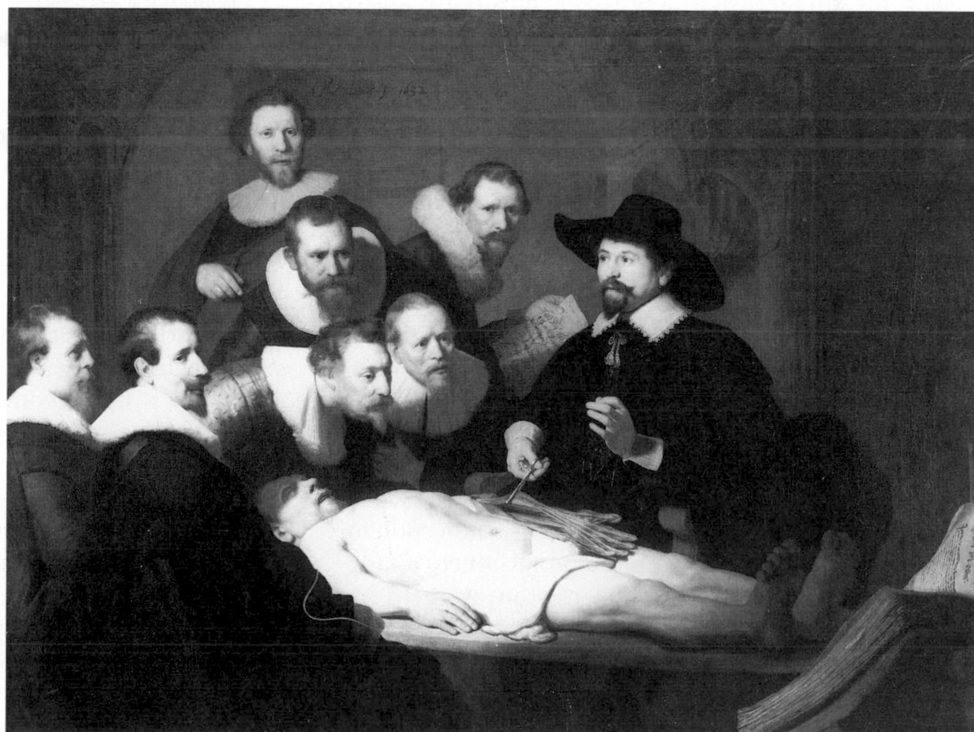

**Figure 30.20** Rembrandt van Rijn, *The Anatomy Lesson of Dr. Nicolaes Tulp*, 1632. Oil on canvas, 5 ft. 3⅜ in. × 7 ft 1¼ in. Mauritshuis, The Hague. Scala/Art Resource, New York.

**Figure 30.21** Winslow Homer, *The War for the Union: A Bayonet Charge*, published in *Harper's Weekly*, July 12, 1862. Wood engraving, 13⅝ × 20⅝ in. The Metropolitan Museum of Art, New York. Harris Brisbane Fund, 1929 (29.88.3 [3]).

world of journalism. Winslow Homer (1836–1910) began his career as a newspaper illustrator and a reporter for the New York magazine *Harper's Weekly*. The first professional artist to serve as a war correspondent, Homer produced on-the-scene documentary paintings and drawings of the American Civil War, which *Harper's* converted to wood-engraved illustrations (Figure **30.21**). Although Homer often generalized the facts of the events he actually witnessed, he never moralized on or allegorized his subjects (as did, for instance, Goya or Delacroix). His talent for graphic selectivity and dramatic concentration rivaled that of America's first war photographer, Mathew B. Brady (see Figure 30.6).

Apart from two trips to Europe, Homer spent most of his life in New England, where he painted subjects that were both ordinary and typically American. Scenes of hunting and fishing reveal Homer's deep affection for nature, while his many genre paintings reflect a fascination with the activities of American women and children. In *The Country School* (Figure **30.22**), Homer combined crisply articulated details and stark patterns of light and shadow to convey the controlled atmosphere of the rural American schoolhouse, a subject dominated by the authoritative figure of the female teacher.

Homer was also interested in the activities of African-Americans in contemporary culture. One of his most enigmatic paintings, *The Gulf Stream*, shows a black man adrift in a rudderless boat surrounded by shark-filled waters which are whipped by the winds of an impending tornado (Figure **30.23**; see also Part Opener, p. 70). While realistic in execution, the painting may be interpreted as a romantic metaphor for the isolation and plight of black Americans in the decades following the Civil War. Homer shared with earlier nineteenth-century artists, including Turner, Melville, and Géricault, an almost obsessive interest in the individual's life and death struggle with the sea. However, compared (for instance) with Géricault's more theatrical rendering of man against nature in *The Raft of the "Medusa"* (see Figure 29.4), Homer's painting is a matter-of-fact study of human resignation in the face of deadly peril.

American audiences loved their realist painters, but, occasionally, critics voiced mixed feelings. The American novelist Henry James (1843–1916), whose novels probed the differences between European and American character, assessed what he called Homer's "perfect realism," with these words:

**Figure 30.22** Winslow Homer, *The Country School*, 1871. Oil on canvas, $21\frac{3}{8} \times 38\frac{3}{8}$ in. The Saint Louis Art Museum. Museum Purchase.

**Figure 30.23** Winslow Homer, *The Gulf Stream*, 1899. Oil on canvas, $28\frac{1}{8} \times 49\frac{1}{8}$ in. The Metropolitan Museum of Art, New York. Catharine Lorillard Wolfe Collection. Catharine Lorillard Wolfe Fund, 1906 (06.1234). © 1984 The Metropolitan Museum of Art.

> He is almost barbarously simple, and, to our eye, he is horribly ugly; but there is nevertheless something one likes about him. What is it? For ourselves, it is not his subjects. We frankly confess that we detest his subjects—his barren plank fences, his glaring, bald, blue skies, his big, dreary, vacant lots of meadows, his freckled, straight-haired Yankee urchins, his flat-breasted maidens, suggestive of a dish of rural doughnuts and pie, his calico sun-bonnets, his flannel shirts, his cowhide boots. He has chosen the least pictorial features of the least pictorial range of scenery and civilization; he has resolutely treated them as if they *were* pictorial, as if they were every inch as good as Capri or Tangiers; and, to reward his audacity, he has incontestably succeeded. It . . . is a proof that if you will only be doggedly literal, though you may often be unpleasing, you will at least have a stamp of your own.*

*Quoted in John W. McCoubrey, *American Art 1700–1960. Sources and Documents*. Englewood Cliffs, N.J.: Prentice-Hall, 1965. 165.

## *Late Nineteenth-Century Architecture*

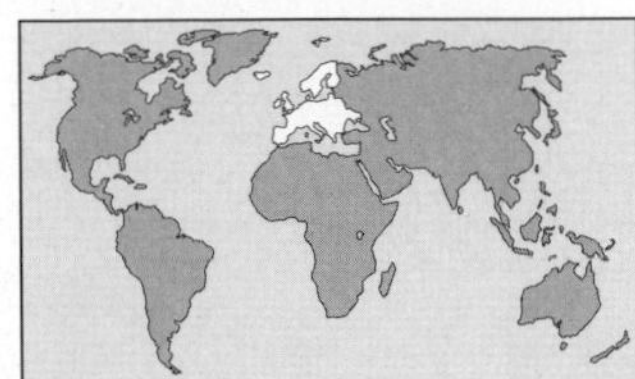

While many nineteenth-century European architects pursued neoclassical and neomedieval revivalism, others were experimenting with the possibilities of an exciting new structural medium: cast iron. The new medium, which provided strength without bulk, allowed architects to span broader widths and raise structures to greater heights than those achieved by traditional stone masonry. Although iron would change the history of architecture more dramatically than any advance in technology since the Roman invention of concrete, European architects were slow to realize its potential. In England, where John Nash had used cast iron in 1815 as the

**Figure 30.24** Joseph Paxton, interior of Crystal Palace, 1851. Cast and wrought iron and glass, length 1,851 ft. Institut für Geschichte und Theorie der Architektur an der ETH, Zürich.

**Figure 30.25** Gustav Eiffel, Eiffel Tower, Paris, 1889. Wrought iron on a reinforced concrete base, original height 984 ft. Photo: Roger-Viollet, Paris.

structural frame for the Brighton Pavilion (see chapter 29), engineers did not begin construction on the first cast-iron suspension bridge until 1836 and not until mid-century was iron used as skeletal support for mills, warehouses, and railroad stations.

The innovator in the use of iron for public buildings was, in fact, not an architect but a distinguished horticulturalist and greenhouse designer, Joseph Paxton (1801–1865). Paxton's Crystal Palace (Figure **30.24**), erected for the Great Exhibition of London in 1851, was the world's first prefabricated building and the forerunner of the "functional" steel and glass architecture of the twentieth century. Consisting entirely of cast- and wrought-iron girders and eighteen thousand panes of glass and erected in only nine months, the 1,851-foot-long structure—its length a symbolic reference to the year of the Exhibition—resembled a gigantic greenhouse. Light entered through its transparent walls and air filtered in through louvered windows. Thousands flocked to see the Crystal Palace; yet most European architects found the glass and iron structure bizarre. Although heroic in both size and conception, the Crystal Palace had almost no immediate impact on European architecture. Dismantled after the exhibition and moved to a new site, however, it was hailed as a masterpiece of prefabrication and portability decades before it burned to the ground in 1930.

Like the Crystal Palace, the Eiffel Tower (Figure **30.25**) originated as a novelty, but it soon became emblematic of early modernism. The viewing tower constructed by the engineer Gustave Eiffel (1832–1923) for the Paris World Exhibition of 1889 is, in essence, a tall (1,064-foot-high) cast-iron skeleton equipped with elevators that offer the visitor magnificent aerial views of Paris. Aesthetically, the tower linked the architectural traditions of the past with those of the future: Its sweeping curves, delicate tracery, and dramatic verticality recall the glories of the Gothic cathedral, while its majestic ironwork anticipated the austere abstractions of international-style architecture (see chapter 32). Condemned as a visual monstrosity when it was first erected, the Eiffel Tower emerged as a positive symbol of the soaring confidence of the industrial age. This landmark of heroic materialism remained for four

**1773** the first cast-iron bridge is built in England
**1851** the first international industrial exposition opens in London
**1856** Henry Bessemer (British) perfects the process for producing inexpensive steel
**1857** E. G. Otis (American) installs the first safety elevator
**1863** the first "subway" (the London Underground) begins operation

**Figure 30.26** Louis Henry Sullivan and Dankmar Adler, Guaranty Building, Buffalo, New York, 1894–1895. Steel frame. Collection, David R. Phillips, Chicago Architectural Photographing Company.

decades (until the advent of the American skyscraper) the tallest structure in the world.

In an age of advancing industrialism, ornamental structures such as the Eiffel Tower and the Crystal Palace gave way to functional ones. Inevitably, the skyscraper was to become the prime architectural expression of modern corporate power. Skyscrapers were made possible by the advancing technology of steel, a medium that was perfected in 1856. Lighter, stronger, and more resilient than cast iron, steel used as a frame could carry the entire weight of a structure, thus eliminating the need for solid weight-bearing masonry walls. Steel made possible a whole new concept of building design characterized by lighter materials, flat roofs, and large windows. In 1868, the six-story Equitable Life Insurance building in New York City was the first office structure to install an electric elevator. By the 1880s, architects and engineers in Chicago combined the new steel frame with the elevator to raise structures of more than ten stories in height. William Le Baron Jenney (1832–1907) built a definitive steel-frame skyscraper, the Home Insurance Building in Chicago, which, ironically, hides its metal skeleton beneath a traditional-looking brick and masonry facade. It fell to his successor, Louis Henry Sullivan (1856–1924), to create multistory buildings, such as the Guaranty Building in Buffalo (Figure **30.26**), whose exteriors proudly reflect the structural simplicity of their steel frames. Within decades, the American skyscraper became an icon of modern urban culture.

## Realism in Music

In Italian opera of the late nineteenth century, a movement called *verismo* (literally, "truth-ism," but more generally "realism" or "naturalism") paralleled the emphasis on reality in literature and art. Realist composers rejected the heroic characters of romantic grand opera and presented the problems and conflicts of people in familiar and everyday—if occasionally somewhat melodramatic—situations. The foremost "verist" in music was the Italian composer Giacomo Puccini (1858–1924). Puccini's *La Bohème*, the tragic love story of young artists (called "bohemians" for their unconventional lifestyles) in the Latin Quarter of Paris, was based on a nineteenth-century novel called *Scenes of Bohemian Life*. The colorful orchestration and powerfully melodic arias of *La Bohème* evoke the joys and sorrows of true-to-life characters. While this poignant musical drama was received coldly at its premiere in 1897, *La Bohème* has become one of the best loved of nineteenth-century grand operas.

Another of Puccini's operas, *Madama Butterfly*, offered European audiences a timely, if moralizing, view of the Western presence in Asia and one that personalized the clash of opposing cultures. The story, which takes place in Nagasaki in the years following the reopening of Japanese ports to the West, begins with the wedding of a young United States Navy lieutenant to a fifteen-year-old *geisha* (a Japanese girl trained as a social companion to men) known as "Butterfly." The American is soon forced to leave with his fleet, while for three years Butterfly, now the mother of his son, faithfully awaits his return. When, finally, he arrives (accompanied by his new American bride) only to claim the child, the griefstricken Butterfly takes the only honorable path available to her: She commits suicide. This tragic tale, which had appeared as a novel, a play, and a magazine story, was based on a true incident. Set to some of Puccini's most lyrical music for voice and orchestra, *Madama Butterfly* reflects the composer's fascination with Japanese culture, a fascination most evident in Puccini's poetic characterization of the delicate Butterfly. And while neither the story nor the music of the opera is authentically Japanese, its *verismo* lies in its frank (if melodramatic) account of the traumas consequent to the meeting of East and West.

## SUMMARY

During the second half of the nineteenth century, as the social consequences of Western industrialism became increasingly visible, realism came to rival romanticism both as a style and as an attitude of mind. Western industrialism and colonialism had a shaping influence on the non-Western world. While the ideologies of liberalism, conservatism, utilitarianism, and socialism offered varying solutions to contemporary problems of social injustice, Marx and Engels called for action in the form of violent proletarian revolution that would end private ownership of the means of economic production. The leading proponent of liberalism, John Stuart Mill, defended the exercise of individual liberty as protected by the state. Mill's opposition to the subjection of women gave strong support to nineteenth-century movements for women's rights.

In the arts, realism emerged as a style concerned with recording contemporary subject matter in true-to-life terms. Such novelists as Dickens in England, Dostoevsky and Tolstoy in Russia, Flaubert and Zola in France, and Twain and Chopin in America described contemporary social conditions sympathetically and with fidelity to detail. Flaubert and Chopin provided alternatives to romantic idealism in their realistic characterizations of female figures. Zola's novels introduced a naturalistic perception of human beings as determined by hereditary and sociological factors. Ibsen pioneered modern drama in his fearless portrayal of class and gender conflicts.

Photography and lithography were invented during the nineteenth century; both media encouraged artists to produce objective records of their surroundings. By the mid-nineteenth century the camera was used to document all aspects of contemporary life as well as to provide artists with detailed visual data for their compositions. In painting, Courbet led the realist movement with canvases depicting the activities of humble and commonplace men and women. Daumier employed the new technique of lithography to show his deep concern for political and social conditions in rapidly modernizing France. Manet shocked art critics by recasting traditional subjects in contemporary terms. In America, realist painters, including Thomas Eakins and Winslow Homer, recorded typically American pastimes in an unembellished, forthright manner. Paxton's Crystal Palace, the world's first prefabricated cast-iron structure, offered a prophetic glimpse into the decades that would produce steel-framed skyscrapers. Though realism did not adapt itself to music in any specific manner, the Italian "verist" Puccini wrote operas that captured the lives of nineteenth-century Europeans with a truth to nature comparable to that in realist novels and paintings. On the whole, the varieties of realism in nineteenth-century cultural expression reflect a profound concern for social and economic inequities and a critical reassessment of traditional Western values.

## GLOSSARY

**capitalist** one who provides investment capital in economic ventures

**entrepreneur** one who organizes, manages, and assumes the risks of a business

**lithography** a printmaking process created by drawing on a stone plate; see Figure 30.10

**proletariat** a collective term describing industrial workers who lack their own means of production and hence sell their labor to live

***verismo*** (Italian, "realism") a type of late nineteenth-century opera that presents a realistic picture of life, instead of a story based in myth, legend, or ancient history

## SUGGESTIONS FOR READING

Baumer, Franklin L., ed. *Intellectual Movements in Modern European History.* London: Macmillan, 1965.

Berlin, Isaiah. *Karl Marx: His Life and Environment.* New York: Oxford University Press, 1978.

Clark, T. J. *The Painting of Modern Life: Paris in the Art of Manet and His Followers.* New York: Knopf, 1984.

Cachin, Françoise. *Manet: The Influence of the Modern,* translated by Rachel Kaplan. New York: Abrams, 1995.

Duncan, Graeme C. *Marx and Mill: Two Views of Social Conflict and Social Harmony.* Cambridge: Cambridge University Press, 1973.

Friedrich, Otto. *Olympia: Paris in the Age of Manet.* New York: Harper, 1992.

Hamilton, G. H. *Manet and His Critics.* New Haven: Yale University Press, 1986.

Johns, Elizabeth. *American Genre Painting: The Politics of Everyday Life.* New Haven: Yale University Press, 1994.

Larkin, Maurice. *Man and Society in Nineteenth-Century Realism, Determinism and Literature.* Totowa, N.J.: Rowman and Littlefield, 1977.

Nochlin, Linda. *Realism.* New York: Penguin, 1971.

Rosen, Charles, and Henri Zerner. *Romanticism and Realism: The Mythology of Nineteenth-Century Art.* New York: Viking, 1984.

Shi, David E. *Realism in American Thought and Culture, 1850–1920.* New York: Oxford University Press, 1993.

Smart, Paul. *Mill and Marx: Individual Liberty and the Roads to Freedom.* New York: St. Martin's, 1991.

# 31
# The Move Toward Modernism

During the last quarter of the nineteenth century, France was the center of most of the important developments in the arts of Western Europe. Especially in Paris, poets, painters, and composers turned their backs on both romanticism and realism. They pursued styles that neither idealized the world nor described it with reforming zeal. Their art was more concerned with sensory experience than with moral purpose, with feeling than with teaching. Unlike their predecessors, these artists had little interest in exalting the noble, the sacred, or the factual; instead, they made art that obeyed purely aesthetic impulses, that—like music—communicated meaning through shape or sound, pattern or color. Their principle was coined by Walter Pater in 1868 in the slogan *l'art pour l'art* or "art for art's sake."

Late nineteenth-century science and technology helped to shape this new approach in the arts. In 1873, the British physicist James Clerk Maxwell (1831–1879) published his *Treatise on Electricity and Magnetism*, which explained that light waves consisting of electromagnetic particles produced radiant energy. In 1879, after numerous failures, the American inventor Thomas Edison (1847–1931) moved beyond scientific theory to create the first efficient incandescent light bulb. Incandescent electric light provided a sharper perception of reality that—along with the camera—helped to shatter the world of romantic illusion. By the year 1880, the telephone transported the human voice over thousands of miles. In the late 1880s Edison developed the technique of moving pictures. The invention of the internal combustion engine led to the production of modern motorcars in the 1890s, a decade that also witnessed the invention of the x-ray and the development of radiotelegraphy. Such developments accelerated the tempo of life and drew attention to the role of the senses in defining experience.

**1877** Thomas Edison (American) invents the phonograph
**1892** Rudolf Diesel (German) patents his internal combustion engine
**1893** Henry Ford (American) test-drives the "gasoline-buggy"

## *Late Nineteenth-Century Thought*

### Nietzsche's New Morality

The most provocative thinker of the late nineteenth century was the German philosopher and poet Friedrich Wilhelm Nietzsche (1844–1900). Nietzsche was a classical philologist, a professor of Greek at the University of Basle, and the author of such notable works as *The Birth of Tragedy* (1872), *Thus Spoke Zarathustra* (1883–1892), and *The Genealogy of Morals* (1887). In these, as in his shorter pieces, Nietzsche voiced the sentiments of the radical moralist. Deeply critical of his own time, he called for a revision of all values. He rejected organized religion, attacking Christianity and other institutionalized religions as contributors to the formation of a "slave morality." He was equally critical of democratic institutions, which he saw as rule by mass mediocrity; instead he lauded the "superman" or superior individual (German, *Übermensch*), whose singular vision and courage would, in his view, produce a "master" morality. Nietzsche did not launch his ideas in the form of a well-reasoned philosophic system, but rather as aphorisms, maxims, and expostulations whose brilliance and visceral force bear out his claim that he wrote "with his blood." Reflecting the cynicism of the late nineteenth century, he asked, "Is man merely a mistake of God's? Or God merely a mistake of man's?"

Nietzsche shared with Dostoevsky the view that European materialism had led inevitably to decadence and decline. In *The Antichrist*, published in 1888, shortly before Nietzsche became insane (possibly a result of syphilis), he wrote:

> Mankind does *not* represent a development toward something better or stronger or higher in the sense accepted today. "Progress" is merely a modern idea, that is, a false ideal. The European of today is vastly inferior in value to the European of the Renaissance: further development is altogether *not* according to any necessity in the direction of elevation, enhancement, or strength.*

The following readings demonstrate Nietzsche's incisive imagination and caustic wit. The first, taken from *The Gay Science* (1882) and entitled "The Madman," is a parable that harnesses Nietzsche's iconoclasm to his gift for prophecy. The others, excerpted from *Twilight of the Idols* (or *How One Philosophizes with a Hammer*, 1888), address the art for art's sake spirit of the late nineteenth century and the fragile relationship between art and morality.

## READING 5.24

## From Nietzsche's *The Gay Science* and *Twilight of the Idols*

*The Madman.* Have you not heard of that madman who lit a lantern in the bright morning hours, ran to the market place, and cried incessantly, "I seek God! I seek God!" As many of those who do not believe in God were standing around just then, he provoked much laughter. Why, did he get lost? said one. Did he lose his way like a child? said another. Or is he hiding? Is he afraid of us? Has he gone on a voyage? or emigrated? Thus they yelled and laughed. The madman jumped into their midst and pierced them with his glances.

"Whither is God" he cried. "I shall tell you. *We have killed him*—you and I. All of us are his murderers. But how have we done this? How were we able to drink up the sea? Who gave us the sponge to wipe away the entire horizon? What did we do when we unchained this earth from its sun? Whither is it moving now? Whither are we moving now? Away from all suns? Are we not plunging continually? Backward, sideward, forward, in all directions? Is there any up or down left? Are we not straying as through an infinite nothing? Do we not feel the breath of empty space? Has it not become colder? Is not night and more night coming on all the while? Must not lanterns be lit in the morning? Do we not hear anything yet of the noise of the gravediggers who are burying God? Do we not smell anything yet of God's decomposition? Gods too decompose. God is dead. God remains dead. And we have killed him. How shall we, the murderers of all murderers, comfort ourselves? What was holiest and most powerful of all that the world has yet owned has bled to death under our knives. Who will wipe this blood off us? What water is there for us to clean ourselves? What festivals of atonement, what sacred games shall we have to invent? Is not the greatness of this deed too great for us? Must not we ourselves become gods simply to seem worthy of it? There has never been a greater deed; and whoever will be born after us—for the sake of this deed he will be part of a higher history than all history hitherto."

Here the madman fell silent and looked again at his listeners; and they too were silent and stared at him in astonishment. At last he threw his lantern on the ground, and it broke and went out. "I come too early," he said then; "my time has not come yet. This tremendous event is still on its way, still wandering—it has not yet reached the ears of man. Lightning and thunder require time, the light of the stars requires time, deeds require time even after they are done, before they can be seen and heard. This deed is still more distant from them than the most distant stars—*and yet they have done it themselves.*"

It has been related further that on that same day the madman entered divers churches and there sang his *requiem aeternam deo*. Led out and called to account, he is said to have replied each time, "What are these churches now if they are not the tombs and sepulchers of God?"

◆

*L'art pour l'art.* The fight against purpose in art is always a fight against the moralizing tendency in art, against its subordination to morality. *L'art pour l'art* means, "The devil take morality!" But even this hostility still betrays the overpowering force of the prejudice. When the purpose of moral preaching and of improving man has been excluded from art, it still does not follow by any means that art is altogether purposeless, aimless, senseless—in short, *l'art pour l'art*, a worm chewing its own tail. "Rather no purpose at all than a moral purpose!"—that is the talk of mere passion. A psychologist, on the other hand, asks: what does all art do? does it not praise? glorify? choose? prefer? With all this it strengthens or weakens certain valuations. Is this merely a "moreover"? an accident? something in which the artist's instinct had no share? Or is it not the very presupposition of the artist's ability? Does his basic instinct aim at art, or rather at the sense of art, at life? at a desirability of life? Art is the great stimulus to life: how could one understand it as purposeless, as aimless, as *l'art pour l'art*?

One question remains: art also makes apparent much that is ugly, hard, and questionable in life; does it not thereby spoil life for us? And indeed there have been philosophers who attributed this sense to it: "liberation from the will" was what Schopenhauer taught as the over-all end of art; and with admiration he found the great utility of tragedy in its "evoking resignation." But this, as I have already suggested, is the pessimist's perspective and "evil eye." We must appeal to the artists themselves. What does the tragic artist communicate of

**The Antichrist*, in Walter Kaufmann, ed. *The Portable Nietzsche*. New York: Viking Press, 1965, 571.

himself? Is it not precisely the state *without* fear in the face of the fearful and questionable that he is showing? This state itself is a great desideratum;[1] whoever knows it, honors it with the greatest honors. He communicates it—*must* communicate it, provided he is an artist, a genius of communication. Courage and freedom of feeling before a powerful enemy, before a sublime calamity, before a problem that arouses dread—this triumphant state is what the tragic artist chooses, what he glorifies. Before tragedy, what is warlike in our soul celebrates its Saturnalia;[2] whoever is used to suffering, whoever seeks out suffering, the heroic man praises his own being through tragedy—to him alone the tragedian presents this drink of sweetest cruelty.

. . . . . . . . . . .

One might say that in a certain sense the nineteenth century *also* strove for all that which Goethe as a person had striven for: universality in understanding and in welcoming, letting everything come close to oneself, an audacious realism, a reverence for everything factual. How is it that the over-all result is no Goethe, but chaos, a nihilistic sigh, an utter bewilderment, an instinct of weariness which in practice continually drives toward a recourse to the eighteenth century? (For example, as a romanticism of feeling, as altruism and hypersentimentality, as feminism in taste, as socialism in politics.) Is not the nineteenth century, especially at its close, merely an intensified, *brutalized* eighteenth century, that is, a century of *decadence*? So that Goethe would have been—not merely for Germany, but for all of Europe—a mere interlude, a beautiful "in vain"? But one misunderstands great human beings if one views them from the miserable perspective of some public use. That one cannot put them to any use, that in itself may belong to greatness. . . .

◆

## Bergson and Intuition

While Nietzsche anticipated the darker side of modernism, the theories of Henri Bergson (1859–1941) presented a more positive point of view. Bergson, the most important French philosopher of his time, offered a picture of the world that paralleled key developments in the arts and sciences of the late nineteenth century and anticipated modern notions of time and space. Bergson viewed life as a vital impulse that evolved creatively, much like a work of art. According to Bergson, two primary powers, intellect and intuition, governed the lives of human beings. While intellect perceives experience in individual and discrete terms, or as a series of separate and solid entities, intuition grasps experience as it really is: a perpetual stream of sensations. Intellect isolates and categorizes experience according to logic and geometry; intuition, on the other hand, fuses past and present into one organic whole. For Bergson, instinct, or intuition, is humankind's noblest faculty, and *duration*, or "perpetual becoming," is the very stuff of reality—the essence of life. In 1889, Bergson published his treatise *Time and Freewill*, in which he explained that true experience is durational, a constant unfolding in time, and that reality, which can only be apprehended intuitively, is a series of qualitative changes that merge into one another without precise outlines.

[1] Something desired as essential.

[2] An orgy, or unrestrained celebration.

# *Poetry in the Late Nineteenth Century: The Symbolists*

Bergson's poetical view of nature had much in common with the aesthetics of many late nineteenth-century artists, including that of the *symbolists*. The symbolists, who included the French poets Paul Verlaine (1844–1896), Arthur Rimbaud (1854–1891), and Stéphane Mallarmé (1842–1898), and the Belgian playwright Maurice Maeterlinck (1862–1949), tried to capture in language the ineffable dimension of intuitive experience. They rejected both the romanticism and the realism/naturalism of nineteenth-century writers and tried to free language from its traditional descriptive and expressive functions. Symbolist poetry evoked the fleeting and incommunicable nature of experience. For the symbolists, reality was a swarm of sensations that could never be described but only translated via poetic symbols—verbal images that, through the power of suggestion, elicited moods and feelings beyond the literal meanings of words. In one of the prose poems from his *Illuminations*, for example, Rimbaud described flowers as "Bits of yellow gold seeded in agate, pillars of mahogany supporting a dome of emeralds, bouquets of white satin and fine rods of ruby surround the water rose."* The symbolists tried to represent nature without effusive commentary, to "take eloquence and wring its neck," as Verlaine put it. In order to imitate the indefiniteness of experience itself, they might string images together without logical connections. Hence, in symbolist poetry, images seem to flow into one another, and "meaning" often lies between the lines.

For Stéphane Mallarmé, the "new art" of poetry was a religion, and the poet-artist was its oracle. Unlike realist writers, who stressed social interaction and reform, Mallarmé withdrew from the world; he held that art was "accessible only to the few" who nurtured "the inner life." Mallarmé's poems are tapestries of sensuous, dreamlike motifs that resist definition and

* *The Norton Anthology of World Literature*, 4th ed. New York: Norton, 1980, 1188.

analysis. To name a thing, Mallarmé insisted, was to destroy it, while to suggest experience was to create it. Such were the principles that inspired his pastoral poem, "L'Après-midi d'un faune" ("The Afternoon of a Faun"). The poem is a reverie of an erotic encounter between two mythological woodland creatures, a faun (part man, part beast) and a nymph (a beautiful forest maiden). As the faun awakens, he tries to recapture the experiences of the previous afternoon. Whether his elusive memories belong to the world of dreams or to reality is uncertain; but, true to Bergson's theory of duration, reality becomes a stream of sensations in which past and present merge. As the following excerpt illustrates, Mallarmé's rhythms are free and hypnotic, and his images, which follow one another with few logical transitions, are intimately linked to the world of the senses.

### READING 5.25

### From Mallarmé's "Afternoon of a Faun"

I would immortalize these nymphs: so bright
Their sunlit coloring, so airy light,
It floats like drowsing down. Loved I a dream?
My doubts, born of oblivious darkness, seem
A subtle tracery of branches grown
The tree's true self—proving that I have known,
Thinking it love, the blushing of a rose.
But think. These nymphs, their loveliness . . . suppose
They bodied forth your senses' fabulous thirst?
Illusion! which the blue eyes of the first,
As cold and chaste as is the weeping spring,
Beget: the other, sighing, passioning,
Is she the wind, warm in your fleece at noon?
No; through this quiet, when a weary swoon
Crushes and chokes the latest faint essay
Of morning, cool against the encroaching day,
There is no murmuring water, save the gush
Of my clear fluted notes; and in the hush
Blows never a wind, save that which through my reed[1]
Puffs out before the rain of notes can speed
Upon the air, with that calm breath of art
That mounts the unwrinkled zenith visibly,
Where inspiration seeks its native sky.
You fringes of a calm Sicilian lake,
The sun's own mirror which I love to take,
Silent beneath your starry flowers, tell
*How here I cut the hollow rushes, well*
*Tamed by my skill, when on the glaucous gold*
*Of distant lawns about their fountain cold*
*A living whiteness stirs like a lazy wave;*
*And at the first slow notes my panpipes gave*
*These flocking swans, these naiads, rather, fly*
*Or dive.*

. . . . . . . . . . .

See how the ripe pomegranates bursting red
To quench the thirst of the mumbling bees have bled;
So too our blood, kindled by some chance fire,
Flows for the swarming legions of desire.
At evening, when the woodland green turns gold
And ashen grey, 'mid the quenched leaves, behold!
Red Etna[2] glows, by Venus visited,
Walking the lava with her snowy tread
Whene'er the flames in thunderous slumber die.
I hold the goddess!
Ah, sure penalty!
But the unthinking soul and body swoon
At last beneath the heavy hush of noon.
Forgetful let me lie where summer's drouth
Sifts fine the sand and then with gaping mouth
Dream planet-struck by the grape's round wine-red star.
Nymphs, I shall see the shade that now you are.

◆

[1]A pipe or flute.

[2]A volcanic mountain in Sicily.

## *Music in the Late Nineteenth Century: Debussy*

It is no surprise that symbolist poetry, itself a kind of music, found its counterpart in music. Like the poetry of Mallarmé, the music of Claude Debussy (1862–1918) engages the listener through nuance and atmosphere. Debussy's compositions consist of broken fragments of melody, the outlines of which are blurred and indistinct. "I would like to see the creation . . . of a kind of music without themes and motives," wrote Debussy, "formed on a single continuous theme, which is uninterrupted and which never returns on itself."

Debussy owed much to Richard Wagner and the romantic composers who had abandoned the formal clarity of classical composition (see chapter 29). He was also indebted to the exotic music of Bali in Indonesia, which he had heard performed at the Paris Exposition of 1889. Debussy experimented with the five-tone scale found in East Asian music and with nontraditional kinds of harmony. He deviated from the traditional Western practice of returning harmonies to the tonic, or "home tone," introducing instead shifting harmonies with no clearly defined tonal center. His rich harmonic palette, characterized by unusually constructed chords, reflects a fascination with tone color that may have been inspired by the writings of the German physiologist Hermann von Helmholtz (1821–1894)—especially Helmholtz's treatise *On the Sensations of Tone as a Physiological Basis for the Theory of Music* (1863). But Debussy found his greatest source of inspiration in contemporary poetry and painting. He was a close friend of many of the symbolist poets, whose texts he often set to music.

Figure 31.1 Vaslav Nijinsky, "Afternoon of a Faun," 1912. Photo: L. Roosen. Courtesy of the New York Public Library. Dance Collection, Astor, Lennox, and Tilden Foundations.

His first orchestral composition, *Prelude to "The Afternoon of a Faun"* (1894),♪ was (in his words) a "very free illustration of Mallarmé's beautiful poem," which had been published eighteen years earlier. Debussy originally intended to write a dramatic piece based on the poem, but he ultimately produced a ten-minute orchestral prelude which shares the dreamlike quality of the poem. (In 1912, Debussy's score became the basis for a twelve-minute ballet choreographed by the Russian dancer Nijinsky, shown in Figure **31.1**; see chapter 32.)

Debussy had little use for the ponderous orchestras of the French and German romantics. He scored the *Prelude* for a small orchestra whose unusual combination of wind and brass instruments might recreate Mallarmé's delicate mood of reverie. A sensuous melody for unaccompanied flute provides the composition's opening theme, which is then developed by flutes, oboes, and clarinets. Harp, triangle, muted horns, and lightly brushed cymbals contribute luminous tonal textures that—like the images of the poem itself—seem based in pure sensation. Transitions are subtle rather than focused, and melodies seem to drift without resolution. Imprecise tone clusters and shifting harmonies create fluid, nebulous effects that call to mind the shimmering effects of light on water and the ebb and flow of ocean waves. Indeed, water—a favorite motif of impressionist art—is the subject of many of Debussy's orchestral sketches, such as *Gardens in the Rain* (1903), *Image: Reflections in the Water* (1905), and *The Sea* (1905).

♪See Music Listening Selection at end of chapter.

# Painting in the Late Nineteenth Century

## Impressionism

What the symbolists sought in poetry, and Debussy pursued in music, the French *impressionists* achieved with paint. Luminosity, the interaction of light and form, subtlety of tone, and a preoccupation with sensation itself were the major features of impressionist art. Impressionist subject matter preserved the romantic fascination with nature and the realist preoccupation with late nineteenth-century French society. But impressionism departed from both the romantic effort to idealize nature and the realist will to record nature with unbiased objectivity. An art of pure sensation, impressionism was, in part, a response to nineteenth-century research in the physics of light, the chemistry of paint, and the laws of optics. Such publications as *Principles of Harmony and the Contrast of Colors* by the nineteenth-century French chemist Michel Chevreul (1786–1889), along with treatises on the physical properties of color and musical tone by Hermann von Helmholtz mentioned above, offered new insights into the psychology of perception. At the same time, late nineteenth-century chemists produced the first synthetic pigments, which replaced traditional earth pigments with brilliant new colors. Such developments in science and technology contributed to the birth of the new art of light and color.

**1879** Edison produces the incandescent light bulb
**1889** Edison invents equipment to take and show moving pictures
**1898** Wilhelm C. Röntgen (German) discovers x-rays

## Monet: Pioneer of Impressionism

In 1874 the French artist Claude Monet (1840–1926) exhibited a work of art that some critics consider the first modern painting. *Impression: Sunrise* (Figure **31.2**) is patently a seascape; but the painting says more about *how* one sees than about *what* one sees. It transcribes the fleeting effects of light and the changing atmosphere of water and air into a tissue of small dots and streaks of color—the elements of pure perception. To achieve luminosity, Monet coated the raw canvas with gesso, a chalklike medium. Then, working in the open air and using the new chemical paints (available in the form of portable metallic tubes), he applied brushstrokes of pure, occasionally unmixed, color. Monet ignored the brown underglazes artists traditionally used to build up form. And, arguing that there were no "lines" in nature, he refused to delineate forms with fixed contours; rather, he evoked form by means of color. Instead of blending his colors to create a finished effect, he placed them side by side, rapidly building up a radiant impasto. In order to intensify visual effect, he juxtaposed complementary colors, putting touches of orange (red and yellow) next to blue and adding bright tints of rose, pink, and vermilion. Monet rejected the use of browns and blacks to create shadows; instead, he applied colors complementary to the hue of the object casting the shadow, thus more closely approximating the prismatic effects of light on the human eye. Monet's canvases captured the external envelope: the instantaneous visual sensations of light itself.

Monet was by no means the first painter to deviate from academic techniques. In defining form, Constable had applied color in rough dots and dabs, Delacroix had occasionally juxtaposed complementary colors to increase brilliance, and Manet had often omitted halftones. But Monet went further by interpreting form as color itself, which, rapidly applied, conveyed a sense of immediacy. Consequently, *Impression: Sunrise* struck the critics as a radically new approach in art. One critic

**Figure 31.2** Claude Monet, *Impression: Sunrise*, 1873. Oil on canvas, 19⅝ × 25½ in. Musée Marmottan, Paris. Scala/Art Resource, New York.

**Figure 31.3** Claude Monet, *Rouen Cathedral, West Facade, Sunlight*, 1894. Oil on canvas, 39½ × 26 in. © 1998 Board of Trustees, National Gallery of Art, Washington, D.C. Chester Dale Collection, 1962.

dismissed the painting as "only an impression," no better than "wallpaper in its embryonic state," thus unwittingly giving the name "impressionism" to the movement that would dominate French art of the 1870s and 1880s.

Monet's early subjects include street scenes, picnics, café life, and boating parties at the fashionable tourist resorts that dotted the banks of the Seine near Paris. However, as Monet found light and color more compelling than Parisian society, his paintings became more impersonal and formless. Wishing to fix sensation, or as he put it, to "seize the intangible," he painted the changing effects of light on such mundane objects as poplar trees and haystacks. Often working on a number of canvases at once, he might generate a series of paintings that showed his subject in morning light, under the noon sun, and at sunset. Between 1892 and 1894, after a trip to England during which he became familiar with the colorist seascapes of Turner (see Figures 27.7, 27.8), Monet produced no less than thirty different versions of the west facade of Rouen Cathedral (Figure **31.3**). As with the other subjects he painted—including the water gardens that he himself created at his summer home in Giverny—Monet seized the thirteenth-century cathedral with his eye rather than with his intellect. This great monument of medieval Christendom, whose surface more resembles a wedding cake than a Gothic church, is rendered not as a sacred symbol but as the site of physical sensation.

Monet may be considered an ultrarealist in his effort to reproduce with absolute fidelity the ever-changing effects of light. His freedom from preconceived ideas of nature prompted his contemporary Paul Cézanne to exclaim that he was "only an eye," but, he added admiringly, "what an eye!" Ironically, Monet's devotion to the physical truth of nature paved the way for modern abstraction—the concern with the intrinsic qualities of the subject, rather than with its literal appearance. Indeed, the panoramic water-garden paintings of Monet's last decades are visionary meditations on light and space.

**Figure 31.4** Pierre-Auguste Renoir, *Le Moulin de la Galette*, 1876. Oil on canvas, 4 ft. 3½ in. × 5 ft. 9 in. Musée d'Orsay, Paris.

**Figure 31.5** Camille Pissarro, *Le Boulevard Montmartre*, 1897. Oil on canvas. Private Collection. Bridgeman Art Library, London.

## Renoir, Pissarro, and Degas

Impressionism was never a single, uniform style; rather, the designation embraced the individual approaches of many different artists throughout Europe and America. Nevertheless, the group of artists who met regularly in the 1870s and 1880s at the Café Guerbois in Paris had much in common. To a greater or lesser extent, their paintings reflected Monet's interest in the urban scene and his stylistic choice of rendering nature in short strokes of brilliant color. Above all, impressionism brought coloristic spontaneity to a celebration of the leisure activities and diversions of modern life: dining, dancing, theater-going, boating, and socializing. In this sense, the most typical impressionist painter might be Pierre-Auguste Renoir (1841–1919). Le Moulin de la Galette, an outdoor café and dance hall located in Montmartre (the bohemian section of nineteenth-century Paris), provided the setting for one of Renoir's most ravishing tributes to youth and informal pleasure (Figure **31.4**). In the painting, elegantly dressed young men and women—artists, students, and lower-middle-class members of Parisian society—dance, drink, and flirt with one another in the flickering golden light of the late afternoon sun.

Renoir's colleague, Camille Pissarro (1830–1903), was born in the West Indies but settled in Paris in 1855. The oldest and one of the most prolific of the impressionists, he exhibited in all eight of the impressionist group shows. Like Monet and Renoir, Pissarro loved outdoor subjects: peasants working in the fields, the magical effects of freshly fallen snow, and sunlit rural landscapes. Late in his career, however, as his eyesight began to fail, he gave up painting out-of-doors. Renting hotel rooms that looked out upon the streets of Paris, Pissarro produced engaging cityscapes (Figure **31.5**)—sixteen of Paris boulevards in 1897 alone. His sensitive, explicit brushstrokes capture the rhythms of urban life; throngs of horse-drawn carriages and pedestrians are bathed in the misty atmosphere that envelops Paris after the rain. Asked by a young artist for advice on "how to paint," Pissarro suggested that one record visual perceptions with immediacy, avoid defining the outlines of things, observe reflections of color and light, and honor only one teacher: nature.

Edgar Degas (1834–1917) regularly exhibited with the impressionists; but his style remained unique, for Degas never sacrificed line and form to the beguiling qualities of color and light. Whether depicting the urban world of cafés, racecourses, theaters, and shops, or the demimonde of laundresses and prostitutes, Degas concentrated his attention on the fleeting and intimate moment (Figure **31.6**). He rejected the traditional "posed" model as a subject, seeking instead to capture momentary and even awkward gestures such as stretching and yawning. Degas' untiring attention to racehorses and ballet dancers mirrored his lifelong fascination with matters of balance and motion (Figure **31.7**). In his efforts to recreate the appearance of physical movement in space, he learned much from the British artist Eadweard Muybridge (1830–1904), whose stop-action photographs of the 1870s and 1880s were revolutionary in their time (Figure **31.8**).

Degas was a consummate draftsman and a master designer. He used innovative compositional techniques which imparted a sense of spontaneity and improvisation. For instance, in *Before the Ballet*, he presents the subject as if seen from below and at an angle that boldly leaves "empty" the lower left half of the composition. He also experimented with asymmetrical compositions in which figures and objects (or fragments of either) might disappear off the edge of the canvas, as if the image were caught at random. Such innovations testify to the influence of photography, with its accidental "slice of life" potential, as well as that of Japanese woodcuts, which began to enter Europe in the 1860s.

**Figure 31.6** Edgar Degas, *The False Start*, ca. 1870. Oil on canvas, 12⅝ × 15¾ in. Yale University Art Gallery. John Hay Whitney, B.A., 1926 Collection.

**Figure 31.7** Edgar Degas, *Before the Ballet*, 1890–1892. Oil on canvas, 15¾ × 35 in.
© 1998 Board of Trustees, National Gallery of Art, Washington, D.C. Widener Collection.

**Figure 31.8** Eadweard Muybridge, *Photo Sequence of Racehorse*, 1884–1885. Photograph. Library of Congress, Washington, D.C.

**Figure 31.9** (above and opposite) Kunisada, triptych showing the different processes of printmaking, early nineteenth century. Japanese woodblock color print. Right: a woman with an original drawing pasted onto a block conversing with another who is sharpening blades on a whetstone. Center: a woman (in the foreground) sizing paper sheets which are then hung up to dry; another is removing areas with no design from the block with a chisel. Left: the printer has just finished taking an impression by rubbing the *baren* (a round pad made of a coil of cord covered by a bamboo sheath) over the paper on the colored block; numerous brushes and bowls of color are visible. Kunisada has made the design more interesting by using women, though the craftsmen were invariably men (information from Julia Hutt, *Understanding Far Eastern Art.* New York: Dutton, 1987, 53). Courtesy of the Trustees of the Victoria and Albert Museum, London.

## Japanese Woodblock Prints and Western Art

The Japanese woodblock prints that were entering Europe (along with other Asian goods) in the late nineteenth century were produced in great numbers in the period between roughly 1660 and 1860. Though the prints were a new commodity for Europeans, they represented the end of a long tradition in Japanese art—one that began declining after Japan was forced to open its doors to the West in the 1860s. Japan's decorative tradition, which looked back to the Heian period (784–1185), came to flower in the magnificent folding screens commissioned by wealthy patrons of the sixteenth and seventeenth centuries. Usually executed on a ground of gold leaf, such screens featured flat, unmodulated colors, undulating lines, and a daring use of "empty" space (see chapter 23). Japanese woodblock prints, the execution of which is depicted in some detail in a set of three prints by Kunisada (1786–1864; Figure **31.9**), shared many of the stylistic attributes seen in such earlier aristocratic artforms. They also often incorporated startling perspective vantagepoints, such as the bird's-eye view seen in Kunisada's compositions. Woodblock prints, however, were often more rapidly produced (most frequently by men, despite Kunisada's rendering). Their subject matter usually came from the everyday life of bustling, urban Edo (now Tokyo)—especially from the *ukiyo,* "the floating (or fleeting) world" of courtesans, actors, and dancers (Figure **31.11**).

During the mid-nineteenth century, Japanese woodblock artists added landscapes to their print repertory. The landscape prints, often produced as a series of views of local Japanese sites, resemble the topographical studies of Turner and Cole (see chapter 27). But they operated out of entirely different stylistic imperatives:

Unlike the European romantics, the Japanese had little interest in the picturesque; rather, they gave attention to bold contrasts and dramatic arrangements of abstract shapes and colors. They also explored unusual ways of layering planes that reduced the sense of continuity between near and far objects. All of these features are evident in one of the most popular mid-nineteenth-century Japanese landscape prints: *Mount Fuji Seen Below a Wave at Kanagawa* (Figure **31.10**), from the series "Thirty-six Views of Mount Fuji" by Katsushika Hokusai (1760–1849).

When Japanese prints arrived in the West, they exercised an immediate impact on fine and commercial art, including the art of the lithographic poster (Figure **31.12**). Monet and Degas bought them (along with Chinese porcelains) in great numbers, and van Gogh, a great admirer of Hokusai, insisted that his work was "founded on Japanese art."

Théodore Duret, a French art critic of the time and an enthusiast of impressionist painting, was one of the first writers to observe the impact of Japanese prints on nineteenth-century artists. In a pamphlet called "The Impressionist Painters" (1878), Duret explained:

**Figure 31.10** (below) Katsushika Hokusai, *Mount Fuji Seen Below a Wave at Kanagawa*, from "Thirty-six Views of Mount Fuji," Tokugawa Period. Full-color woodblock print, width 14¾ in. Courtesy, Museum of Fine Arts, Boston. Spaulding Collection.

> We had to wait until the arrival of Japanese albums before anyone dared to sit down on the bank of a river to juxtapose on canvas a boldly red roof, a white wall, a green poplar, a yellow road, and blue water. Before Japan it was impossible; the painter always lied. Nature with its frank colors was in plain sight, yet no one ever saw anything on canvas but attenuated colors, drowning in a general halftone.
>
> As soon as people looked at Japanese pictures, where the most glaring, piercing colors were placed side by side, they finally understood that there were new methods for reproducing certain effects of nature.*

*Japonisme,* the influence of Japan on European art, proved to be multifaceted: The prints sparked the impressionist interest in casual urban subjects (especially those involving women) and inspired fresh approaches to composition and color. At the same time, the elegant naturalism and refined workmanship of Asian *cloisonné* enamels, ceramics, lacquerwares, ivories, silks, and other collectibles were widely imitated in the arts and crafts movements that flourished at the end of the century.

*Quoted in Linda Nochlin, *Impressionism and Post-Impressionism 1874–1904.* Englewood Cliffs, N.J.: Prentice-Hall (1966), 8–9.

**Figure 31.11** (above) Torii Kiyonobu, *Actor as a Monkey Showman.* Woodblock print, 13¼ × 6¼ in. The Metropolitan Museum of Art, New York. Rogers Fund, 1936 (JP 2623). © 1994 The Metropolitan Museum of Art.

**Figure 31.12** Henri de Toulouse-Lautrec, *Jane Avril,* 1899. Lithograph, printed in color, 22 × 14 in. The Museum of Modern Art, New York. Gift of Abby Aldrich Rockefeller. Photograph © 1997 The Museum of Modern Art, New York.

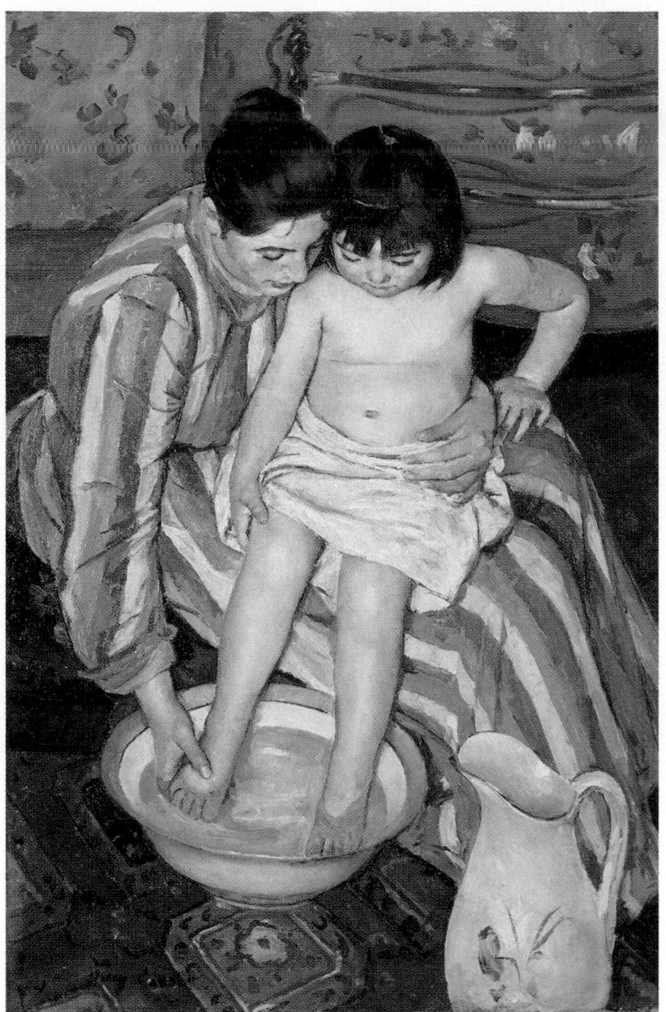

## Cassatt and Toulouse-Lautrec

One of the most notable artists to come under the influence of Japanese prints was the American painter Mary Cassatt (1844–1926). Cassatt spent most of her life in Paris, where she became a friend and colleague of Degas, Renoir, and other impressionists, with whom she exhibited regularly. Like Degas, she painted mainly indoors, cultivating a style that combined forceful calligraphy, large areas of unmodulated color, and unusual perspectives—the major features of the Japanese woodcuts—with a taste for female subjects. Cassatt brought a unique sensitivity to domestic themes that featured mothers and children enjoying everyday tasks and diversions (Figure **31.13**). These gentle and optimistic images appealed to American collectors and did much to increase the popularity of impressionist art in the United States.

A far less gentle spirit pervades the paintings of Henri de Toulouse-Lautrec (1864–1901). Toulouse-Lautrec, the descendant of an aristocratic French family, practiced many of the stylistic principles of impressionism, but his choice of subject matter was often so intimate that members of his own family condemned his work as unacceptable to "well-bred people." The art of Toulouse-Lautrec shows a more seamy side of Parisian life—the life of cabaret dancers and prostitutes who, like Zola's Nana, lived on the margins of middle-class society (Figure **31.14**; see also Frontispiece, p. ii). Toulouse-Lautrec self-consciously mocked traditional ideas of

**Figure 31.13** (above) Mary Cassatt, *The Bath*, 1891–1892. Oil on canvas, 39½ × 26 in. Photograph © 1998, The Art Institute of Chicago. All Rights Reserved. Robert A. Waller Fund (1910.2).

**Figure 31.14** Henri de Toulouse-Lautrec, *At The Moulin-Rouge*, 1893–1895. Oil on canvas, 4 ft. ⅜ in. × 4 ft. 7¼ in. Photograph © 1993, The Art Institute of Chicago. All Rights Reserved. Helen Birch Bartlett Memorial Collection (1928.610).

beauty and propriety. He stylized figures—almost to the point of caricature—in bold and forceful silhouettes. Fleshtones might be distorted by artificial light or altered by the stark white makeup (borrowed from Japanese theater) that was current in European fashion.

Toulouse-Lautrec pioneered the art of poster design. In his color lithographs of the voluptuous pleasures of Parisian nightlife, he used bright, flat colors, sinuous lines, and startling juxtapositions of positive and negative space (see Figure 31.12)—stylistic features that reflect the direct influence of eighteenth-century Japanese kabuki prints (see Figure 31.11).

## *Art Nouveau*

The posters of Toulouse-Lautrec bear the seductive stamp of *art nouveau* (French for "new art"), an ornamental style that became enormously popular in the late nineteenth century. *Art nouveau* artists shared with members of the English Arts and Crafts movement a high regard for the fine artisanship of the preindustrial Middle Ages, an era that achieved an ideal synthesis of the functional and the decorative in daily life. The proponents of the new style also prized the arts of Asia and Islam, which tended to favor bold, flat, organic patterns and semi-abstract linear designs. Acknowledging the impact of the Japanese woodcut style, one French critic insisted that Japanese blood had mixed with the blood of *art nouveau* artists.

**Figure 31.16** Eugène Grasset, Comb. ca. 1900. 6¼ × 2¾ in. Musée Galliera, Paris. Photo: Bulloz, Paris.

**Figure 31.15** Victor Horta, Tassel House, Brussels, 1892–1893. © Bastin & Evrard Photodesigners.

*Art nouveau* originated in Belgium among architects working in the medium of cast iron, but it quickly took on an international reach that affected painting, as well as the design of furniture, textiles, glass, ceramics, and jewelry. The Belgian founder of *art nouveau*, Victor Horta (1861–1947), brought to his work the Arts and Crafts veneration for fine craftsmanship and the symbolist glorification of the sensuous and fleeting forms in nature. A distinguished architect and a great admirer of Eiffel's 1,064-foot-high tower (see Figure 30.25), Horta translated the serpentine lines and organic rhythms of flowers and plants into magnificent glass and cast-iron designs for public buildings and private residences (Figure 31.15).

"Art in nature, nature in art" was the motto of *art nouveau*. The sinuous curves of blossoms, leaves, and tendrils, conceived in iron and immortalized in such notable monuments as the Paris Métro (the subway), also showed up in wallpaper, poster design, book illustration, tableware, and jewelry. In *art nouveau*, as in late nineteenth-century literature and in impressionist painting, women were a favorite subject: The female, often shown with long, luxuriant hair, might be

**Figure 31.17** Tiffany Glass and Decorating Co., peacock vase, 1892–1902. Iridescent "favrile" glass, blues and greens with feather and eye decorations, height 14⅛ × 11½ in. The Metropolitan Museum of Art, New York. Gift of H. O. Havemeyer, 1896 (96.17.10). © 1987 The Metropolitan Museum of Art.

pictured as seductress or enchantress. She might appear as a fairy or water nymph (Figure **31.16**), a poetic, sylphlike creature. In *art nouveau* pins, bracelets, and combs, she is the living counterpart of vines and flowers fashioned in delicately crafted metal armatures and semiprecious stones. Such images suggest that *art nouveau,* although modern in its effort to communicate meaning by way of shapes, patterns, and decoration, was actually the final expression of a century-long romantic infatuation with nature.

In America, *art nouveau* briefly attracted the attention of such architects as Louis Sullivan (see chapter 30), who embellished parts of his otherwise austere office buildings and department stores with floral cast-iron ornamentation. It also inspired the magnificent glass designs of Louis Comfort Tiffany (Figure **31.17**). The son of Charles L. Tiffany, founder of the famed New York jewelry house, Louis was a great admirer of Chinese *cloisonnés* and ancient glass techniques. His innovative studio methods included assembly-line production, the use of templates, and the employment of female artisans who received the same wages as males—a policy that caused great controversy in Tiffany's time. Tiffany's inventive glass designs, which featured floral arabesques and graceful geometric patterns, made him one of the masters of the international *art nouveau* style.

## *Sculpture in the Late Nineteenth Century*

### Degas and Rodin

While *art nouveau* artists brought organic naturalism to decorative design, the two greatest European sculptors of the late nineteenth century, Edgar Degas and Auguste Rodin (1840–1917), captured a similar vitality in three-dimensional, figural form. Like the impressionists, Degas and Rodin were interested in movement and the sensory effects of light. To catch these fleeting qualities,

**Figure 31.18** Edgar Degas, *Little Fourteen-Year-Old Dancer,* 1880–1881. Probably cast in bronze, tulle skirt and satin hair ribbon, height 3 ft. 3 in. The Metropolitan Museum of Art, New York. H. O. Havemeyer Collection. Bequest of Mrs. H. O. Havemeyer, 1929. (29.100.370 View #2). © 1981 The Metropolitan Museum of Art.

they modeled their figures rapidly in wet clay or modeling wax. The bronze casts made from these originals preserve the spontaneity of the additive process. Indeed, Degas' sculptures bear the imprints of his fingers and fingernails.

Degas executed all of his seventy-four sculptures as exercises preliminary to his paintings. Throughout his life, but especially as his vision began to decline, the artist increasingly turned to making wax and clay "sketches" of racehorses, bathers, and ballerinas—his favorite subjects. Only one of these sculptures, the *Little Fourteen-Year-Old Dancer*, was exhibited as a finished artwork during Degas' lifetime. The reddish-brown wax original, made eerily lifelike by the artist's addition of a tutu, stockings, bodice, ballet shoes, ribbons, and real hair (embedded strand by strand into the figure's head), was the subject of some controversy in the Parisian art world of 1881 (a world that would not see such mixed-media innovations for another half-century). The bronze version of Degas' *Dancer* (Figure **31.18**), whose dark surfaces contrast sensuously with the fabric additions, retains the supple grace of the artist's finest drawings and paintings.

Like Degas, Rodin was keenly interested in movement and gesture. In hundreds of drawings, he recorded

**Figure 31.19** Auguste Rodin, *Dancing Figure*, 1905. Graphite with orange wash, $12\frac{7}{8} \times 9\frac{7}{8}$ in. © 1998 Board of Trustees, National Gallery of Art, Washington, D.C. Gift of Mrs. John W. Simpson.

**Figure 31.20** Auguste Rodin, *The Age of Bronze*, 1876. Bronze, $25\frac{1}{2} \times 9\frac{5}{16} \times 7\frac{1}{2}$ in. © Detroit Institute of Arts. Gift of Robert H. Tannahill (69.304).

**Figure 31.21** Isadora Duncan in *La Marseillaise.* Collection of the Library of Congress, Washington, D.C.

the dancelike rhythms of studio models whom he bid to move about freely rather than assume traditional, fixed poses (Figure **31.19**). But it was in the three-dimensional media that Rodin made his greatest contribution. One of his earliest sculptures, *The Age of Bronze* (Figure **31.20**), was so lifelike that critics accused him of forging the figure from plaster casts of a live model. In actuality, Rodin had captured a sense of organic movement by recreating the fleeting effects of light on form. Here, as in his later works, he heightened the contrasts between polished and roughly textured surfaces, deliberately leaving parts of the piece unfinished. "Sculpture," declared Rodin, "is quite simply the art of depression and protuberance."

But Rodin moved beyond naturalistic representation to wring from volume (as the symbolists wrung from language) specific states of feeling. Taking the modernist turn, he used expressive distortion to convey a mood or mental disposition. He renounced formal idealization and gave his figures a nervous energy and an emotional intensity that were lacking in both classical and renaissance sculpture. "The sculpture of antiquity," he explained, "sought the logic of the human body; I seek its psychology." In this quest, Rodin was joined by his close friend, the American dancer Isadora Duncan (1878–1927). Duncan, who rebelled against the rules of classical ballet by dancing with bare feet, introduced a new style of dance characterized by free form, personalized gestures, and movements that were often fierce, earthy, and passionate (Figure **31.21**). "I have discovered the art that has been lost for two thousand years," claimed Duncan.

**Figure 31.22** Auguste Rodin, *The Gates of Hell*, 1880–1917. Bronze, 20 ft. 8 in. × 13 ft. 1 in. Philadelphia Museum of Art. Gift of Jules E. Mastbaum.

**Figure 31.23** Auguste Rodin, *The Kiss*, 1886–1898. Marble, over life-size. Musée Rodin, Paris.

As in Duncan's choreography, so in Rodin's greatest pieces, a particular psychological condition might inspire sculptural form. Such is the case with Rodin's most famous work of art, *The Gates of Hell* (Figure **31.22**), a set of doors designed for the projected Paris Museum of Decorative Arts. Loosely modeled after Ghiberti's *Gates of Paradise* (see chapter 17), the portal consists of a swarm of powerful images that represent the tortured souls of Dante's *Inferno* (see chapter 12). These images, which melt into each other without logical connection, operate by intuition and suggestion, like the imagery in a Mallarmé poem or a Monet landscape. For eight years Rodin added and deleted figures, modeling the Gates section by section. Although he never completed the commission, he remained compelled by its contents, recasting many of the figures individually in bronze and in marble. The most famous of these individual sculptures are *The Kiss* (Figure **31.23**) and *The Thinker*. The latter—one of the best known of Rodin's works—originally represented Dante contemplating his creation of the underworld from atop its portals.

## *Africa, Oceania, and Primitivism*

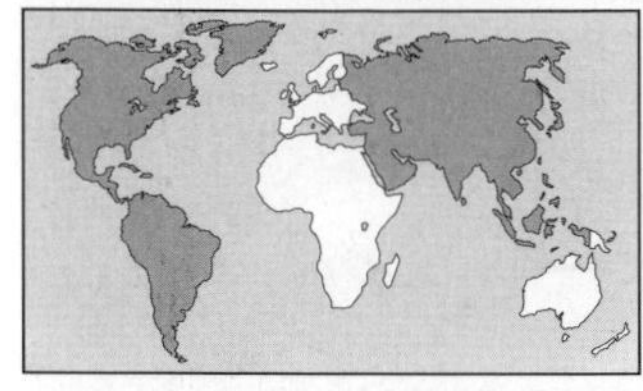

While Degas and Rodin gave new expression to Western sculptural tradition, it remained for their followers to develop a radically new vocabulary of form—one inspired by the tribal arts of non-Western cultures. *Primitivism,* a term used here to describe the late nineteenth-century movement that embraced the artforms of a wide variety of tribal peoples,* was a positive force in advancing the move toward modernism: The opening of Western eyes to the beauty and power of non-Western artforms forged an aesthetic bond among artists of different cultures, races, and religious beliefs. Although late nineteenth-century critics often lumped together or confused the arts of Africa and Oceania, they intuitively grasped the potential of these two regions for altering the course of world art history.

The visual arts of nineteenth-century Africa and Oceania (the islands of the South and Central Pacific) reflect long-established cultural styles and traditions, many extending back over a thousand years. For the most part they were unknown and uncelebrated outside of their own specific geographic locales. While no dramatically new artforms emerged in nineteenth-century Africa or Oceania, in both regions traditional kinds of wood and stone carving (along with other forms of artistic expression) flourished until, and in some cases even following, the intrusion of Western colonialists and collectors. Such sculpture, marked by stylistic and regional diversity, but startlingly different in both form and function from Western academic art, came to have an enormous impact on the West. Ironically, although Europeans described the non-naturalistic and generally abstract artforms of Africa and Oceania as "primitive" (implying simplicity and lack of sophistication by Western academic standards), this art introduced a fresh and direct vision of the world that powerfully influenced the modernist turn.

Nineteenth-century Africa and Oceania were essentially preindustrial and preliterate. Their social organization was tribal, their economies agricultural, their gods and spirits closely associated with nature and natural forces (see chapter 19). In most of these societies, members of the clan or tribe revered their deceased ancestors, the gods, sacred animals, and natural forces; they preserved the spirits of each in elaborately carved and ornamented reliquaries, masks, and cult figures (Figure 31.24). These objects, which local artists created as vessels for powerful spirits, were essential to traditional religion—especially rites of passage and rituals ensuring the success of the harvest. The value of such magico-religious figures lay not in their narrative or representational authority, nor necessarily in their aesthetic appeal, but, instead, in their ability to channel or transmit spiritual energy. Expressive simplification, exaggeration, and distortion (often generating a fierce intensity) served a sacred, communal function, rather than a mundane, personal vision.

African and Oceanic cultures came into the Western purview with the onset of European expansion and colonialism. In the eighteenth century, the French philosopher Jean-Jacques Rousseau (see chapter 24) had glorified "exotic" cultures for their freedom from the taint of civilization. Nineteenth-century romantics and world-weary industrialized Europeans followed suit by exalting "the primitive." The *Exposition Universelle* (World's Fair), held in Paris in 1889, contributed to the interest in foreign cultures by bringing to public view, along with the arts of Asia, the native arts of Africa and Oceania. Reconstructions of villages from the Congo and Senegal, Japan and China, Polynesia and other South Sea islands introduced the non-Western world to astonished Europeans. Remote societies and their artistic achievements quickly became objects of research for the new disciplines of anthropology (the science of humankind and its culture) and ethnography (the branch of anthropology that studies preliterate peoples or groups). In 1890, the Scottish anthropologist Sir James Frazer (1854–1941) published *The Golden Bough,* a pioneer study of magic and religion as reflected in ancient and traditional folk customs. Tragically, however, it was often the case that even as these cultures were coming to be known by ethnographers and their art collected and installed in Western museums, their brilliance, originality, and output began to wane. The French painter Paul Gauguin (1848–1903), who recorded his impressions of Tahiti in his romanticized journal *Noa Noa,* observed:

> The European invasion and monotheism have destroyed the vestiges of a civilization which had its own grandeur. . . . [The Tahitians] had been richly endowed with an instinctive feeling for the harmony necessary between human creations and the animal and plant life that formed the setting and decoration of their existence, but this has now been lost. In contact with us, with *our school,* they have truly become "savages" . . .*

*See William S. Rubin, ed., *"Primitivism" in Twentieth Century Art: Affinity of the Tribal and the Modern.* New York: Museum of Modern Art, 1984.

*From Paul Gauguin, *Noa Noa,* translated by O. F. Theis. New York: Noonday Press, 1964, 106.

The appeal of the primitive among late nineteenth-century figures such as Gauguin reflected a more than casual interest in the world beyond the West. It constituted a rebellion against Western sexual and societal taboos—a rebellion that would become full-blown in the primitivism of early modern art (see chapter 32).

# *Postimpressionism*

The group of Western artists who followed the impressionists—loosely designated as "postimpressionists"—are linked by their modernist direction: Pursuing an art for art's sake aestheticism, they prized pictorial invention over and above pictorial illusion. The postimpressionists were largely uninterested in satisfying the demands of public and private patrons; they made only sporadic efforts to sell what they produced. Although strongly individualistic, they were all profoundly concerned with the formal language of art and its capacity to capture sensory experience. Like impressionism, postimpressionism can be seen as an intensification of romantic artists' efforts to share their subjective responses to the real world. But unlike the romantics (and the impressionists), the postimpressionists made a conscious effort to bring order to the world of pure sensation. These pioneers of modern art put into practice the point of view of the French artist and theorist Maurice Denis (1870–1943): Denis believed that a painting was not first and foremost a pictorial reproduction of reality but was essentially "a flat surface covered with shapes, lines, and colors assembled in a particular order." This credo, as realized in postimpressionist painting, would drive most of the major modern art movements of the early twentieth century (see chapter 32).

## Van Gogh and Gauguin

The Dutch artist Vincent van Gogh (1853–1890) was a passionate idealist whose life was marred by loneliness, poverty, psychological depression, and a hereditary mental illness which ultimately drove him to suicide. During his career as an artist, he produced over seven hundred paintings and thousands of drawings, of which he sold less than a half-dozen in his lifetime. Influenced by Japanese prints, van Gogh painted landscapes, still lifes, and portraits in a style that featured flat, bright colors, a throbbing, sinuous line, and short, choppy brushstrokes. His heavily pigmented surfaces were often manipulated by a palette knife or built up by

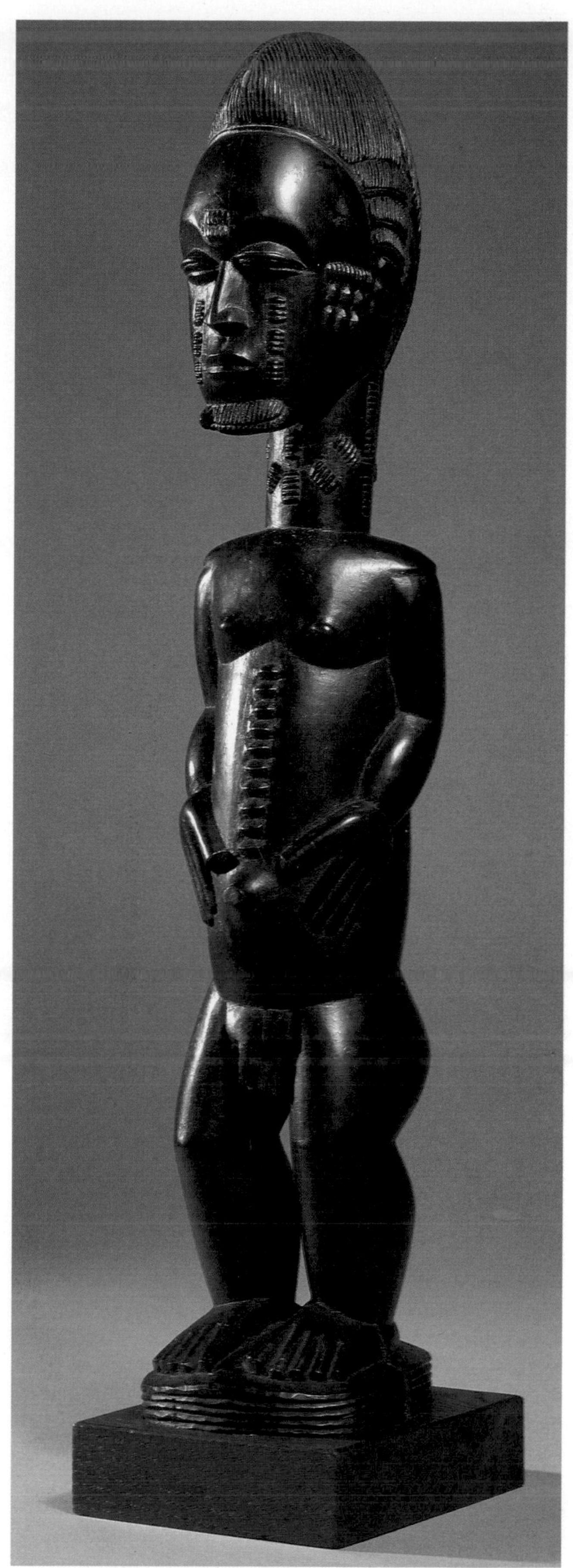

**Figure 31.24** Ancestor figure from Baule, Ivory Coast, Africa. Wood, height 20½ in. British Museum, London. The incisions on the face and body represent ritual scarification—marks of honor and distinction.

**Figure 31.25** Vincent van Gogh, *The Starry Night*, 1889. Oil on canvas, 29 × 36¼ in. The Museum of Modern Art, New York. Acquired through the Lillie P. Bliss Bequest. Photograph © 1997 The Museum of Modern Art, New York.

applying paint directly from the tube. Deeply moved by music (especially the music of Wagner), van Gogh shared with the romantics an attitude toward nature that was both inspired and ecstatic. His emotional response to an object, rather than its mere physical appearance, often determined his choice of colors, which he likened to orchestrated sound. As he explained to his brother Theo, "I use color more arbitrarily so as to express myself more forcefully." Van Gogh's painting *The Starry Night* (Figure **31.25**), a landscape view of the small French town of Saint-Rémy, is electrified by thickly painted strokes of white, yellow, orange, and blue. Cypresses writhe like tongues of flame, stars explode, the moon seems to burn like the sun, and the heavens heave and roll like ocean waves. Here, van Gogh's expressive use of color invests nature with visionary frenzy.

In his letters to Theo (an art dealer by profession), van Gogh pledged his undying faith in the power of artistic creativity. In 1888, just two years before he committed suicide, van Gogh wrote: "I can do without God both in my life and in my painting, but I cannot, ill as I am, do without something which is greater than I, which is my life—the power to create. And if, defrauded of the power to create physically, a man tries to create thoughts in place of children, he is still part of humanity." Assessing his own creativity, van Gogh claimed that making portraits allowed him to cultivate what was "best and deepest." "Altogether," he explained, "it is the only thing in painting which moves me to the depths, and which more than anything else makes me feel the infinite."* For van Gogh, the challenge of portraiture lay in capturing the heart and soul of the model. In his many portraits of friends and neighbors, and in the twenty-four self-portraits that he painted between 1886 and 1889, van Gogh raised the mood of romantic subjectivity to new levels of confessional intensity. In the *Self-Portrait* of 1889 (Figure **31.26**), for instance, where the pale fleshtones of the head are set against an almost monochromatic blue field, the skull takes on a forbidding, even spectral presence—an effect enhanced by the lurid green facial shadows and the blue-green eyes, slanted deliberately (as he related to Theo) so as to make himself look Japanese. Van Gogh's brushstrokes, similar to those that evoke the coiling heavens in *The Starry Night*, charge the surface with undulating rhythms that sharply contrast with the immobile human figure. This visual strategy underscores the artist's alienation from his surroundings; it becomes more meaningful in light of van Gogh's confession (to Gauguin) that he saw himself in this portrait as a simple Buddhist monk.

If van Gogh may be said to have apprehended an inner vision of nature, Paul Gauguin tried to embrace nature in its unblemished state. Abandoning his wife, his children, and his job as a Paris stockbroker, this prototype of the modern bohemian traveled to Martinique in the West Indies, to Brittany in Northwest France, and to Southern France before finally settling on the island of Tahiti in the South Seas. Gauguin, in his self-conscious effort to assume the role of "the civilized savage," shared the fascination with unspoiled nature that characterized the writings of Rousseau and Thoreau. And in this sense, Gauguin's bohemianism represented the "last gasp" of romanticism. But Gauguin's flight to the South Seas was also typical of the search for a lost Eden and the fascination with non-Western cultures that swept through the intellectual community of late nineteenth-century Europe.

Gauguin took artistic inspiration from the folk culture of Brittany, from the native arts of the South Sea islands, and from dozens of other nonacademic sources. What impressed him was the self-taught immediacy and authenticity of folk and tribal artforms, especially those that made use of powerful, totemic abstraction (Figure **31.27**). His own style, nurtured in the symbolist environment and influenced by Japanese woodcuts and photographs of Japanese temple reliefs on view at the Paris Exposition, featured flat, often distorted and brightly colored shapes that seem to float on the surface of the canvas. In *The Day of the God* (Figure **31.28**), bright blues, yellows, and pinks form rhythmic tapestry-like patterns reminiscent of Japanese prints and *art nouveau* posters. Like the verbal images of the symbolist poets, Gauguin's colored shapes evoke a mood and imply ideas that lie beyond literal description. For example, the languid, organic shapes in the foreground pool of water and the fetal positions of the figures lying on the shore are suggestive of birth and regeneration—images appropriate to the totemic figure (pictured at top center of the canvas), who resembles the creator god and supreme deity of Maori culture (compare Figure 31.27).

**Figure 31.26** Vincent van Gogh, *Self-Portrait*, 1889. Oil on canvas, 25½ × 21¼ in. Musée d'Orsay, Paris.

Gauguin's figures cast no shadows, and his bold, unmodeled colors, like those of van Gogh, often bear little relationship to visual appearance. (The blues in the background of *The Day of the God*, for instance, are of the same intensity as those in the foreground.) Gauguin joined van Gogh at Arles in the fall of 1888, and for a brief time the two artists lived and worked side by side. Volatile and temperamental, they often engaged in violent quarrels, and during one of van Gogh's psychotic episodes (which ended in his cutting off part of his own ear), he even attempted to kill Gauguin. But despite their intense personal differences, van Gogh and Gauguin were fraternal pioneers in the search for a provocative language of form and color.

*In Irving Stone, ed., *Dear Theo: The Autobiography of Vincent van Gogh*. New York: New American Library, 1937, 382, 370.

**Figure 31.27** Fragment of a Maori doorpost, from New Zealand. University of Pennsylvania Museum, Philadelphia (neg. S4134161).

**Figure 31.28** (below) Paul Gauguin, *The Day of the God* (*Mahana no Atua*), 1894. Oil on canvas, 27$\frac{3}{8}$ × 35$\frac{5}{8}$ in. Photograph © 1998, The Art Institute of Chicago. All Rights Reserved. Helen Birch Bartlett Memorial Collection (1926.198).

**Figure 31.29** Georges Seurat, *Sunday Afternoon on the Island of La Grande Jatte*, 1884–1886. Oil on canvas, 6 ft. 9½ in. × 10 ft. ⅛ in. Photograph © 1998, The Art Institute of Chicago. All Rights Reserved. Helen Birch Bartlett Memorial Collection (1926.224).

## Seurat and Cézanne

Extending the techniques of the impressionists in a different direction, the postimpressionist French painter Georges Seurat (1859–1891) treated color as analytically as a modern laboratory technician. Seurat was trained academically and, like the academicians Poussin and David, he brought balance and order to his style. The forms in his compositions, for instance, seem plotted along an invisible graph of vertical and horizontal lines that run parallel to the picture plane. A similar fervor for order may have inspired Seurat's novel use of tiny dots of color (in French, *points*), which he applied side by side (and sometimes one inside another) to build up dense clusters that give the impression of solid form—a style known as *pointillism*. Seurat arrived at the technique of dividing color into component parts after studying the writings of Chevreul and other pioneers in color theory. Leaving nothing to chance (Gauguin called him "the little green chemist"), Seurat analyzed color into its component tints. He applied each tint so that its juxtaposition with the next would produce the desired degree of vibration to the eye of the beholder. Although Seurat shared the impressionists' fascination with light and color, he shunned spontaneity, and though he made his sketches out-of-doors, he executed his paintings inside his studio, usually at night and under artificial light.

Seurat's monumental *Sunday Afternoon on the Island of La Grande Jatte* shows a holiday crowd of Parisians relaxing on a sunlit island in the River Seine (Figure **31.29**). Although typically impressionistic in its subject matter—urban society at leisure—the painting (along with the twenty-seven preparatory panels on the same theme) harbors little of the impressionist's love for intimacy and fleeting sensation. Every figure is isolated from the next as if each were frozen in space and unaware of another's existence. One critic railed, "Strip his figures of the colored fleas that cover them; underneath you will find nothing, no thought, no soul." Seurat's universe, with its atomized particles of color and its self-contained figures, may seem devoid of human feeling, but, at the same time, its exquisite regularity provides a comforting alternative to the chaos of experience. Indeed, the lasting appeal of *La Grande Jatte* lies in its effectiveness as a symbolic retreat from the tumult of everyday life and the accidents of nature.

More so than Seurat, Paul Cézanne (1839–1906) served as a bridge between the art of the nineteenth century and that of the twentieth. Cézanne began his career as an impressionist but his traditional subjects—such as landscapes, portraits, and still lifes—show a greater concern for the formal aspects of the painting than for its subject matter. His effort to "redo nature after Poussin," that is, to find the enduring forms of nature that were basic to all great art, made Cézanne the first modernist artist.

Cézanne's determination to invest his pictures with a strong sense of three-dimensional form (a feature often neglected by the impressionists) led to a method of building up form by means of small, flat planes of color, larger than (but not entirely unlike) Seurat's colored dots. Abandoning the intuitive and loosely organized compositions of the impressionists, Cézanne also sought to restore to painting the sturdy, formal structure of academic composition. His concern for pictorial unity inspired him to take bold liberties with form and perspective, and, ultimately, to modify traditional methods of reproducing the appearance of physical objects in space: He might, for instance, tilt and flatten surfaces; reduce (or abstract) familiar objects to such basic geometric shapes as cylinders, cones, and spheres; or depict various objects in a single composition from different points of view. Cézanne's still lifes are not so much likenesses of tempting apples, peaches, or pears as they are architectural arrangements of colored forms (Figure **31.30**). In short, where narrative content often seems neglected, form itself has meaning.

Cézanne's mature style developed when he left Paris and returned to live in his native area of Southern France. Here he tirelessly painted the local landscape: Dozens of times he painted the rugged, stony peak of Mont Sainte-Victoire near his hometown of Aix-en-Provence. Among Cézanne's last versions of the subject is a landscape in which trees and houses have become an abstract network of colored facets of paint (Figure

**Figure 31.30** Paul Cézanne, *The Basket of Apples*, ca. 1895. Oil on canvas, 25¾ × 32 in.
Photograph © 1998, The Art Institute of Chicago. All Rights Reserved. Helen Birch Bartlett Memorial Collection (1926.252).

**Figure 31.31** Paul Cézanne, *Mont Sainte-Victoire*, 1902–1904. Oil on canvas, 27½ × 35¼ in. Philadelphia Museum of Art. George W. Elkins Collection (Acces. E'36–1–1).

31.31). By applying colors of the same intensity to different parts of the canvas—note the bright green and rich violet brushstrokes in both sky and landscape—Cézanne challenged traditional distinctions between foreground and background. In Cézanne's canvases, all parts of the composition, like the flat shapes of a Japanese print, become equal in value. Cézanne's methods, which transformed an ordinary mountain into an icon of stability, led the way to modern abstraction.

## *SUMMARY*

Art for art's sake was neither a movement nor a style but rather a prevailing spirit in European and especially French culture of the last quarter of the nineteenth century. In all of the arts, there was a new attention to sensory experience rather than to moral and didactic purpose. At the same time, advances in optics, electricity, and other areas of science and technology brought attention to matters of motion and light. Paralleling the radical changes in technology and art, the German iconoclast Nietzsche questioned the moral value of art and rallied superior individuals to topple old gods—that is, to reject whatever was sentimental and stale in Western tradition. Amidst new theories of sensation and perception, the French philosopher Bergson stressed the role of intuition in grasping the true nature of durational reality. The symbolist poets devised a language of sensation that evoked feeling rather than described experience. In Mallarmé's "L'Après-midi d'un faune," images unfold as sensuous, discontinuous fragments. Similar effects occur in the music of Debussy, where delicately shaded harmonies gently drift without resolution.

The French impressionists, led by Monet, were equally representative of the late nineteenth-century interest in sensation and sensory experience. These artists tried to record an instantaneous vision of their world, sacrificing the details of perceived objects in order to capture the effects of light and atmosphere. Renoir, Degas, Cassatt, and Toulouse-Lautrec produced informal and painterly canvases that offer a glimpse into the pleasures of nineteenth-century European urban life. Stop-action photographs and the flat, linear designs of Japanese prints influenced the style of the impressionists. Japanese woodcuts also anticipated the decorative style known as *art nouveau,* which dominated architecture, poster design, and Western arts and crafts in the last decades of the century. In sculpture, the works of Degas and Rodin reflect a common concern for figural gesture and movement. Rodin's efforts to translate inner states of feeling into expressive physical form were mirrored by Isadora Duncan's innovations in modern dance.

The visual intensity of such Western artforms seemed dim, however, in the light of those artifacts newly arrived in the West from the cultures of Africa and Oceania. Primitivism would come to play a major part in the move to modernism that occurred in the last decade of the nineteenth century. The postimpressionists van Gogh, Gauguin, Seurat, and Cézanne renounced the impressionist infatuation with the fleeting effects of light to devise new pictorial strategies. Van Gogh and Gauguin used color not as an atmospheric envelope but as a tool for personal and visionary expression. Seurat and Cézanne reacted against the formlessness of impressionism by creating styles that featured architectural stability and solid, simplified forms. On the threshold of the twentieth century, artists would escape the naturalistic bias of both romanticism and realism by boldly shedding their former roles as idealizers and imitators of nature.

## SUGGESTIONS FOR READING


Berger, Klaus. *Japonisme in Western Painting from Whistler to Matisse,* translated by David Britt. New York: Cambridge University Press, 1992.

Gogh, Vincent van. *Van Gogh's Diary: The Artist's Life in His Own Words and Art.* New York: Morrow, 1971.

Goldwater, Robert. *Symbolism.* London: Allen Lane, 1979.

Herbert, Robert L. *Impressionism: Art, Leisure and Parisian Society.* New Haven: Yale University Press, 1988.

Kroegger, M. E. *Literary Impressionism.* New Haven: Yale University Press, 1973.

Masur, Gerhard. *Prophets of Yesterday: Studies in European Culture, 1890–1914.* New York: Macmillan, 1961.

Rewald, John. *Cézanne: A Biography.* New York: Abrams, 1986.

——. *The History of Impressionism.* New York: New York Graphic Society, 1980.

Schmutzler, Robert. *Art Nouveau.* New York: Abrams, 1962.

Silverman, Deborah. *Art Nouveau in Fin-de-Siècle France: Politics, Psychology, and Style.* Berkeley, Calif.: University of California Press, 1989.

Solomon, Robert. *Reading Nietzsche.* New York: Oxford University Press, 1988.

Whitford, Frank. *Japanese Prints and Western Painting.* New York: Macmillan, 1977.


## MUSIC LISTENING SELECTION

**Cassette II Selection 15** Debussy, *Prélude à "L'Après-midi d'un faune,"* 1894.

# Credits

# Selected General Bibliography


Anderson, Bonnie S., and Judith P. Zinsser. *A History of Their Own: Women in Europe from Prehistory to the Present*. Vol. 2. New York: Harper, 1988.

Arnason, H. H. *History of Modern Art: Painting, Sculpture, Architecture, Photography*, 3rd ed. Englewood Cliffs, N.J.: Prentice-Hall, 1986.

Artz, F. B. *From the Renaissance to Romanticism: Trends in Style in Art, Literature, and Music, 1300–1830*. Chicago: University of Chicago Press, 1962.

Austin, William. *Music in the Twentieth Century from Debussy through Stravinsky*. New York: Norton, 1966.

Barzun, Jacques. *Darwin, Marx, and Wagner*, 2nd ed. New York: Columbia University Press, 1981.

Boorstin, Daniel. *The Creators: A History of Heroes of the Imagination*. New York: Random House, 1993.

Bridenthal, Renate, and Claudia Koonz, eds. *Becoming Visible: Women in European History*. Boston: Houghton Mifflin, 1977.

Bronowski, Jacob, and Bruce Mazlish. *The Western Intellectual Tradition: From Leonardo to Hegel*. New York: Harper, 1960.

Brown, Calvin S. *Music and Literature: A Comparison of the Arts*. Hanover, N.H.: University Press of New England, 1987.

Bugner, Ladislas, ed. *The Image of the Black in Western Art*. Vol. 3, *From Sixteenth-Century Europe to Nineteenth-Century America*. Cambridge, Mass.: Harvard University Press, 1986.

Bullock, Alan, and Stephen Trombley. *The Harper Dictionary of Modern Thought*. New York: Harper, 1988.

——, and R. B. Woodbridge, eds. *Modern Culture: A Biographical Companion*. New York: Harper, 1984.

Canaday, John. *Mainstreams of Modern Art*, 2nd ed. New York: Holt, Rinehart and Winston, 1981.

Chadwick, Whitney. *Women, Art and Society*. New York: Norton, 1991.

Chang, H. C. *Chinese Literature: Popular Fiction and Drama*. New York: Columbia University Press, 1973.

Clark, Kenneth. *Civilisation: A Personal View*. New York: Harper, 1970.

Clarke, Mary, and Clement Crisp. *The History of Dance*. New York: Crown, 1981.

Collier, Peter, and Robert Lethbridge, eds. *Artistic Relations: Literature and the Visual Arts in Nineteenth-Century France*. New Haven: Yale University Press, 1994.

Copland, Aaron. *What to Listen for in Music*, rev. ed. New York: New American Library, 1963.

Craven, Roy C. *Indian Art*. London: Thames and Hudson, 1976.

Driskel, Michael P. *Representing Belief: Religion, Art, and Society in Nineteenth-Century France*. University Park, Pa.: Pennsylvania State University, 1992.

Eitner, Lorenz, ed. *Neoclassicism and Romanticism, 1750–1850: An Anthology of Sources and Documents*. New York: Harper, 1989.

Fitzgerald, C. P. *The Horizon History of China*. New York: American Heritage, 1969.

Fleming, William. *Concerts of the Arts: Their Interplay and Modes of Relationship*. Gainesville, Fla.: University of West Florida Press, 1990.

——. *Musical Arts and Styles*. Gainesville, Fla.: University of West Florida Press, 1990.

Goodenberger, Jennifer. *Subject Guide to Classical Instrumental Music*. Metuchen, N.J.: Scarecrow Press, 1989.

Harman, Carter. *A Popular History of Music*, rev. ed. New York: Dell, 1973.

Johnson, Paul. *The Birth of the Modern: World Society 1815–1830*. New York: Harper, 1991.

Kaufmann, Walter. *Discovering the Mind*. 3 vols. New York: McGraw-Hill, 1980.

Kostoff, Spiro. *A History of Architecture: Settings and Rituals*. New York: Oxford University Press, 1985.

Lee, Sherman E. *A History of Far Eastern Art*. New York: Abrams, 1964.

Mackenzie, John. *Orientalism: History, Theory and the Arts*. New York: St. Martin's Press, 1995.

Nelson, Lynn H., and Patrick Peebles, eds. *Classics of Eastern Thought*. San Diego: Harcourt, 1991.

Newhall, Beaumont. *The History of Photography: From 1839 to the Present*, rev. ed. New York: Museum of Modern Art, 1982.

Novak, Barbara. *American Painting of the Nineteenth Century: Realism, Idealism, and the American Experience*. New York: Praeger, 1969.

Orr, Clarissa S., ed. *Women in the Victorian Art World*. New York: St. Martin's, 1995.

Orrey, Leslie. *Opera: A Concise History*. London: Thames and Hudson, 1968.

Pevsner, Nikolaus. *An Outline of European Architecture*, 6th ed. Baltimore, Md.: Penguin, 1960.

Prendergast, Christopher. *Paris and the Nineteenth Century*. Oxford: Blackwell, 1992.

Raynor, Henry. *A Social History of Music: From the Middle Ages to Beethoven*. New York: Schocken Books, 1972.

Russell, Bertrand. *A History of Western Philosophy*, 2nd ed. New York: Simon and Schuster, 1984.

Sadie, Stanley, ed. *The New Grove Dictionary of Music and Musicians*. New York: Macmillan, 1980.

Sorrell, Walter. *The Dance Through the Ages*. New York: Grosset and Dunlap, 1967.

Spence, Jonathan D. *The Search for Modern China*. New York: Norton, 1990.

Sterling, Charles. *Still Life Painting from Antiquity to the Twentieth Century*, 2nd rev. ed. New York: Harper, 1981.

Stromberg, Roland N., ed. *Realism, Naturalism and Symbolism: Modes of Thought and Expression in Europe, 1848–1914*. New York: Walker, 1968.

Sypher, Wylie. *Rococo to Cubism in Art and Literature*. New York: Random House, 1960.

Trowell, Margaret, and Hans Nevermann. *African and Oceanic Art*. New York: Abrams, 1968.

Weiss, Piero, and Richard Taruskin. *Music in the Western World: A History in Documents*. New York: Schirmer, 1984.

Wiener, Philip P., ed. *Dictionary of the History of Ideas*. New York: Scribners, 1973.

Willet, Frank. *African Art: An Introduction*. London: Thames and Hudson, 1993.


## BOOKS IN SERIES


*Great Ages of Man. A History of the World's Cultures*. New York: Time-Life Books, 1965–1969.

*Library of Art Series*. New York: Time-Life Books, 1967.

*Time-Frame*. 25 vols. (projected). New York: Time-Life Books, 1990–.

# Index

**Numbers in bold refer to figure numbers. Text excerpts are indicated by (quoted).**

## N



## O



## P



## R